A Hospice in Change

I0882758

A Hospice in Change: Applied Social Realist Theory reports upon a study into aspects of the ways in which structural and organisational developments, professional cultures and 'bedside' or patient focused clinical practice interact within a single UK institution. While the findings of this study are time and context specific, the events and social processes being described may nonetheless resonate closely with the experience of healthcare practitioners at other hospices both within and without the UK. The work examines themes and ideas that hospice and palliative care practitioners, as well as those involved or interested more broadly in 'end of life issues', may find relevant.

It is argued that differential morphogenesis can be identified between structures (social and cultural) and agents (individual and group) at an independent healthcare charity in southern England. *A Hospice in Change* connects theory and philosophy with concrete research practice to provide a worked example of Margaret Archer's realist social theory.

Martin Lipscomb is Senior Lecturer at the University of the West of England.

Critical realism: interventions

Other titles in this series:

(Mis)recognition, Social Inequality and Social Justice
Nancy Fraser and Pierre Bourdieu
Edited by Terry Lovell

After International Relations
Critical realism and the (re)construction of world politics
Heikki Patomäki

Being and Worth
Andrew Collier

Beyond East and West
Roy Bhaskar

Capitalism and Citizenship
The impossible partnership
Kathryn Dean

Critical Realism and Marxism
Edited by Andrew Brown, Steve Fleetwood and John Michael Roberts

Dictionary of Critical Realism
Edited by Mervyn Hartwig

A Social Theory of the Nation-State
The political forms of modernity beyond methodological nationalism
Daniel Chernillo

Rethinking Marxism
From Kant and Hegel to Marx and Engels
Jolyon Agar

Transcendence
Critical realism and God
Margaret S. Archer, Andrew Collier, and Douglas V. Porpora

Maurice Mandelbaum and American Critical Realism
Edited by Ian F. Verstegen

Contradictions of Archaeological Theory
Engaging critical realism and archaeological theory
Sandra Wallace

Integrating knowledge Through Interdisciplinary Research
Problems of theory and practice
Dominic Holland

A Hospice in Change
Applied social realist theory
Martin Lipscomb

A Hospice in Change

Applied social realist theory

Martin Lipscomb

Routledge
Taylor & Francis Group
LONDON AND NEW YORK

First edition published 2014
by Routledge
2 Park Square, Milton Park, Abingdon, Oxfordshire OX14 4RN

and by Routledge
711 Third Avenue, New York, NY 10017

First issued in paperback 2016

Routledge is an imprint of the Taylor & Francis Group, an informa business

© 2014 Martin Lipscomb

The right of Martin Lipscomb to be identified as the author of this work has been asserted by him in accordance with sections 77 and 78 of the Copyright, Designs and Patents Act 1988.

All rights reserved. No part of this book may be reprinted or reproduced or utilised in any form or by any electronic, mechanical, or other means, now known or hereafter invented, including photocopying and recording, or in any information storage or retrieval system, without permission in writing from the publishers.

Trademark notice: Product or corporate names may be trademarks or registered trademarks, and are used only for identification and explanation without intent to infringe.

British Library Cataloguing in Publication Data
A catalogue record for this book is available from the British Library

Library of Congress Cataloging-in-Publication Data
Lipscombe, Martin.
A hospice in change: applied social realist theory/Martin Lipscombe.–
Lipscomb, Martin.
A hospice in change: applied social realist theory/Martin Lipscomb. –
First edition.
pages cm. – (Critical realism: interventions)
Includes bibliographical references and index.
1. Hospice care–Research. 2. Critical theory. I. Title.
R726.8.L57 2014
616.02′9–dc23

2013014180

ISBN 13: 978-1-138-23328-7 (pbk)
ISBN 13: 978-0-415-62251-6 (hbk)

Typeset in Times New Roman
by Wearset Ltd, Boldon, Tyne and Wear

For Kath, Harry and Ella – the nicest people.

Contents

Acknowledgements

I must thank the hospice as an organisation and the individuals who work within it for agreeing to help me in this study. Without the openness of this organisation and the kindness and patience of those individuals this book would now conclude.

I would also like to express my gratitude to Professor Margaret Miers and Doctor Theresa Mitchell for their respective and much valued contributions. Thank you.

1 Introduction

Critical realist philosophy and social theory are here combined to structure an investigation into what might colloquially be termed 'change at a hospice'.[1] To this end the realist social theory of Margaret Archer (awkwardly termed 'morphogenetic-morphostatic methodology') directs a study into developments at a hospice in Southern England. The book therefore presents a worked example of realist social research[2] and, since critical and social realists claim that philosophy and theory must both ultimately be judged according to use value, if this example productively offers insights that alternative approaches might not have generated, then the value of Archer's realism is demonstrated. More generally it is proposed that critical realist philosophy and social theory have much to offer healthcare workers, researchers and theorists with an interest in healthcare, healthcare organisation and health related behaviours. This book hopefully illustrates the nature, benefits and scope of at least elements of this "offering".

And so to begin – although it is not always considered good form to reveal results in advance of an explanation of how those results were generated, in synopsis the research findings presented here run as follows: comments and behaviours made or performed by participating study site personnel suggest that relations between the hospice and what were perceived to be hostile external institutions (e.g. the NHS and Department of Health) created unease among senior hospice staff. This presumption of external threats generated a logic of interests that pushed managerial staff at the hospice to re-designate the organisation a specialist palliative care unit. Re-description or re-designation catalysed the development of pre-existing long-term trends in organisational practice. It also exacerbated tensions among clinical staff (notably nurses and doctors) some of whom can be identified with pro- and anti-change groups. Tensions between these groups are expressed or evidenced as conflicting beliefs about the purpose and form of organisational activity. More concretely, disagreement focused on admission policy (who should be included and excluded from care) as well as the types and 'intensity' of clinical treatments offered (i.e. the sort of care provided). Tentative suggestions are made concerning the reasons or factors underpinning agential dissonance.

To present and develop the case outlined above this book has a very simple structure. Chapter 2 provides an overview of Margaret Archer's theoretical assumptions and methodology. This outline should 'make sense' of morphogenesis for newcomers to social realism. However, one person's helpful overview is another's incomprehensible gibberish and despite its utility there is no escaping the fact that Archer's work is both conceptually challenging and jargon 'rich'. Alternatively, since the deeper theoretical nuances of realist social theory are not here explored, seasoned realists may be disappointed with the level of detail and critique provided. For readers who think that either too much or too little theory is presented a short bibliography at the close of this work suggests just a few of the now numerous and excellent texts that exist on this subject.

Chapter 3 introduces contextualising information about the study and study site. It details how ethical and procedural issues were handled and it describes how and why particular research methods were chosen to complement morphogenetic-morphostatic methodology. Chapter 4, the longest section of this book, presents the results of this study. The work concludes with Chapter 5, a synopsis and critique of aspects of the research presented in Chapter 4.

Since it in part aims to problematise or raise questions about the soundness or validity of the research being presented, the last chapter might be seen as something of an anomaly. However, to excuse this oddity I would bring to readers' attention a key realist tenant, namely the unavoidability of theoretical concerns for practicing researchers. Thus critical realists argue that witting or, more often, unwitting presumptions or background theories about causality or the nature and powers of society and people are inevitably embedded within and influence social explanation. This suggests that theory cannot be sidestepped and, for example, critical realists emphasise and seek to make overt what they see as the logical ties binding ontology (ideas about 'what is' or the nature of being) with epistemology (ideas about knowledge and/or what can be known) and methodology (ideas about how we might investigate the world). And, while the strength of these bonds or ties can be questioned – they can be over-egged – relentlessly focusing upon these sorts of difficult or problematic issues, particularly when understandings of the social world are contemplated, is a major strength of the realist approach.

The final chapter therefore critiques aspects of the methodology and philosophic assumptions that inform the study being described. As suggested this might seem foolish since, having argued that realist social theory usefully directs researchers to construct understandings that non-realist approaches may miss, potential weaknesses in the study are then exposed. Nonetheless, this sort of 'to-and-fro' between research practice and theory is a recognised part of realist explanation and, the point I would stress, thinking about a research project need not cease when that project formally concludes.

A personal commentary

The study described in this work grew out of or embodies three distinct personal interests and, since these interests influenced the way in which the study was conducted (the way in which realist social theory was interpreted and applied), as well as my relationship with or to realism, these interests need to be recognised. The introduction seems an appropriate place to do this.

First, I was initially attracted to realist social theory and critical realism more generally because these approaches (and it is probably best to think of them in the plural) appeared to offer the possibility that deficiencies in my own understanding of the social realm might be remedied. Specifically, I began the study with a desire to better comprehend the nature of causality in social explanation and engaging with this thorny issue seemed necessary if I was to progress my ability to explain events at the organisation, the hospice, in which I worked.

The difficulty and indeed disputed merit of establishing causality in social explanation is a perennial conundrum. It may be that questions connected with this issue are ultimately irresolvable or, at least, they may be 'irresolvable' if by resolution we mean that widespread consensus about the form, nature and plausibility of descriptions of social causation can be achieved. Nevertheless, causation came to my attention as a problem when, in an earlier work, I became aware that I was using causally implicative descriptors such as 'produced', 'led to', 'prompted' or 'encouraged' (this list can easily be extended) without adequately explaining or justifying the links between events or concepts thus associated.

For example, I was not always clear about how or in what way one happening or set of happenings 'led to' or 'produced' another happening. I did not detail whether the explanatory descriptors being employed captured necessary or contingent relations. And I failed to make clear how much one happening caused another. Thus while precise quantification is almost always impossible (and it may be unnecessary or undesirable), when I stated that 'x prompted y', did I mean that 'x prompted y' 'entirely' or 'a lot' and if 'a lot' what did that mean? Further, what motor, power, force or mechanism drives or lies behind social causation? Achinstein (2010) recognises that these terms are especially difficult to describe and, yet, when we say that 'x' prompted 'y', what is it about 'x' that does this thing? What enables 'x' to prompt 'y'?

Failure to clarify what is meant by causation in social explanation is not unusual. However, lack of clarity is of signal importance to the status and validity of explanation. Descriptive imprecision influences and often limits the sorts and strength of belief that can be derived from social explanation and this aspect of the way we present ideas adversely affects the informative or action guiding potential of explanation.

Serendipitously when considering these matters I chanced upon Roy Bhaskar's early works *A Realist Theory of Science* (1997 – first published in 1975) and *The Possibility of Naturalism: A Philosophical Critique of the Contemporary Human Sciences* (1998 – first published in 1979). These two books have been hugely influential within the modern realist movement. Miller (2002) states that "the nature and plausibility of realism is one of the most hotly debated issues in contemporary philosophy" and, as a part of this debate, Collier (1994) enthusiastically describes Bhaskar's critical realism as "the most exciting development in Anglophone philosophy in this half-century" (p. ix). Collier (ibid.) probably overstates Bhaskar's importance. However, as Groff (2004) notes,

Bhaskar's critical realism offers "a point of entry into epistemology and metaphysics for practicing social scientists" (p. 23) and it was this 'entry' that I found intriguing.

Further reading led me to, among others, Margaret Archer and her texts *Realist Social Theory: The Morphogenetic Approach* (1995) and *Culture and Agency: The Place of Culture in Social Theory* (1996 – first published 1988). The account of social investigation presented in these works undergird or scaffold the study described in this book and they do so because, picking up on the point made by Groff (2004), Archer (1995) is, in these texts, keenly interested in connecting philosophy or theory with research practice. Indeed, as she says: "The practical analyst of society needs to know not only *what social reality is*, but also *how to begin to explain it*, before addressing the particular problem under investigation" (p. 5 – italicisation in original).

Realist writers did not ultimately answer or resolve my questions (that would be to expect too much). However, critical realism and realist social theory did at least take those questions seriously and, moreover, in becoming familiar with the realist corpus I broadened my interest from causality – now redefined as 'tendencies' – to the ontological stature of social phenomena and the nature of social explanation in general. Further, realism, especially the realism of Margaret Archer, enabled me to articulate what had hitherto been a merely intuitive reticence towards some forms of alternative non-realist perspective.

That said, unsurprisingly, my relationship with realism is not static and, while I was attracted in the first instance towards the works of Bhaskar and Archer because they offer a clear advance on alternative systems of explanation as well as some admittedly tentative methodological guidance; retrospectively, I now question several of the claims and suggestions of both theorists. Positively, the issues and problems highlighted by critical realists are important and, to their credit, the realist 'way' is worthy of considerable attention. Yet I would now position myself as someone interested in and favourably disposed towards realist explanation rather than a critical or social realist cheerleader. I suspect that significant elements of realism, for example, the version of free will apparently endorsed by Bhaskar and Archer is not necessary for realist theory and, like Dean (2006), I believe that to adequately inform research practice, realist insights require considerable support from non-realist theories.

Despite this reappraisal and notwithstanding qualification, the realisms of Bhaskar and Archer remain, in my opinion, an attractive option for healthcare workers, researchers and theorists operating in the health and social care fields. And, moreover, even people opposed to realism have much to gain from thinking through critical realist challenges to non-realist forms of explanation. Supporting and justifying these claims is a major objective of this book.

The second personal factor or influence upon the study stems from my position within (and now 'without') the hospice study site. Thus I am by trade a nurse. I qualified in 1993 and joined a professorially led combined haematology, oncology and bone marrow transplant unit in a newly built hospital on the South coast of England. This high tech and (then) generously resourced facility, part sponsored by a cancer charity, was considered to be one of the UK's most innovative and research active centres. Nevertheless, at any one time up to a fifth of in-patients might be dying and, although the care given to these patients was of a very good standard, this eventful and at times frenetic clinical environment could be considered an inappropriate place in which to die. For, not only was the facility unceasingly busy (activity continued around the clock) but, in addition, medical enthusiasm for curatively orientated interventions was sustained, on occasion, up until the point of death. When this occurred, feelings of disquiet were often voiced by colleagues and an interest in palliative care was kindled during this period.

Several years and posts later I went to work at a charitably funded hospice in Southern England (the study site). This organisation provides outstanding care to those in its charge and comparisons between it and NHS hospitals with which I am familiar cast those hospitals in an unfavourable light. In particular, hospice staff spend more time with patients and families, specialist expertise is greater, equipment and facilities are superior and more attention is paid to comfort and emotional support than appears feasible within the state sector.

Nonetheless, 'hands-on' experience as a staff nurse led me to query aspects of clinical and organisational practice and clarifying and addressing these questions provides the focus for this study. Specifically, in conversation, staff expressed divergent interpretations of what their work is or should be and, importantly, these contrasting interpretations, translated into clinical actions, directly influence the nature and quality of care provided. Colleagues with whom I spoke were often aware of actual and potential instances of friction associated with these differing understandings and conversations regarding such matters and their impact upon care occupied a part of many daily activities. Yet explanations regarding the causes of ideational dissonance were mixed (when forthcoming).

In exploring these issues a review of hospice and palliative care scholarship neither provided the answers I sought nor described the situation in which I worked. Indeed, despite the existence of a flourishing, sophisticated and increasingly analytical literature (see, e.g. Lawton, 2000; Cobb, 2001; Seymour, 2001; Sandman, 2005; Randall and Downie, 2006; and Woods, 2007 – to name but a few) controversy continues as regards the nature and future of hospice and palliative care provision.

Understanding how staff at the study site interpret or understand their work and the organisation in which they function – i.e. as a hospice *and/or* specialist palliative care unit – forms the basis of this study and motivation for performing the research described in this book comes from the simple desire to 'study up' (Nader, 1972) the organisation in which I worked.

And here I insert two asides. My position as a staff nurse at the study site combined with a pre-hospice background in interventionist clinical practice will inevitably have played a part (for good and ill) in all aspects of the research. Questions or issues generated by my position in and influence on the study are therefore addressed at various points in the text. Also, I generally refer to the study site as a hospice throughout this work and yet, as previously mentioned, the organisation re-designated itself a specialist palliative care unit. This might seem confusing. However, study site staff and those they cared for continued to use the descriptor hospice and this colloquial habit was maintained even by the senior staff who sanctioned re-designation. Hopefully, this terminological issue will not prove disruptive.

The third personal "driver" for this work derives from a concern with the determinedly (one might say obstinately) untheoretical nature of much health and social care scholarship. This observation complements realist concerns with lucidity and it is an interest informed by my professional identity.

As noted realists presume that argumentative coherence relies, in part, upon making explicit the mutually implicative logical ties that connect ontological, epistemological and methodological reasoning (Danermark *et al.*, 2002; Bergene, 2007). Where a focus on this linkage aids, or can potentially aid, argumentative coherence then it is a laudable goal. However, the demands being placed upon researchers and scholars by this claim should not be underestimated.

Focusing upon argumentative structure, upon logic, may and often does appear needlessly abstract to researchers who are grappling with complex real world issues. Indeed, when the object of study concerns health and/or social care, the pressing need to swiftly generate 'evidence' that can help others will, perhaps inevitably, limit the amount of time that researchers can or want to devote to what might, in caricature, be termed philosophic navel gazing (Foss and Ellefsen, 2002).

The "metaphysical paradigm" or theoretical emphasis that critical realists endorse is thus rejected by Morgan (2007, p. 62) on pragmatic grounds (i.e. it is seen as impractical and unnecessary). And it must be granted that scholars and scientists can and do operate effectively without developed philosophic understandings (Rose, 2006; Achinstein, 2010). Nonetheless, as Leplin (2004) states, while there "is no *a priori* stance from which philosophy can assume to dictate the standards and methods for acquiring knowledge. Philosophical assumptions are ineliminable from the reasoning by which science fixes its ontological commitments" (p. 118 – italicisation in original).

Leplin (ibid.) rather than Morgan's (2007) position is thus here commended and, yet, certainly within nursing scholarship – though the point applies widely across many and possibly most professional/research health and social care literatures – reluctance to engage with philosophic or theoretical issues of substance can be sustained by the perception that practitioners and researchers must maintain a "person-centred" (McCormack, 2003, p. 179) focus on concrete, outcomes based or (loosely) 'bed-side' or 'hands-on' care. This focus is of course understandable. However, where Newell and Burnard (2006) argue that nursing (and by implication health related) research "should have immediate consequences for patient care" (p. 4) the concomitant view that philosophy and theory's contribution to explanation is intangible, distancing and superfluous ought, I suggest, to be resisted.

Rather than simply dismissing theory, Simons (2007), in an argument aimed at mixed method investigators – an approach that is becoming increasingly popular in health and social care – calls upon researchers to be sensitive to other "conceptions of knowledge and reflect on their position in relation to the range of possibilities" (p. 73). This seems sensible and yet reflection can and perhaps should prompt *all* researchers to consider the intertwined nature of philosophy, theory and scientific practice for, self-evidently, the existence of competing forms of explanation necessitates that researchers make choices and these choices include ontological, epistemological and methodological considerations (Willmott, 2003). Moreover, as Collier (1994) notes, "part of the answer to the question 'why philosophy?' is that the alternative to philosophy is not *no* philosophy but *bad* philosophy" (p. 16 – italicisation in original) – i.e. bad reasoning.

Explicitness and clarity are easily compromised when a careless approach to methodological use is combined with an indifferent attitude towards theoretical dispute and the philosophic questions (broadly defined) that this dispute articulates (Rose, 2006). For example, Rycroft-Malone *et al.* (2004) pragmatically suggest that researchers should use "whatever approach(es) are relevant to the clinical problem and resultant research question" (p. 88). This 'pick-n-mix' attitude to method and methodological choice is not unusual (see also, for example, Weaver and Olson, 2006), it may even prove 'serviceable'; however, it is also potentially problematic.

Methodologies rest upon and embody theories stemming from diverse and occasionally incommensurable philosophic traditions. The danger of incommensurability can be and often is overdramatised. Nonetheless, while method and methodological promiscuousness may be appropriate or acceptable where the extended linkages of ontological and epistemological reasoning are understood and respected; when sundry methods or methodologies are employed without careful consideration, incoherence and irrationality can ensue (Hedström, 2005).

Despite this Bryman (2007) notes, again in relation to mixed studies, that "epistemological and ontological issues have been marginalized to a significant extent as pragmatism has emerged as a major orientation to combining quantitative and qualitative research" (p. 17). And a literature review by Kinn and Curzio (2005) into researchers' use of mixed qualitative and quantitative methods concluded that although the combination of approaches is "not always appropriate" (p. 330) strong "enthusiasm amongst researchers" (p. 331) for this activity is apparent.

Researchers who mix methods and/or the methodologies associated with them rarely address the rigour of study forms combined and unreflective scholars may rely on "a 'sense of evidence', or a feeling of plausibility" (Hempel, 1945, p. 8) in deciding whether evidence successfully supports a study's hypothesis (study question/problem), finding(s) or conclusion. The difficulty with this approach is of course that it involves "a confusion of logical and psychological considerations" (ibid., p. 8). Researchers and scholars who accept or reject evidence on the basis of subjective criteria – i.e. criteria that rest on a psychological *sense of evidence* – expose themselves to logical or conceptual confusion. They also ignore, for example, both the directive role that theoretic assumptions play in sensitising researchers to study topics or problems and the influence exerted by theory on the form that investigation and analysis subsequently takes (Cruickshank, 2003b; Achinstein, 2010).

Authorial interests as well as the object and purpose of study inevitably and properly determine the emphasis or balance given to theoretic concerns in research and scholarly papers. However, all research incorporates ontological, epistemological and methodological assumptions (Hammersley, 2005b) and, while the balance given to these elements in explanation varies between reports, no element of this triptych can be disposed of since they are all always 'in play'.

Realists assert that unless researchers are prepared to examine the relationship between philosophy, theory and research practice then their outputs – regardless of clinical, patient or client/user focus – risk lacking robustness. The danger in this approach is, for realists, that more is asked of philosophy and theory than can reasonably be expected. Philosophy and theory then gets in the way of explanation or, worse, they become exclusionary, righteous, sectarian and inward looking whereon, as Seale (1999) warns, the: "Readers of theory may feel immersed in a self sustaining literary fantasy" (p. 87). The opposite danger is that indifference spawns and sustains explanatory muddle. In relation to this study and where research investigates care from a social perspective:

> The view [of social science] I wish to commend presupposes a certain conception of philosophy. So, however irrelevant it may at first appear, a discussion of philosophy is an *essential* part of the argument.
>
> (Winch, 1958, p. 2 – italicisation in original)[3]

The work therefore includes a substantial philosophic and theoretic component and to justify this inclusion I here quote and agree with Margaret Archer's statement that:

> what society is held to be also affects how it is studied. Thus one of the central theses of this book is that any given social ontology has implications for the explanatory methodology which is (and in consistency can be) endorsed.
>
> (Archer, 1995, pp. 2–3)

To conclude this introduction, while more questions than answers are inevitably generated by studies of this sort I would like to think that, in some small way, this book productively furthers the literature on hospice/palliative care *and* contributes to the realist literature.

Notes

1 The study described in this book is a 'collapsed' version of what was, originally, a PhD thesis. Like most such things this object slumbers untouched and not a little dusty in an infrequently visited corner of a university library. Indeed, a £5 note tucked inside the front cover of the thesis remains sadly undisturbed not a few months after it was put there. Snappily titled: *The Theory and Application of Critical Realist Philosophy and*

Morphogenetic Methodology: Emergent Structural and Agential Relations at a Hospice, the thesis can be downloaded from the British Library. However, you do not then get to find the £5! This book also makes use (particularly Chapters 1 and 4) of material originally published elsewhere – notably Lipscomb, 2006a, 2006b, 2008, 2010a and 2010b (see reference list).

2 The descriptors *realist* and *realism* are often employed loosely and this slipshod approach to explanation continues here. Unless otherwise stated these terms refer to the realist philosophies and theories of Roy Bhaskar, Margaret Archer and other 'critical' realists. However, readers should be mindful of the fact that many varieties of realism exist and not all of these take the form described here.

3 Fay (2000) suggests that this quotation echoes sentiments originally expressed by Wittgenstein in *Philosophical Investigations* (1976 [1953]). The citation captures the link between philosophic theory and social scientific practice that Roy Bhaskar and Margaret Archer promote or maintain. Critical realists however would distance themselves from the *certain conception of philosophy* advanced by Winch and Wittgenstein.

2 Margaret Archer's morphogenetic-morphostatic methodology

Critical realist philosophy has, depending on how one defines that thing, a long, complex and circuitous history. However, in recent decades the role played by Roy Bhaskar in bringing this particular form of realism to wide attention cannot be underestimated. Two of Bhaskar's early works, *A Realist Theory of Science* and *The Possibility of Naturalism*, have already been referred to (in the Introduction). And these texts, along with later works, have proven hugely significant. Bhaskar's realism challenged established orthodoxies across a number of disciplines. He kick-started what is now a self-conscious movement in both the humanities and social sciences (Engholm, 1999) and critical realism now inspires work throughout an increasingly varied range of academic fields.

That said Bhaskar presents a philosophy of ontology rather than a methodology for research and researchers who want to 'do' realist research therefore need to find ways of bridging the hiatus or gap that exists between abstract philosophical ideas and practical or manifest methodology. This requirement may irritate those who just want to 'get on with' applying realism. Yet, as Wight notes:

> There is simply no way to move directly from critical realism (as philosophy) to substantive methodological development. The need to engage in in-depth philosophical groundwork can frustrate practicing social scientists, who are keen to employ it in substantive research without getting bogged down in complex philosophical speculation. Yet, the fact that critical realism places ontology at the heart of analysis means that there can be no specification of methods in an ontological vacuum. Critical realism as a philosophy cannot be directly 'plugged' into social research.
>
> (Wight, 2006, p. 33)

Like Wight (ibid.), Carter (2000) similarly claims that any "distinctively *sociological* realism requires some considerable refinement of Bhaskar's *philosophical* naturalism" (p. 65 – italicisation in original) and, to meet this need, realist sociologies owing a considerable debt to Bhaskar have been advanced by authors such as Pawson (1989, 2006), Layder (1990, 1994, 1997), Pawson and Tilley (1997), Sayer (2000), and Danermark *et al.* (2002).

Margaret Archer's morphogenetic-morphostatic methodology is used in this study since it is, arguably, the most developed and nuanced realist methodology currently available. And, yet, in producing work aimed at researchers, Archer understandably fails to describe the philosophic underpinnings or background to her thinking in the detail or at the level that Bhaskar provides. Bhaskar's ideas are therefore introduced at various points throughout this study to clarify and occasionally add to Archer's methodology.

Margaret Archer and realist social theory

Margaret Archer is a major theorist whose "accomplishment cannot be overstated" (Potter, 2003, p. 161). Together with Bhaskar, Collier, Lawson and Norrie, she edits two realist Routledge book series, *Critical Realism: Interventions* and *Studies in Critical Realism.* She is a member of the editorial advisory committee for the *Journal of Critical Realism* and a Trustee of the Centre for Critical Realism. However, Archer's influence and prestige extend far beyond her contribution to realist scholarship. For example, she edited *Current Sociology* (1972–1982), she chaired the International Sociological Association's Publications Committee (1982–1986), she was elected first woman President of the International Sociological Association (1986–1990) and, in 1994, Margaret Archer became a founder member of the Pontifical Academy of Social Sciences and the Academy of Learned Societies in the Social Sciences. A member of the editorial board of the *Journal of Classical Sociology* and Emerita Professor of Sociology at the University of Warwick, in 2011 Archer took up the position of Professor of Social Theory and Directrice du Centre d'Ontologie Sociale at the Ecole Polytechnique de Lausanne. She has been nominated by the British Sociological Association for the prestigious Balzan prize.

This study is informed by Archer's *Realist Social Theory* (1995) and, to a lesser extent, *Culture and Agency* (1996). Other of her books such as *Being Human: The Problem of Agency* (2000), *Structure, Agency and the Internal Conversation* (2003a) and *Making our Way through the World* (2007) are fascinating publications that advance upon and develop the texts used here. However, these more recent works are not integral to this study.

As the title suggests *Realist Social Theory* (1995) is an overtly realist text; indeed, the frontispiece claims it is "the sociological complement of transcendental realism" (which is another way of describing critical realism) and the social theory it advances is "the practical methodological embodiment of the realist social ontology" (p. 16). *Culture and Agency* (1996) is, on the other hand, curiously reticent about acknowledging its antecedents. Bhaskar provides much of the philosophic scaffolding that Archer builds upon in both books. Yet despite Archer's sustained and intimate involvement in the realist movement, Bhaskar's name is absent from the main index of *Culture and Agency* (1996) and realism's significance is not specifically mentioned until page 275 of the revised edition.

Archer's relationship with realism is therefore intriguing. She occasionally uses Bhaskarian terms without clarification,[1] her developed theory evidences input from non-realist sources and, as she acknowledges, realist themes are occasionally introduced in *Realist Social Theory* (1995) without being exploited. For example, Archer follows but does not develop arguments from Bhaskar's *The Possibility of Naturalism* (1998b) when she states that: "In any field of study, the nature of what exists cannot be unrelated to how it is studied. This is a strong realist statement, which I endorse, but cannot explore here" (Archer, 1995, p. 16). Since Archer is, as stated, writing for researchers rather than philosophers, realist concepts such as emergence, stratification, open system explanation and the impossibility of experimental social closure remain relatively underdeveloped in *Realist Social Theory* (1995) and *Culture and Agency* (1996). In consequence, critical realist terminology is occasionally introduced in this work to clarify meaning where Archer points towards but does not necessarily use Bhaskarian nomenclature. It might be suggested that this misrepresents Archer (though, hopefully, this is not the case). However, more pressingly, insofar as these terms may not be familiar to all readers, and to prevent this work from becoming overly bogged down in explanatory digressions, readers are directed to the glossary of terms provided by Danermark *et al.* (2002).

To structure this chapter I begin by offering a short overview or snapshot of morphogenetic-morphostatic methodology. A slightly more leisurely review is then detailed that places Archer's work in a broader socio-historical context. To conclude, key morphogenetic-morphostatic concepts are outlined. These concepts inform and direct data collection and analysis in Chapter 3. They also underpin and give form to the 'results' presented in Chapter 4.

Throughout this and subsequent sections of the book a relatively large number of direct quotations are presented. When overused, citations can be intrusively irksome. However, first, little benefit accrues from précising work where that work is clear and succinct and, second, quotations are deployed here in a protective manner. Morphogenesis can be variously interpreted and this outline will inevitably differ from alternative readings. Reference back to source material is thus one means by which this particular interpretation can be sustained. Lastly, henceforth, when citing *Realist Social Theory* (1995) the abbreviation *RST* is used. *Culture and Agency* (1996) is identified as *CAA*. To avoid painful repetition, publication dates are omitted from references to the main texts (already introduced) by Archer and Bhaskar.

Morphogenetic-morphostatic methodology: an overview

In key respects *Realist Social Theory* and *Culture and Agency* both begin by mirroring the structure of Bhaskar's *A Realist Theory of Science* and *The Possibility of Naturalism*. All of these books commence by debunking the direction and implications of non-realist theory and, in this process, Archer is, like Bhaskar, concerned with, among other things, the nature of causal reasoning in social explanation. To this end *Realist Social Theory* begins by lambasting alternative types of social inquiry. These 'types' and their critique are described as being "identical" (*RST*, p. 139) with the models of explanation found in Bhaskar's

The Possibility of Naturalism and Archer therefore recognises and opposes epiphenomenal and elisionary social theories.

Epiphenomenalism exists, Archer suggests, in two forms. Top down epiphenomenal models describe theories that overly emphasise social structure at the expense of agency. These models discount the ability of agents (individuals or groups) to change or affect social structures and, for theorists operating under top down assumptions, structure is paramount. Bottom up epiphenomenal models on the other hand reduce society to the activities of agents (generally individuals) and, from this perspective, society is merely the aggregate outcome or epiphenomena of agential behaviours. Elisionary models in contrast are proposed by theorists who recognise inherent deficiencies in epiphenomenal explanation but who, in an attempt to overcome these deficiencies, simply elide or collapse both approaches. Elisionists therefore combine the weaknesses of top down and bottom up epiphenomenal forms. They do not however surmount them (Lipscomb, 2006b).

To avoid epiphenomenalism and elisionism Archer brings together Lockwood's (1964) concept of analytic dualism with critical realist philosophy to produce, following Buckley's (1967) terminology, the morphogenetic-morphostatic model of social interaction. For Archer, the morphogenetic-morphostatic model (morphogenesis or morphogenetic theory) clothes or gives practical form to realist social ontology and, in making this move, analytic dualism is "the basis of the morphogenetic approach" (*RST*, p. 165).

Analytic dualism treats structure (cultural and social[2]) and agents as distinct entities. This enables Archer to argue that sociological description need not privilege the causal significance of either society's 'parts' or 'people' on a priori grounds (i.e. neither takes precedence in social explanation). In contrast to epiphenomenal and elisionist theories, morphogenesis emphasises and makes use of the "explanatory power" (*RST*, p. 171) that derives from dealing separately with society's features. Moreover, Archer maintains that ontological substance accompanies and is implicit in these analytic divisions so that, rather than being simply heuristic devices, the things described possess discrete essences – i.e. they exist (though Engholm, 1999, for example, disagrees).

Notwithstanding the emphasis placed upon Lockwood by Archer, it may be argued that he is unnecessary to morphogenesis since analytic dualism (his contribution) is, as Archer acknowledges, presupposed within critical realism where "separability is indispensable to realism" (*RST*, p. 70). Nevertheless, ignoring this quibble, the centrality of analytic dualism and critical realism is apparent in the two founding principles of morphogenetic-morphostatic methodology; namely – first, that "structure necessarily pre-dates the action(s) leading to its reproduction or transformation [and second] that structural elaboration necessarily post-dates the action sequences which give rise to it" (*RST*, p. 15).[3] It could at this point be suggested that recognising the historical pre-existence of structure inadvertently undercuts analytic dualism by downgrading agency. However, the *sui generis* emergent powers that are inherent in agents (i.e. the ability of, for example, people to exercise free will and escape structural constraints) preclude determinism and Archer would not therefore countenance this objection.

In their developed form (to be discussed) these two principles sustain a three part explanatory cycle, i.e. "structural conditioning → social interaction → structural elaboration" (*RST*, p. 16). Analogues of this 'cycle' exist for social and cultural structures, as well as primary and corporate forms of agency (these terms are defined later in this chapter). And, as will be described, this cycle generates or underpins as its final product a narrative or "analytical *history* of emergence" (*RST*, p. 91 – italicisation in original).

Several key realist and analytically dualist themes are suggested or introduced by these cycles that enable mophogenetic theory to evade explanatory conflation while, simultaneously, recognising the stratified, open and nomic[4] nature of social reality and causation. For example, temporality, which is a core or intrinsic element in critical realist philosophy (Dean *et al.*, 2006a) "is incorporated as sequential tracts and phases rather than simply as a medium through which events take place" (*RST*, p. 89). And it is thus in or through the medium of time that distinct processes of generative activity and their elaborative "emergent consequences" (*RST*, p. 62) happen or function. Similarly, analytic dualism is necessary to the idea that structural or agential histories can be told apart from the entities they interact and overlap with and, in consequence, morphogenetic-morphostatic theory makes it possible for researchers to theorise about the differential morphogenesis (genesis = birth, origin, source or change) or morphostasis (stasis = standing still or non-change) occurring between structures and agents over time.

Another way of describing this is that agential or cultural- or socio-structural developments need not take place synchronously (i.e. at the same time). Thus cultural- or socio-structural as well as agential change (or non-change) may occur in any order and at any pace. This form of causal reasoning, this form of explanation, is denied to epiphenomenalists and it is extremely problematic for elisionists. It can only comfortably be accommodated by emergentist theories such as that proposed by Archer.

Emergence is a hotly disputed concept in philosophy and it is often counterpoised against or alongside supervenience or supervening theories in, for example, discussions about the nature and form of group agency (e.g. List and Pettit, 2011). Emergence is also a key realist concept. For critical realists emergence occurs when new objects are created or develop from pre-existing objects and these new objects are known or recognised by their effects – i.e. they are known or are knowable insofar as they evidence novel "structures, powers and mechanisms" (Danermark *et al.*, 2002, p. 205).

Emergence cannot be countenanced by upward conflationists or bottom up epiphenomenalists (individualists) since they are committed both to rebutting the suggestion that structure may in some instances be unaffected by agential change as well as the assumption that structural change could precede or promote agential change. This perspective on the nature of social reality cannot accept these possibilities because society and its structures are, for bottom up epiphenomenalists, simply a reflection of agential activity (structure is not granted *sui generis* status). Alternatively, downward conflationists (top down epiphenomenalists or collectivists) discard the idea that agents may be unaffected by structural developments since agents, as anonymous *träger*, from this perspective merely instantiate and objectify structure. Elisionists, who by definition conjoin or merge structure with agency, effectively deny the possibility that their interplay can be separately investigated or differentially described, for, if that was possible, why elide them?

Morphogenesis develops critical realist social theory and philosophy in three ways. First, it elaborates upon and updates Bhaskar's critique of non-realist social theory (e.g. by redirecting Bhaskar's attack upon elisionism towards Anthony Giddens). Second, it exposes and improves upon deficiencies in Bhaskar's Transformation Model of Social Activity (developed in *The Possibility of Naturalism*) as well as a later version of this model in *Reclaiming Reality* (Bhaskar, 1989). Third, while accepting realist arguments concerning emergence, openness and the impossibility of prediction, Archer outlines the beginning of a practical methodology for use. She therefore emphasises society's potential comprehensibility and the feasibility of explanation.

Morphogenetic theory: socio-historical context

Archer couples claims that social explanation inevitably involves ontological and epistemological assumptions with the idea that methodological theory (the means by which such issues are made concrete) must usefully guide research practice if it is to be of genuine value. Indeed, "methodology, broadly conceived of as an explanatory programme, is the necessary link between social ontology and practical theory" (*RST*, p. 5). Archer follows Bhaskar in arguing that abstract theories about what is admissible in or for explanation are ineffectual unless they can fruitfully inform research so that more accurate accounts of reality are developed (progress being an aspirational objective rather than a guaranteed outcome) and theory is therefore purposeful: "It is never an end in itself but a tool for the working social analyst which gives explanatory purchase on substantive social problems, through supplying the terms or framework for their investigation" (*RST*, pp. 12–13). Indeed:

> Social theory has to be useful and usable. The vexatious fact of society has to be tackled *in* and *for* practice. These two tasks cannot be separated, for were practical utility to be the sole criterion we would commit ourselves to instrumentalism – to working with theoretically ungrounded rules of thumb. Conversely, a purely theoretical taming of the vexing beast may give a warm inner glow of ontological rectitude but is cold comfort to practical social analysts.
>
> (*RST*, 1995, p. 135 – italicisation in original)

Archer therefore sketches in *Realist Social Theory* and, to a lesser extent, *Culture and Agency*, a methodology for practical social theorising. She acknowledges that her work "remains at a high level of theoretical abstraction and at certain points becomes purely speculative for want of appropriate data" (*CAA*, p. xxviii). Morphogenesis, presented in *Realist Social Theory*, therefore describes orientating principles for social research. It is *about* method but it is not *a* method (New, 2001). And, as will be seen, abstractness and the provisional nature of realist social theory mean that Archer's work is susceptible to criticism. Nevertheless, morphogenesis provides researchers with some basic guidance – if not a detailed map – to help them proceed and hers is therefore a work (to borrow from a rival theoretician):

> about 'method' in the sense in which Durkheim used it in his *Rules of Sociological Method.* That is to say, it is not a guide to 'how to do practical research', and does not offer any specific research proposals. It is primarily an exercise in clarification of logical issues.
>
> (Giddens, 1976, p. 8)

Archer is contrite in acknowledging that realist theory is underdeveloped, "a mess [with] few worthwhile offerings" (*RST*, p. 136). And while much has changed since she penned these words her response to underdevelopment is that the "only thing to do is admit it, confront it, and hope to do something about it" (*RST*, p. 136). As part of this response she emphasises that social explanation's theoretical underpinnings must be acknowledged head-on.

> no social theory can be advanced without making some assumptions about what kind of reality it is dealing with and how to explain it. All social theory is ontologically shaped and methodologically moulded even if these processes remain covert and scarcely acknowledged by the practitioner.
>
> (*RST*, pp. 57–58)

Social reality ought therefore "to regulate how we explain it" (*RST*, p. 21) and Archer agrees with Bhaskar that "what social reality is held to be cannot but influence how society is studied [since] there is always a connection between social ontology and explanatory methodology" (*RST*, p. 13). Ontology, epistemology and methodology are thus mutually implicative. ("An ontology without a methodology is deaf and dumb; a methodology without an ontology is blind", *RST*, p. 28 – the aphorism is Kant's). However, within this triptych ontology dominates. Primacy emanates from ontology's ability to regulate and "govern *those concepts which are deemed admissible* in explanation as in description" (*RST*, p. 20 – italicisation in original). It is "both gatekeeper and bouncer for methodology" (*RST*, p. 22).

Archer's focus on ontology (here the nature of 'being' or existence in the social realm) as well as ontology's relationship with epistemology and methodology plays out in her critique of individualist and collectivist forms of epiphenomenalism as well as elisionism. For Sawyer (2002), the debate between individual and collectively orientated perspectives "occurs at two levels: an ontological level, concerning arguments about what entities and properties exist in the world, and a methodological or epistemological level, concerning the proper way to proceed in scientific practice" (p. 537). Archer engages with both of these levels. Yet whereas Bhaskar begins *A Realist Theory of Science* and *The Possibility of Naturalism* with a frontal assault upon the legacy of Hume and Kant, Archer commences her critique (in *Realist Social Theory*) by introducing the work of Alexander *et al.* (1987). This is not however a radical departure for it permits her to stick with familiar Bhaskarian themes.

She suggests (following Alexander *et al.*, ibid.) that debates within social science about society and the individual, voluntarism versus determinism, micro-macro levels of analysis and/or structure and agency, can *all* be understood or explained as re-descriptions of a fundamentally similar problem, namely: the persistent and tenacious conflict between individualistic and collectivist theories. Archer thus trails Bhaskar in critiquing those forms of social causal reasoning that *The Possibility of Naturalism* describes as Humean or Durkheimian collectivist or downwards conflationary and Kantian or Weberian individualist or upwards conflationary. The essential 'problem' with both variants is, as has been stated, that: "In the heritage of Individualism it was 'structure' which became the inert and dependent element, whilst Collectivism fostered instead the subordination or neglect of 'agency'" (*RST*, p. 33). Obvious difficulties accompany the collapse or reduction of different and nuanced non-realist theories into a simple and possibly simplistic opposition (i.e. individualism vs collectivism) and distortion by generalisation is an ever present danger when this sort of 'collapse' takes place. Nonetheless, differentiating between ideational protagonists in this way enables Archer to assert, following Bhaskar, that it is an uncritical "rooting in empiricism" (*RST*, p. 8) which ultimately grounds and bedevils, by realist criteria, the historic failure of both epiphenomenal traditions. Thus while UK theorists discussed and wrangled over the problem of structure and agency, and North Americans scrutinised scope or micro-macro sociology, "it is empiricism which bedevils both standpoints" (*RST*, p. 28). Accordingly, empiricism or the supposed need to base explanation in observables (behaviour or speech) provided:

> individualists with their trump card (for who could doubt the existence of flesh-and-blood people) and the collectivists with their stumbling block (since how could they validate the existence of any property unless they could translate it into a series of observational statements about people). The American debate was even more unabashed in its positivism, since its defining terms, the 'micro-' and the 'macro-' necessarily dealt only with an observable property, that is *size*.
>
> (*RST*, p. 8 – italicisation in original)

Archer instead argues that this micro-macro distinction (and by analogy the agency-structure debate) is more usefully and 'correctly' conceptualised in terms of *relations* rather than *bulk*. However, before outlining the role of relational theorising in morphogenetic methodology, the historical significance of the absence of this dynamic within epiphenomenal and elisionary reasoning is re-emphasised.

Archer argues that individualist and idealist social methodological theories or approaches (e.g. approaches associated with phenomenology and/or hermeneutics) fail adequately to address and therefore underestimate – indeed, they frequently ignore – the enabling possibilities and constraining realities that society and its structures generate for agents. Thus despite protestations to the contrary, theorists with individualist and/or idealist orientations are prone to minimise or overlook the significance and influence of exterior structural (social or cultural) factors when describing concrete or real-world micro interactions and 'understandings'. Downplaying the impact of structural factors in social explanation allows and encourages agency to assume unwarranted freedoms. This occurs, Archer suggests, because individualist theories erroneously privilege or accentuate the demonstrably objective and empirically verifiable nature of face-to-face interactions that occur between small groups of people. And although morphogenetic-morphostatic methodology provides scant guidance as to how particular interpretations of reality and abstract social theory are to be reconciled, it is important that researchers avoid or are wary of over-emphasising personal (respondent) understandings in explanation for, as Archer notes:

> To the social realist there is no 'isolated' micro world – no *lebsenswelt* 'insulated' from the socio-cultural system in the sense of being uncontrolled by it, nor a hermetically sealed domain whose day-to-day doings are guaranteed to be of no systemic 'import'.
>
> (*RST*, p. 10 – italicisation in original)

Structuralists and collectivists are also scolded by Archer for failing to draw the appropriate ontological conclusion which – if "a causal criterion of existence is acceptable" (*RST*, p. 23) – their explanations permit. Archer thus asserts that, historically, theorists such as Mandelbaum (1959) and Gellner (1968) correctly recognised and identified links between causation and ontological veracity as well as the role that emergence plays in this process. However, at the time when they wrote, the "framework of empiricism" (*RST*, p. 50) created a "brick wall" (*RST*, p. 52) since non-observables, which collectivists accurately identified as influencing social life, could not "be 'pointed to' in the sense in which we can point to material or organic objects, or to their qualities or activities" (*RST*, p. 52). Structural explanations therefore failed to meet empiric criteria for existence/acceptability.

Mirroring Bhaskar's argument, Archer asserts that what had yet to be discerned was that agreeing to "play a purely methodological game according to Humean rules undermines the Collectivist programme" (*RST*, p. 55) because, for "most of the time, in open social systems, regularities at the level of events are just what emergent features do not generate" (*RST*, p. 54). Disagreement between individualist or idealist and structural or collectivist perspectives were, however, both then and now, often sidestepped or hidden and the "unsatisfactory" (*RST*, p. 58) nature of social theory often bypassed researchers who continued in:

> a state of inarticulate unawareness … at one extreme interpretive sociologists undertook small-scale interactional studies and simply placed a big etc. after them, implying that the compilation of enough sensitive ethnographies would generate an understanding of society by aggregation. At the other, large scale multivariate analysis pressed on towards some predictive goal without reference to the interactional processes generating their variables.
>
> (*RST*, p. 58)

This is an important and powerful statement and the claims presented here remain, I suggest, applicable and pertinent to many researchers currently involved in health and social care. Thus the generators of small scale interpretative studies presumably imagine that they are in some way contributing to a larger edifice of understanding; for, if this was not the case, then their outputs must be considered unique and isolated productions of questionable use or informative value. On the other hand, the creators of big empiric quantitative works continue to sidestep serious engagement with the complex processes and mechanisms which at a 'deep' level influence and steer the reductive observations that they map. And, despite the development of various elisionisms (described below), traditional approaches to understanding – approaches often crudely juxtaposed as qualitative vs quantitative – frequently continue without reference to or acknowledgement of 'the other' or its challenge.

Archer does not examine in any substantive sense why the *state of inarticulate unawareness* that she identifies had to end. However, having outlined the historical forms taken by antagonistic epiphenomenalisms, she proposes that "idealist" (*RST*, p. 60) neo-phenomenological and symbolic interactionists, by merging structure with agency, were the first to attempt to surmount or dodge the limitations associated with traditional individualist and collectivist approaches. Subsequently, "mutual constitution" (*RST*, p. 60) or conflation developed in the sociological literature until it became a "distinctive theoretical orientation" (*RST*, p. 60) and, for Archer, Giddens's (1976) Structuration Theory represents what might be termed the apogee of this type of elisionist thinking.

For Bhaskar, Peter Berger and his associates (e.g. Berger and Luckman, 1991) personified elisionist social explanation. Archer acknowledges Berger's influence. However, she primarily critiques elisionism through an attack on Structuration Theory which, she asserts, illegitimately conjoins structure and agency to preclude "examination of their interplay, of the effects of one upon the other and of any statement about their relative contribution to stability and change at any given time" (*RST*, p. 14). Structuration Theory is, Archer claims, falsely premised on the idea that language is or can be used as a valid metaphor for society and, just as Bhaskar criticised Winch (1958, 1970) for perpetrating what he defined as the linguistic fallacy, so Archer lambasts Giddens for committing an essentially identical offence. Thus having justifiably and correctly noted that "many elements of syntax are mutually implicative" (*RST*, p. 95), Structuration Theory illicitly, in Archer's view, over-eggs the linguistic metaphor to assert that within society "every aspect of 'structure' is held to be activity-dependent in the present tense and equally open to transformation, and [thus the] causal efficacy of structure is dependent upon its evocation by agency" (*RST*, p. 60). Structuration Theory is equated by Archer with the "phonological revolution" (*CAA*, p. 43) which, in her opinion, denies analytic dualism by discounting the separateness and temporal autonomy of structure and agency: "Because 'structure' is inseparable from 'agency' then, *there is no sense in which it can be either emergent or autonomous or pre-existant or causally influential*" (*RST*, p. 97 – italicisation in original). Archer argues that elisionist theories of one sort or another gained in popularity because their adherents naively believed that, in taking this approach to social explanation, they thereby circumvented or sidestepped the now passé "old debate" (*RST*, p. 61) between individualism and collectivism. However, while elisionists correctly realised that epiphenomenalism was inadequate and misguided, they were mistaken in their remedial prescription and, just as sociologists once had to choose between individualism and collectivism so, today, those engaged in social explanation must continue to take sides in a battle between two distinct and competitive world views:

> 'Elision' (the term used for those grouping themselves around Structuration theory) and 'Emergence' (those exploring the interface between transcendental realism and social theory) are based upon different ontological conceptions, related to disparate methodological injunctions and thus have quite distinct implications for practical social theorizing.
>
> (*RST*, pp. 60–61)

Morphogenetic-morphostatic methodology: key concepts

In *Realist Social Theory* Archer acknowledges that Bhaskar is the primary influence on developed morphogenetic-morphostatic methodology. She states that Bhaskar's "ontological realism, premised explicitly upon emergence, is used to develop the framework of a social theory which seems set fair to navigate a passage between Individualism and Holism" (*RST*, p. 136). She also notes that Bhaskar's Transformational Model of Social Activity and morphogenetic-morphostatic methodology are in "objective and approach very close indeed" (*RST*, p. 137).[5] That said, Archer recognises that Bhaskar's work can be variously interpreted;[6] she acknowledges the existence of non-Bhaskarian ideas in morphogenetic theory and unacknowledged influences may also be discernable.[7]

An alternative to size orientated assumptions concerning the micro-macro metaphor was, as noted, advanced by Alexander *et al.* (1987) and this edited work contains an influential review by Münch and Smelser (1987). This review positions micro-macro descriptors as relational distinctions that are "analytic rather than concrete" (ibid., p. 357) and Archer makes considerable use of this distinction. She interprets it as applying equally to the agency-structure debate and its significance, for her, is that if micro-macro or agency-structure links are relational then actual group or unit size becomes immaterial. Defining these concepts in relational terms complements critical realist attempts to explain interaction within and between emergent strata. It is a viewpoint which does not assume "that observable differences in the size of groups automatically means that they constitute distinct levels of social reality" (*RST*, p. 9) and it allows for forms of explanation wherein "a given stratum can be 'micro' to another and 'macro' to a third" (*RST*, p. 9).

Archer asserts "complete agreement" (*RST*, p. 9) with Alexander *et al.* (1987) that there "can be no empirical referents for micro or macro as such. They are analytical contrasts, suggesting emergent levels within empirical units, not antagonistic empirical units themselves" (*RST*, p. 9). From this, Archer concludes that relational descriptors rely upon or are authorised by the existence of emergent properties that are size independent. Further, these properties, normically expressed as tendencies rather than invariant happenings, possess relational components which are "internal and necessary" (*RST*, p. 173) albeit that external and contingent relations may also influence each other "reciprocally or asymmetrically" (*RST*, p. 174).

Morphogenesis, in contrast to elisionist and epiphenomenalist theory, therefore uses relational metaphors to explore the temporal interplay of links between and within agency and structure (or the micro and the macro). This exploration involves the examination of specific historical interactions and Archer thereby avoids "*sinking*" (*RST*, p. 65 – italicisation in original) either element – parts or people – into the other (Lipscomb, 2006b). More formally she follows Lockwood (1964) in analytically distinguishing social from system integration to differentiate "the orderly or conflictual relations maintaining between groups of actors from the orderly or conflictual relations prevailing between parts of the social structure" (*RST*, p. 67). Analytic dualism, thus defined, allows Archer, contra Giddens, to untie structure from agency so that their respective emergent powers or tendencies can be identified and examined.[8] She grants structure an ontological status that is distinct from agency. However, to support this position Archer must demonstrate how structures can be identified "independently of their occupants and incumbents, yet of showing its effects upon them (establishing the reality of structures via the causal criterion)" (*RST*, p. 167) and, to this end, morphogenesis amalgamates critical realist ideas about emergence, temporality (interplay), reason as cause and proofs of existence by effect.

Moreover, Archer claims that while cultural and social structures differ from each other, serendipitously, they each "raise identical difficulties and the method by which these can be resolved turns out to be exactly the same" (*CAA*, p. xi). This alleged homogeneity allows Archer to model cultural and social structure using the same descriptive morphogenetic sequences. In this process Archer emphasises that:

> *all* structural influences (i.e. the generative powers of SEPs [structural emergent properties] and CEPs [culturally emergent properties]) work through shaping the situations in which people find themselves. It is the situations to which people respond which are mediatory because they condition (without determining) different courses of action for those differentially placed, by supplying different reasons to them. This is the basic manner in which I conceive of the mediation of the tendential powers inherent in material and ideational structures to agents, who, in their turn, represent necessary mediators if structural powers are to be realized.
>
> (*RST*, p. 201 – italicisation in original)

To demonstrate how structural influences *work through* the situations in which agents operate, the ontological status and place in morphogenetic methodology of structure (social and cultural) and positioned agency (individual and group) is now explored and their respective morphogenetic-morphostatic sequences and propositional models are described.

Analytic dualism and the relational yet contingent nature of emergence are modelled through the 'morphogenetic sequence'. Figure 2.1 (below) illustrates this sequence as a three stage orderly progression that begins at T^1 (T=time) with pre-existent social structures (SS) that constrain and enable but do not determine the social interaction (SI) of agents who evidence between T^2 and T^3 independent emergent properties which, at T^4, transform and elaborate (morphogenesis) or reproduce (morphostasis) but never create *ex nihilo* the structures that initially confronted them at T^1.[9]

Describing a complete cycle – i.e. T^1 to T^4 – articulates an analytic history and, at the end of this history, T^4 (of history 1) becomes T^1 for a successor (history 2) cycle. A double morphogenesis of structure and agency is narrated by analytic histories in which all components (parts and people) "*emerge*, *intertwine* and *redefine* one another" (*RST*, p. 76 – italicisation in original) and, importantly, the concept of double morphogenesis denies or rejects the idea that structures and/or agents need maintain stable identities. Indeed, morphogenesis accepts that the objects of study (structures and agents) not only may but often will alter through time and thus:

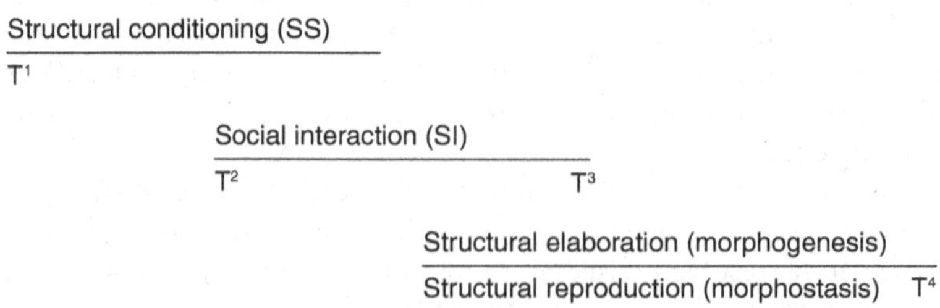

Figure 2.1 Social structure and the morphogenetic-morphostatic sequence (source: adapted from *RST*, pp. 157 and 193).

> at the end of a transformational [double morphogenetic] sequence, not only is structure transformed, but so is agency as part and parcel of the same process. As it re-shapes structure, agency is ineluctably reshaping itself, in terms of organization, combination and articulation, in terms of its powers and these in relation to other agents.
>
> (*RST*, p. 74)

Historically, social structures at T^1 are the product of innumerable past sequences of antecedent agential and structural interactions each of which was, in turn, the product of still earlier analytic cycles. In the present tense social structures (at T^1) precede and shape the situations in which agents are located and the ontological status of these structures (i.e. the proof of their reality) is demonstrated through the emergent causal powers that they evidence in providing or suggesting *interests* to agents. Social structures thus have powers which are unattributable to the actions of current agents[10] and Archer claims these are identifiable: "because of their irreducible character, autonomous influence and relatively enduring character this means that they pre-date any particular cohort of occupants/encumbants" (*RST*, p. 168). Structure thus provides agents (individuals and groups) with interests (i.e. "frustrating or rewarding contexts", *RST*, p. 90) in relation to the social roles or positions that they occupy.[11] Social interaction (occurring between T^2 to T^3) is thereby structurally conditioned. However, the possession by agents of emergent volitional properties (crudely 'free will') means actions are "never structurally determined" (*RST*, p. 90).

Interests, which provide *reasons* for actions, can be variously interpreted by agents. There is no requirement that interests generate 'singular', homogenous, consistent or even logical responses and they can initiate "action patterns" (*RST*, p. 90) aimed at change or entrenchment that may be explained but never predicted.[12] Thus, as both Bhaskar and Archer make clear, augury is inappropriate in open social systems where emergent powers are instantiated as interacting tendencies and, for example, deliberate attempts by agents to maintain or reform structures are frequently unlikely to meet individual or group expectations. Indeed, the outcome of structural elaboration is generally "unintended" (*RST*, p. 91).

Social structures describe or capture relations pertaining between stratified or differentiated classes, ethnic groupings, occupational roles and societal positions as well as relations between organisations/institutions.[13] And although agential interaction can modify or maintain structure, interaction does not, to repeat, create structure. Pulling this all together, Archer's propositional social structure/ social interactional model (2.1) is detailed below. As will be seen, this model mirrors that proposed for cultural structures and socio-cultural interaction.

In *Culture and Agency* Archer argues that social structures are better understood than their cultural counterparts and, accepting this claim, more attention is given here (and again later in Chapter 5) to the description of culture as structure. As can be seen (Figure 2.2 below) the morphogenetic-morphostatic sequence for cultural structure (defined as the cultural system or CS) and agential

- i there are internal and necessary relations within and between social structures (SS);
- ii causal influences are exerted by social structure(s) (SS) on social interaction (SI);
- iii there are causal relationships between groups and individuals at the level of social interaction (SI);
- iv social interaction (SI) elaborates upon the composition of social structure(s) (SS) by modifying current internal and necessary structural relationships and introducing new ones where morphogenesis is concerned. Alternatively, social interaction (SI) reproduces existing internal and necessary structural relations when morphostasis applies.

Model 2.1 The propositional model of social structure (SS) and social interaction (SI) interaction (source: *RST*, pp. 168–169).

socio-cultural (S-C) interaction exactly reflects that depicting the morphogenetic sequence outline above (i.e. the T^1 to T^4 SS/SI cycle already described). Similarly, cultural system socio-cultural interaction (CS/S-C) interplay gives rise to propositional model 2.2 that mirrors its SS/SI counterpart.

To sustain the ontological distinctness of cultural structure, Archer offers a very particular definition of culture that distinguishes culture in total (i.e. everything that might be understood) from the cultural system which describes that part of total culture that has been or is capable of translation into propositional statements. Here Archer follows Bhaskar in viewing ideas in the cultural system as

- i there are internal and necessary logical relationships between components of the Cultural System (CS);
- ii causal influences are exerted by the Cultural System (CS) on Socio-Cultural interaction (the S-C level);
- iii there are causal relationships between groups and individuals at the Socio-Cultural (S-C) level;
- iv there is elaboration of the Cultural System (CS) due to Socio-Cultural interaction (S-C) modifying current logical relationships and introducing new ones, where morphogenesis is concerned. Alternatively, Socio-Cultural interaction (S-C) reproduces existing internal and necessary cultural relationships when morphostasis applies.

Model 2.2 The propositional model of cultural structure/conditioning (CS) and socio-cultural (S-C) interaction (source: *RST*, p. 169).[14]

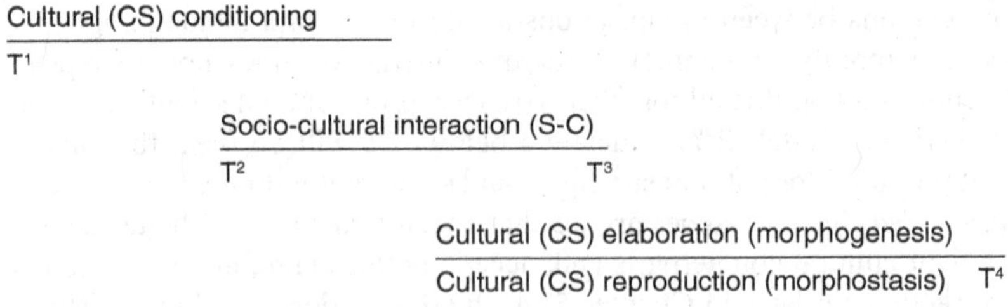

Figure 2.2 Cultural System/structures (CS) and the morphogenetic-morphostatic sequence (source: adapted from *RST*, p. 193).

"essentially specific *forms* of the material world, or [as being] qualitatively specific material social entities in their own right" (Dean *et al.*, 2006a, p. 3 – italicisation in original). And, significantly, culture is not therefore "understood in its conventional sense as something that expresses the identity of a community" (Carter, 2000, pp. 22–23), but rather:

> culture as a whole is taken to refer to all intelligibilia, that is to any item which has the dispositional capacity of being understood by someone. Within this I then distinguish the Cultural System, which is that sub-set of items to which the law of contradiction can be applied. These are propositions, for only statements which assert truth or falsity can be deemed to be in contradiction or to be consistent with one another. In turn this means that the Cultural System is restricted to the propositional register of society at any given time. The justification for defining the CS in this way rests partly on the fact that it meets the criterion of methodological workability, but partly, too, on the self-evident importance of those things held to be true or false in society at any given time and place.
>
> (*CAA*, p. xviii)

By justifying her definition of the cultural system, in part, upon the grounds of *methodological workability*, Archer might be accused of allowing pragmatism (contrary to assertions elsewhere – e.g. *RST*, p. 135) to usurp ontological theory. However, Archer can equally be complimented for attempting to clarify the meaning of descriptors such as 'culture' where many other theorists abrogate precision. Moreover, she is aware of the limitations surrounding this definition and the model within which it sits.

> Obviously we do not live by propositions alone (any more than we live logically); in addition, we generate myths, are moved by mysteries, become rich in symbolics and ruthless in manipulating hidden persuaders. But all of these elements are precisely the stuff of Socio-Cultural interaction. For they are all matters of interpersonal influence, whether we are talking at one extreme of hermeneutic understanding (including religious experience at the furthest extremity) or of the manipulative assault and battery of ideas used ideologically. All those other non-propositional things to which we assent or over which we dissent – such as tastes and preferences, likes and dislikes, affinities and animosities, patriotism and prejudice – lie in between.
>
> (*CAA*, pp. xviii–xix)

Morphogenesis thus focuses predominantly upon the interplay of ideas within the cultural system rather than culture as *all intelligibilia*. And in this capacity it may be noted that Archer associates culture with interlinked Bhaskarian themes concerning the relation between transitive and intransitive forms of knowledge, the idea that knowledge is produced from knowledge-like antecedents and proof of emergence by effect.

> If we think of culture then all knowledge was certainly activity dependent for its genesis and elaboration. Nevertheless, once recorded it constitutes knowledge without a current knowing subject. It is knowledge because it retains the dispositional character to be understood, though it persists unrecognized, sustaining potential powers (of contradiction and complementarity with other cultural items) which remain unexercised. *Ontologically it exists* and if the theory it states is true, if the technique it describes works, or if the belief it articulates is justifiable, these remain the case quite independently of current actors knowing it, using it or believing it. We know that they are real by virtue of their realisable effects.
>
> (*RST*, p. 144 – italicisation added)

In this statement Archer possibly conflates knowledge with true or justifiable knowledge, a position that problematises the ontological status of factually erroneous or unvalidated knowledge claims/beliefs vis-à-vis agential action. Nevertheless, despite this caveat, Archer here advances major claims for the ontological substance and power of the cultural system, propositionally expressed, to inform sociological enquiry. Specifically, Archer argues that cultural system propositions coexist within a matrix of four ideal logical relations which generate, for agents, as role and position occupants, a series of interest bearing situational logics. This matrix of logical relations and the situated logics (influences) they generate/articulate is integral to the claim that the cultural system 'register' pre-exists agency's ability to transform or reproduce it.

Table 2.1 lists the structural relationships (cultural system and social structures – CS and SS) that, Archer claims, pertain at T^1 as well as the situated logics that they present to agents as interests in socio-cultural and social interactions (S-C and SI) between T^2 and T^3. And, importantly, if cultural and social structural (CS/SS) logical relationships exist then they exist *regardless* of whether agents recognise, adopt, make use of or misuse them. Agents are thus free to

Table 2.1 Cultural Emergent Properties (CEP) and Structural Emergent Properties (SEP) – logical relations and situational logics

	Contradictions		*Complementarities*	
	Necessary	*Contingent*	*Necessary*	*Contingent*
(Situational logic)	(Correction)	(Elimination)	(Protection)	(Opportunism)
CEP				
CS level	Syncretism	Pluralism	Systematisation	Specialisation
S-C level	Unification	Cleavage	Reproduction	Sectionalism
SEP				
SS level	Compromise	Competition	Integration	Differentiation
SI level	Containment	Polarisation	Solidarity	Diversification

(Source: adapted from *RST*, p. 303).

identify or not-identify, observe or ignore the interests inherent in situational logics. However, exercise of this freedom carries a price since failure to identify or meet the expectations that interests describe, for whatever reason, potentially incurs material penalties.

Each of the four relations of contradiction and complementarity that give rise to agentially situated logics is hereafter explained in turn. To avoid duplication only CS/S-C level interaction is described and the process is not repeated for SS/SI relations or logics (overt similarities in cultural- and socio-structural modelling make duplication unnecessary). Importantly, Archer recognises that concrete instances of the relationships detailed in Table 2.1 will be complex and, in reality, ambiguous; nevertheless, she asserts that the schema presented above provides ontologically existent if idealised illustrations of relations between propositional and agentially situated logics.

Sketched exemplars of the four permutations are now outlined. In these examples the same descriptors (*A* and *B*) are used to signify both cultural system (CS) propositional sets and their sponsoring socio-cultural (S-C) group interactions. As will be seen in Chapters 3 and 4, cultural and structural emergent properties (logical and situated relations) play a key part in describing and explaining changing external relationships between the hospice and what were perceived to be hostile institutions as well as internally between 'factions' within the study site.

Necessary complementarities describe situated logics of *protection*. In such instances it is supposed that agents who advance cultural system proposition (belief, theory, idea or idea set) *A* within the socio-cultural realm also and inevitably invoke proposition *B*. Further, it is assumed that *B* reproduces, reinforces or promotes *A*. Supporters of *A* and *B* therefore have no reason to contradict or hinder each other (indeed they can become over time a single or unitary group) and a protective, supportive or defensive association may develop between the two agential groups as well as the ideational sets (propositions) in question (i.e. distinct propositional sets may become enmeshed and arguments may be erected against their mutual corruption). This cosy environment is not an unalloyed benefit, however, since protection deters critical and challenging debate and agential and propositional positions may thus become entrenched, embedded and incapable of reform or development.

Necessary contradictions, on the other hand, describe situated logics of *correction*. In this instance, rather than reciprocal support, it is supposed that agential groups with (potentially) differing political or social power hold mutually implicative and co-dependent but disputational cultural system (CS) propositions that are at variance (so bringing either CS proposition into play necessarily implicates the co-dependent other). Thus, for example, if proposition *B* is supported by politically more powerful individuals or groups than *A* and if in advancing the politically weaker proposition (*A*) the contradictory other is inevitably invoked, then, in consequence, individuals or groups holding and advancing *A* will seek syncretism at the cultural system level and unification at the socio-cultural level. Initially, though not necessarily subsequently, unification will be attempted in regard to either or both ideational sets by group *A* (assuming that neither individual or group is willing simply to concede the field). However, as described, this is not a 'fair' fight and syncretism will be variously contested according to the cultural and material resources that each group can martial within the socio-cultural realm. Three options are available for the groups involved and, as will be noted, the outcome of each option differentially favours the advocates of each propositional set. The available options are:

1 $A \leftarrow B$, i.e. correcting *B* so that it becomes consistent with *A*.
2 $A \leftrightarrow B$, i.e. correcting both *A* and *B* so they become mutually consistent.
3 $A \rightarrow B$, i.e. correcting *A* so that it becomes consistent with *B*.

(*RST*, p. 233 – adapted)

Contingent contradictions are associated with the situated logic of *elimination*. Here the logical relation is that of doctrinal incompatibility between mutually oppositional propositional sets. In this instance co-dependence is absent and relations between agents whose interests orientate them to 'take up' the antagonistic propositional sets are, whatever their relative political powers in the socio-cultural realm, anti-syncretic and incommensurable. Rejecting syncretism, agents in socio-cultural interaction become and remain hostile towards each other. Combative parties now have everything to gain and nothing to lose from engaging in activities that seek to annihilate their opponents in argument or otherwise. However, in this process, even if it is assumed that advocates of one proposition in some sense 'win', propositional cultural system knowledge cannot be eliminated and, as long as a rump of adherents remain, the battle continues. Further, the consequence of hostilities are both the conscription of primary agents (unattached individuals) to corporate agency (organised groups), as well as the splintering of corporate agents to form new groups that may be partisan, insensible, agnostic or antagonistic towards the initiating fray. As can be seen, co-dependence between propositions at the cultural system level and the ability or willingness of agents in socio-cultural interaction to seek adjustment between or reformulate logical ideational relations differentiates contingent from necessary incompatibilities.

The fourth and final form of relation is termed contingent complementarity. It is linked with *opportunism* and in this instance the advocates of proposition *A* when confronted by proposition *B* (and its advocates) in the socio-cultural realm are at liberty to employ, ignore or dispute the alternative proposition without restraint (all options are equally open). However, once a course of action is initiated, it may become difficult to change or alter course at a later date. Thus: "Only the contingent complementarity is free from Socio-Cultural manipulation, designed to induce *avoidance* or *adoption* or *aversion*" (*RST*, p. 244 – italicisation in original).

To recap, Archer asserts that four forms of cultural system logical relation potentially exist at T^1 independently of agents realising or caring to make use of them. However, to be known or identified, real people are required in historically contingent socio-cultural interactions to utilise or deploy contradictory or complementary propositional knowledge for their own interest informed but not determined purposes (this occurs between T^2 and T^3). Socio-cultural activity is therefore needed to register the ontological reality of cultural system propositional knowledge (ontological existence is demonstrated through effect). And, within the analytic cycle, the outcome of socio-cultural interaction determines the cultural system register at T^4 so that, relative to T^1 the cultural system at T^4 can be modified through a process of morphogenesis or, morphostatically maintained. In Archer's words:

> As an emergent entity the CS [cultural system] has an objective existence and autonomous relations amongst its components (theories, beliefs, values or more strictly between the propositional formulations of them) in the sense that these are independent of anyone's claim to know, to believe, to assent or to assert them. At any moment the CS is the product of historical S-C [socio-cultural] interaction, but having emerged then *qua* product, it has properties of its own. Like structure, culture is a human product but it too escapes its makers to act back upon them. The CS contains constraints (like the things that can and cannot be said in a particular natural language), it embodies new possibilities and it introduces new problems through the relationships between the emergent entities themselves (the clash of theories), between these and the physical environment and between these and human agents (makers and openers of Pandora's box).
>
> (*RST*, pp. 180–181 – italicisation in original)

Described thus, the cultural system demonstrates its ontologically intransitive character by predating and shaping the environment wherein human (mediating) activity thereafter affects it. As an emergent entity the cultural system occupies a rung within the stratified system of reality that Bhaskar described in *A Realist Theory of Science*. The cultural system grounds and is anterior to socio-cultural interaction. It supplies agents with conditioning but non-determining interests. Yet mutability in the face of socio-cultural action illustrates culture's plastic quality as well as the peculiarly interactive nature of the various 'strata'.

Although known through its effects, the cultural system need not produce effects. Logical relations may exist, using Bhaskarian terminology, unexercised and unrecognised within the realm of the unactualised real. Indeed, the cultural system can be imagined as conditioning socio-cultural interaction along a metaphorical continuum. Thus, its influence might be unacknowledged or misunderstood, partially recognised or understood and fully recognised and understood. Viewed in this way Bhaskar's theory of knowledge domains and objects as well as auxiliary concepts such as powers and normative tendencies can be seen to underpin Archer's claims regarding the ontological status of cultural system propositions (though Archer does not always make these connections explicit).

Analytic dualism is integral to the morphogenetic-morphostatic model of cultural elaboration since cultural system propositions at T^1 and their instantiation in the socio-cultural realm between T^2 to T^3 remain distinct. Wittingly or unwittingly, agents develop or preserve the cultural system initially present at T^1 in the period T^2 to T^3. Yet agential freedom regarding development or preservation of the cultural system is enabled and constrained by at least two closely related factors. First, historically pre-existent circumstances (e.g. role or position occupancy or prior exposure to and acceptance of a belief system) suggest that agents enter at T^2 with inherited interests that predispose them to favour certain contextually defined cultural system ideas over others. Thus, agents do not enter T^2 as *tabula rasa*. Agents do not take up cultural system propositions whimsically. Second, assuming that agents seek at a psychological level to maintain at least a modicum of logical coherence between the most significant conscious ideas that they hold, agents are encouraged to orientate themselves towards achieving elaborated outcomes that enable coherence to be maintained with pre-existing logical cultural system relations and the situated logics (interests) to which these relations give rise. It is in promoting these outcomes that the ontological reality of cultural system propositional logics makes itself known. And thus, as Archer states: "Systematic relationships (logical) impress themselves (causally) on S-C action.... This is the element of truth in downwards conflation" (*RST*, p. 246).

A lot has already been said about the concept of agency in morphogenetic theory. Nevertheless, it is necessary to briefly restate Archer's argument on voluntarism and determinism vis-à-vis agency in order that the linked concepts of persons and roles and primary and corporate agency can be developed.

For Archer (1990) the place and significance of agency: "stalks through the history of sociological theory" (p. 73). In contrast to epiphenomenal downwards conflationary theories, critical realists grant that while pre-existing cultural and social structures provide agents with orientating interests (reasons for behaving), actions are not determined by structures. Agents often lack "discursive penetration" (*RST*, p. 252) into their condition or situation and in such instances they may act without overt (or accurately perceived) structural guidance. Further, agents can deliberately and knowingly act against structurally generated interests albeit that a charge or penalty may be incurred for doing so. Indeed, agency's voluntaristic capacity depends upon their ability to act intentionally and this power (allowing both that reasons can be causes and that reasons may override structural interests) "demarcates agency from structure" (*RST*, p. 153) and demonstrates humanity's (psychological) emergent ontological status.

Alternatively, in contrast to epiphenomenal upwards conflationary theories, morphogenesis allows that structural interests at T^1 enable and constrain the actions of free individuals. Actions "presuppose an already existing set of structures" (Sayer, 2000, p. 18 – commenting on Archer's work) and historically situated structural interests thus allow agents to formulate reasons or desires for certain actions and debar, as negative realities, the articulation of alternative intentions.[15]

Archer illustrates agency's emergent status by distinguishing between "the 'human being', 'social agent' and 'social actor'" (*RST*, p. 249) as well as primary and corporate forms of agency.[16] In this schema, persons beget agents who father actors "both phylogenetically and ontogenetically" (*RST*, p. 255). Persons provide "the needed reflexive quality and generalized ability for innovation" (*RST*, p. 256). However, persons, as singular bodies, lack interests and the concept of agency is therefore introduced. For Archer agents are always

> agents *of* something. Baldly, they are agents of the socio-cultural system into which [as persons] they are born (groups or collectivities in the same position or situations) and equally they are agents of the systemic features they transform (since groups and collectivities are modified in the process).
>
> (*RST*, p. 257 – italicisation in original)

Agency is however a complex entity. Corporate agency includes or describes "self-conscious vested interest groups, promotive interest groups, social movements and defensive associations [and their] common denominators are articulation and organization" (*RST*, p. 258). Primary agents, on the other hand, do not intentionally engage in structural change, albeit that "dumb numerical pressure" (*RST*, p. 262) can force corporate agents to accept unplanned or unintended structural morphogenesis or morphostasis. And persons can be simultaneously primary and corporate agents at any specific time (T^2) depending on the type of structure (cultural or social) under consideration.

Actors, like persons, always exist in the singular. Actors embody roles and roles occur in relational role-sets. These can be internal and necessary (e.g. "a pupil requires a teacher" *RST*, p. 275) or, asymmetrical and dependent (e.g. a "schools inspector [implies] teachers, but not vice versa", *RST*, p. 276). Actors personify roles insofar as they bring their "own ideals and objectives, skill and incompetence, dedication or distancing, inflexibility or creativeness to the roles they occupy" (*RST*, p. 187). Personification links individual psychology to or with social expectation. Roles pre-exist and are autonomous of the individuals who occupy them. However, by interrogating the interplay between actor and role it is possible to "account for why some roles are personified in routinized ways whilst others can be cumulatively transformed in the hands of their incumbents" (*RST*, p. 187). Thus it is possible to plot the double morphogenesis or stasis of roles and their occupants over time.

The three analytic cycles proposed by Archer (cultural and social structural and agential) operate coterminously and are linked through their T^2/T^3 'mediating' or 'middle element'. Yet each cycle can and to some extent must be described separately if the relative autonomy of agency and structure is to be respected. Diagrams 2.1 and 2.2 (below) indicate in idealised forms how this 'overlap' might be envisaged.

As illustrative "extreme instances" (*RST*, p. 308), Diagram 2.1 depicts uniform structural (social) and cultural morphostasis, while Diagram 2.2 indicates concurrent structural (social) and cultural morphogenesis. Each element may however experience stasis or genesis non-synchronously and it is thus perfectly feasible, according to morphogenetic theory, for morphogenesis to occur in one element of one cycle, or one part of a cycle, while stasis describes another element. Indeed, non-uniform or non-synchronous developmental histories are equally or more likely to occur than those depicted below. For example, structural morphogenesis and cultural morphostasis *or* structural morphostasis and cultural morphogenesis may pertain and diagrams 2.1 and 2.2 thus represent "rarities in reality" (*RST*, p. 308).

Archer argues that the value of theory is synonymous with its explanatory power. In Chapters 3 and 4 realist social (morphogenetic) theory determines "the conceptual structures of explanation" (Pawson, 1989, p. 192). These conceptual structures frame, coordinate and give meaning to data and evidence regarding aspects of hospice practice. In Chapter 5, the usefulness of morphogenetic theory in social explanation is critiqued.

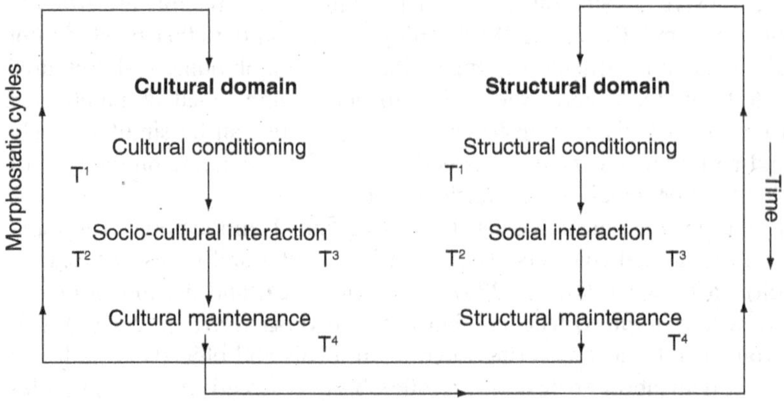

Diagram 2.1 Cultural and structural configurations generating morphostasis in society and agency (source: reproduced from Archer, 2000, p. 271).[17]

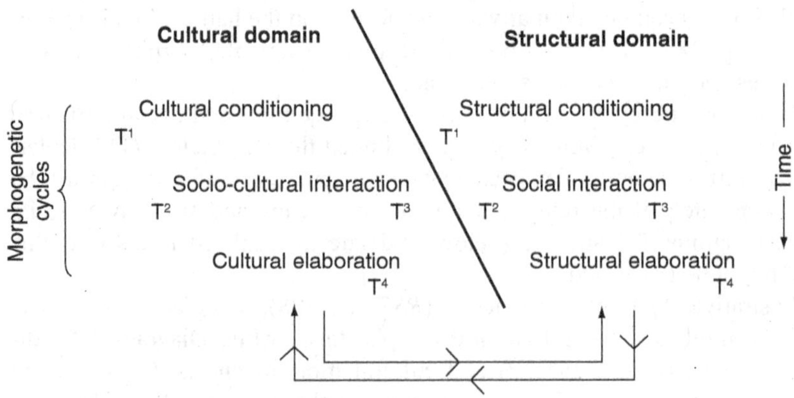

Diagram 2.2 Cultural and structural configurations generating morphogenesis in society and agency (source: reproduced from *RST*, p. 323).

Notes

1 For example, Archer states that her theory "makes no leap from the real to the actual" (*RST*, p. 175). In context these descriptors (real or actual) should be understood as part of Bhaskar's theory of domains and knowledge forms (see also *RST*, p. 343). Other examples concern the impossibility of prediction in open systems (*RST*, p. 159) and retroduction/retrodiction (*RST*, p. 327).

2 Archer uses the terms social structure and cultural system throughout *Realist Social Theory* and *Culture and Agency*. Moreover, she often distinguishes structure from culture. However, Archer also makes it clear in both *Realist Social Theory* and *Culture and Agency* that since: "Culture is approached analytically in exactly the same way as structure it is just as appropriate to speak of cultural as of social structures" (*RST*, p. 179). In this work, unless otherwise stated, the term structure refers to both cultural and social structures. No violence is done to Archer's work by this usage. Carter (2000) also references "cultural and social structures" (p. 93).

3 Slightly differently worded versions of this two part propositional statement appear throughout *Realist Social Theory*, see, for example, pages 76 and 89–90.

4 Nomic statements are the "indicative form" of normic statements (*RTS*, p. 51).

5 Referring to Bhaskar's *Reclaiming Reality* (1989), Archer notes that: "With minor alterations the TMSA [Transformational Model of Social Activity] and M/M [Morphogenetic-Morphostatic] diagrams now readily combine" (*RST*, p. 157).

6 Archer quotes Outhwaite (1990, p. 366) approvingly stating that: "realist metatheory is clearly compatible with a wide variety of theoretical and methodological approaches" (cited *RST*, p. 136).

7 For example, although Stuart Hampshire is uncited in *Culture and Agency* and *Realist Social Theory*, it might be argued that overlaps exist between Archer's use of analytic dualism and the manner in which Hampshire (1960) maintains distinctions between internal mental states and external influences and environments (in which such states may, but need not, be evidenced). Naturally, in drawing this potential parallel it is necessary to place caveats around the differences that separate their works. However, the links between both theorists are striking. It may also be noted that Bhaskar (1998b) obliquely refers to Hampshire in relation to the axiological imperative – i.e. the idea that: "beliefs are necessitated by the condition that what I am to do can never be reduced to, or discovered by scrutiny of the antecedents of, what I will do" (p. 87). Further, aspects of Hampshire's thought on causal reasoning appear, again with caveats, to resemble Bhaskarian ideas concerning nomic tendencies. (Hampshire's *Thought and Action* was originally published in 1959.) Alternatively, points of contact between Archer and Norbert Elias are worth considering (Byrne, 2004, quotes Elias favourably). Again, bar a single cursory reference on p. 281 of *Culture and Agency*, Archer does not mention Elias. However, Elias's (1978) focus on social explanations that incorporate a temporal dimension, unintended consequences, the importance of differential dispositional power relations between individuals and groups in the framing and resolution of conflict and 'game' modelling match, to some degree, Archer's theory of ideational relations and the situated logics they give rise to. Conjecture upon potential influence can easily spiral off towards consideration of a preposterously large number of tangentially related possibilities. Yet speculation on the development of Archer's thinking serves two purposes. First, that Archer independently traversed the theoretical terrain that Bhaskar subsequently mines may explain or account for the form in which she exploits his ontological insights (e.g. *RST*, p. 69). And, in this respect, it is interesting to note that as early as 1972 (i.e. three years *before* the publication of *A Realist Theory of Science*), Archer outlined relations between student groups, educational ideals, social structures and late 1960s political unrest using a form of logical modelling and argumentation that embodies or heralds significant elements of morphogenetic reasoning (Archer, 1972). Second, noting that

theorists from varying perspectives were and are similarly engaged with 'critical realist' issues or questions is a corrective to overly extravagant realist presumptions. That non-critical realist theorists such as Rosenberg (2001) can reach similar conclusions from disparate beginnings is important.

8 Archer (*RST*, p. 98) asserts that, for Giddens, structure lives only as memory traces within individuals and this, she points out, places a heavy burden on memory.

9 Archer recognises similarities between her nomenclature and that of Bhaskar when she states that: "Morphogenesis and morphostasis are very close indeed to the notions of transformation and reproduction, and all four terms only make sense as processes which come 'after' something which existed 'before' them" (*RST*, p. 140).

10 Archer states that:

> In short, when we talk about structural properties and their effects from the morphogenetic perspective, we are endorsing the realist notion of emergence and its causal powers. Thus we accept that the results of past actions have effects in their own rights later on, as constraining or facilitating influences upon actors, which are not attributable or reducible to the practices of other agents.
>
> (*RST*, p. 90)

Structures therefore exert "systematic causal effects on subsequent action" (*RST*, p. 167).

11 Interests produce experiences of problems "or benefits [which] condition different situational interpretations and dissimilar action patterns [so that] groups experiencing exigencies seek to eradicate them (thus pursuing structural change) and those experiencing rewards try to retain them (thus defending structural stability)" (*RST*, p. 90). Implicit within this schema is the assumption that actors "are not responsible for creating the distributions, roles and associated interests with which they live" (*RST*, p. 152).

12 The connection between interests and reasons is made by Archer when she notes that structure influences human action by "supplying *reasons* for different courses of action to those who are differentially positioned" (*RST*, p. 154 – italicisation in original). However, reasons are not necessarily synonymous with interests since actors may formulate reasons to ignore or act against their positional interests.

13 Note, however, first, Carter (2000, 2003) denies the ontological veracity of race as a sociological concept and, second, Archer fails to explore the potential conditioning impact of geography (though other social realist sympathisers do – e.g. Sayer, 2000).

14 Subtle differences distinguish claims regarding cultural system and socio-cultural interaction in *Realist Social Theory* (e.g. see p. 169) and *Culture and Agency* (e.g. p. 143).

15 If structure exerts its influence upon social interaction by predating, ordering or enabling the context in which agents act (i.e. the 'mechanisms/powers' they are exposed to), then structure can be described as a positive reality. However, negative realities may also have or exert influence by constraining or limiting agential options. Archer acknowledges the possible reality and significance of negative powers. Yet it is left to Collier (1999) to develop the concept more fully (in relation to moral reasoning). See also Engholm (1999). Negative realities describe breaks or blocks upon agential thought or action that result from ideational or material *absences*. Thus, for example, historic failure to invest in certain forms of health or illness care inevitably means these forms of care are unavailable to patients in the present (though with varying degrees of ease, investment can generate future provision). However, despite this potential, the absence of specific forms of care, conjoined with materially existing substitutes (and the rationalisations that accompany substitutes) may and probably will act to prevent agents recognising that alternatives to current provision (i.e. the absent form of care) could become a viable or attractive future option. The ontological status of negative realities is, as ever in critical realist thinking, given by their causal

effects. From a non-critical realist perspective Howson (2000) recognises the problematic nature of the concept and states that philosophers have long "worried about the existence of negative facts" (p. 129). The potential place and importance of negative realities in social theory requires further development.

16 Archer recognises that: "Undoubtedly there are further strata, such as the linking level of individual psychology or personality, itself emergent from 'consciousness', which in turn emerges from 'mind', which is emergent from 'matter' etc." (*RST*, pp. 254–255). These *further strata* are not explored in *Realist Social Theory*. However, Archer returns to examine aspects of these postulated relationships in *Being Human: The Problem of Agency* (2000), *Structure, Agency and the Internal Conversation* (2003a) and *Making our Way through the World* (2007).

17 A slightly different version of this diagram appears on p. 309 of *Realist Social Theory*.

3 Realist social theory applied

This book presents a worked example of realist social theory. Chapter 2 introduced Margaret Archer's morphogenetic-morphostatic methodology and in Chapter 3 this methodology is used to direct an investigation into aspects of hospice activity. A number of appendices are referred to in this chapter. These appendices supply supporting detail and information about the study. Chapter 4 describes the results or findings of this investigation.

Permission to proceed (gaining formal access)

I was employed as a full-time staff nurse at the study site (hospice) before permission to proceed with the research outlined here was requested or granted. Occupying a staff position within the organisation being investigated clearly had an impact on the study. Yet in the first instance being an 'insider' undoubtedly eased the process of obtaining formal/agreed access or permission to proceed.

Approval to conduct the study came from two sources. First, approval was provided by a local University (where the research was 'registered') and, second, at the study site, permission was granted by senior managerial and clinical staff. Before approval was given discussions took place at the hospice regarding possible disruption to clinical practice, anticipated findings/conclusions, confidentiality/anonymity and the protection of organisational 'reputation'. Informal assurances were provided that some sensitive issues regarding staff performance would not be explored. These issues were not germane to this study. However, see below (p. 40).

Following approval, hospice staff were notified in broad terms about the study's aims and methods at an open meeting and via internal hospice publications. The study did not require NHS ethics committee approval. The hospice is an independent charity, only a small fraction of its income comes from statutory sources, no patients were involved and the work was 'privately' funded.

Ethics and methods

Interviews with clinical, administrative and managerial hospice staff provide the bulk of study data. Interview recruitment, conduct and data handling/use generate ethical responsibilities for researchers and method choice thereby influences or creates the ethical questions that researchers thereafter address. Ethical responsibilities must be acknowledged and met. However, decisions regarding ethical issues also influence research findings when those decisions have method and/or methodological consequences. The interlinked or co-dependent nature of ethical decision making and research practice is not always fully recognised.

In this study purposeful recruitment was employed to access a diverse range of staff (see 'Interview list', p. 46). However, problematically, because I was a work colleague, some people may have felt obliged to agree to participate. Imbalances in power relations between researchers and those researched or, in this instance, the demands of friendship can generate ethical complications if putative participants feel unable to refuse the invitation to participate (Stevens *et al.*, 2003; Arraf *et al.*, 2004; Mueller, 2004; Liamputtong, 2007). Hopefully in this particular instance no one felt compelled to agree to be interviewed and it could be the case that familiarity with the researcher, a co-worker, would facilitate anyone who wanted to decline to do so. One person did decline to participate when asked and, after I left the hospice, nobody withdrew from the study despite being reminded of their 'right' to do so. If it is the case that obligatory or coercive relations dissipate following the withdrawal of researchers from study sites then the willingness of interviewees to remain in this study following my departure might suggest that coerced recruitment was not an issue.

Participants were re-informed about the study on two occasions. First, an information sheet was given to participants before written consent was obtained. Second, discussion about the study formed part of the interview process. Interviewees were made aware that they could withdraw from the study at any time and, post-interview and following transcription, a printout of the discussion was offered to participants. This transcript enabled interviewees to identify comments that, upon reflection, they might wish to withdraw, amend or 'clarify'. In practice hardly any alterations were made and, when changes were suggested, they concerned minor typographical errors rather than matters of substance. Nonetheless, providing participants with an opportunity to check and review comments may have enhanced participant confidence in the research process if or insofar as this suggested that interviewee interests were being respected. Checking transcripts in this manner might arguably bolster descriptive data validity or factual precision (but not interpretive validity). However, transcription inevitably distorts and reduces data complexity and richness (Sjöström, 2002) and, therefore, it is mischievous to imagine that a correct or accurate transcript is possible since factually unassailable transcription is a chimera (Cohen *et al.*, 2000). Recordings were destroyed following data analysis.

From a researcher perspective it was desirable that interviewee remarks could be associated with role or position descriptors. For example, I wanted to be able to say that the Ward Manager said 'x' or that the General Manager said 'y'. Indeed, given Margaret Archer's nuanced description of agents (see Chapter 2) this sort of linkage is necessary if morphogenetic theory is to fulfil its potential.

However, in a small organisation, participants might easily occupy roles or positions that are unique or held by comparatively few people and the possibility that anonymity might be compromised where roles are associated with quotations had to be acknowledged and addressed.

The danger here was that despite maintaining formal anonymity (i.e. not naming names) quotations might identify speakers to anyone aware of the identity of role-position occupants. This possibility was brought to the attention of interviewees, those at the hospice charged with granting permission for the study to proceed and the sponsoring University.

The moderate size of the hospice and the specificity or distinctiveness of UK hospices in general (Clark *et al.*, 1997; Connor, 1998; Lawton, 2000) also contributes to difficulties in maintaining organisational and interviewee anonymity. Thus descriptions of the hospice, however circumspect, can yield data that might enable informed readers to locate the study site and, hence, participants. Again, the possibility and implications of site and therefore individual identification was brought to the attention of those charged with granting permission for the study to proceed as well as prospective interviewees.

To safeguard participants from embarrassment (or worse) associated with unwitting identification and regardless of 'formal' anonymity, interviewees were asked to imagine that they were at all times speaking to a public audience which included work colleagues and, where applicable, senior staff. Thus as a defensive measure participants were asked to speak in a considered manner that presumed identification. Interviewees were also made aware that comments could have a wide audience if embedded in texts such as this. As a last measure, participants were informed that quotations would only be linked with role or position descriptors when, in the researcher's opinion, no harm to them would occur. Interviewees were thus asked to trust that the interviewer would endeavour to protect them. Reliance on subjective criteria such as researcher 'opinion' is clearly problematic. However, at root all or almost all procedural safeguards ultimately rest upon interpretation and trust.

Overtly highlighting the danger of interviewee identification was deemed necessary to protect participants' interests and protection of this sort is generally considered ethically desirable. As noted ethical decisions have method and methodological implications and, in this instance, emphasising the danger of 'breaching' confidentiality undoubtedly had an effect upon the interview process (and thus data collection). The size of this effect cannot be calculated. However, it is probably sensible to assume that there will have been some loss of data 'richness'.

Even more imponderably, while the interacting personalities, expectations and understandings of researcher and interviewees inevitably inform, influence and steer data collection, these 'socio-psychological' factors remain unassessed (and they may in practice be largely unassessable). Despite this it is recognised that prior familiarity, collegiality and in many instances friendship between researcher and participants was both a benefit and potential draw upon data collection and, thereafter, analysis.

Positively, cordial relations between interviewers and interviewees engender trust, help negotiate access to participants, reduce anxiety regarding the interview process (e.g. surrounding the recording of dialogue) and enable communication as abbreviations, slang and exemplar stories are easily understood and shared (an example of this sort of positive benefit is described shortly). Negatively, "familiarity" (Hammersley and Atkinson, 1995, p. 103) and preconceived expectations on the part of the researcher regarding participants may be associated with assumptions that naive or unfamiliar researchers would avoid and, in consequence, the interview process may be unproductively distorted. Alternatively and contrariwise, prior familiarity and preconceived expectations on the part of interviewees regarding interviewer beliefs might lead participants to talk about or indeed curtail utterances in a manner that would not have occurred were an unknown researcher present.

Since it is not possible to fully or even substantively establish how interviewer-interviewee relations affected the interview process, all that can be said is that interviewees may have revealed or disclosed more or less about their thoughts and feelings to a known researcher than they would have done had an unknown interviewer been present. Yet this statement is clearly 'unhelpful'. It merely recognises that a vital element or part of the interview process remains unknown or unaccounted for and, where participant expectations and assumptions result, during interviews, in restraint or reticence, then these expectations and assumptions are clearly a threat to research (such as this) that relies upon frank disclosure. This aspect of interviewer-interviewee relations requires further consideration.

Interviews were not conducted with patients or their families/friends or hospice volunteer workers and their anonymity is maintained absolutely. However, despite requesting that interviewees not use patient names or the names of non-clinical or non-professional staff such names were sometimes mentioned. When this happened it was occasionally possible to replace the identifier with a pseudonym so that meaning was preserved. However, since hospice personnel might read outputs from the study, since the incident being described could be rare or distinctive and since, in a small organisation, most staff have a good overview of what occurs, it could not be guaranteed that pseudonyms safeguarded anonymity and, to ensure that patients, families/friends or other non-participants are not identified to hospice staff or anyone else it was in some instances appropriate, despite the loss of data, to omit transcript passages in which names or suchlike appeared.

Once again, ethical considerations here impact on data collection and ethical decisions thus have method or methodological implications. Yet in practice the amount and significance of data loss was not burdensome and a very large body of data remained despite the losses described. As will become clear (Chapter 4), this data clearly evidences the robustness of views expressed by interviewees on a range of issues.

In addition to interview data, the researcher, as participant observer, kept observational notes. These notes tended to be reflective rather than procedural or descriptive and individuals were not identified in these writings. When procedural or descriptive notes were taken and when these notes involved staff, the individuals concerned were informally (verbally) asked whether they objected to anonymised note taking – none did. Following Seale (1999), distinctions between procedural, descriptive and interpretive records were maintained. However, distinctions between these sorts of category are generally of degree rather than kind.

Post-study reflection on the researcher-participant and researcher-organisational relationship suggests that, despite the benefits accruing from 'insider status', the pursuit of some critical lines of investigation was marginally hampered by three factors. First, the need to gain permission to proceed probably encouraged overly prescriptive assurances to be given as regards the study's remit. For example, it was as noted tacitly agreed that some forms of sensitive personnel and role difficulties would not be pursued. These particular issues had no direct bearing on the study. Nonetheless it is feasible that foreclosing on study 'lines' in this way had unforeseen knock-on effects as allied or linked questions were thereafter out of bounds and some of these kindred or ancillary issues might have been worth exploring. Second, individual friendships with participants as well as personal loyalty to the hospice probably restricted the candour with which problems or issues are identified. This will on occasion have occurred unwittingly. At other times I was aware of 'pulling punches' and thus, in contrast to Lawton (2000), the research presented here lacks an outsider's critical gaze. Third, prior professionalisation into the role of nurse probably influenced the manner in which ethical obligations were recognised and met. As has been stressed, ethical decisions often have method and methodological impacts and, since the approach to ethical decision making taken here can be challenged, the importance of prior professionalisation (the significance of background assumptions) must be recognised (see Lipscomb, 2010b).

Data, evidence and theory

Data and evidence recognition and theory informed analysis or interpretation are intimately linked. It is therefore important to clarify the relationship between data, evidence and theory.

It might be proposed that data (here derived from interview transcripts, observation or indeed 'the literature') becomes evidence of or 'for something' (i.e. an interpretation, proposal/proposition or hypothesis) through or via processes of analysis. This claim is not unreasonable. However, it may be somewhat simplistic. For example, the claim perhaps presupposes an overly firm distinction between data and evidence. It also underplays or ignores the role of theory in data/evidence identification and assemblage. More accurately then, data becomes evidence of or for something only in relation to – only through the lens of – theory. And, from this perspective, neither data nor evidence exists in any meaningful sense apart from theory. Theory thus directs the identification and ordering of data and evidence. The world or 'what is' places limits upon what theorists can sensibly or reasonably suggest. So reality – including the reality of our limitations – places 'brakes' upon speculation. However, in this process, boundaries need not be placed on the sources theory utilises (Cruickshank, 2003a).

What then is theory or, more simply (a different question), what is theory in this study? Here theory carries five distinct appellations. First, theory refers to high level philosophical discourse (e.g. Bhaskar's critical realist philosophy). Second, theory refers to high level methodological discourse (e.g. Archer's morphogenetic-morphostatic theory). Third, theory describes 'middle range' emergent research generated theories or theoretical proposals regarding structural and agential interaction at the study site (this is the main focus of Chapter 4). Fourth, in this chapter, interview transcript data coding and organisation can be designated 'low level' theory (i.e. theory about the meaning and interrelation of individual participant statements).[1] And, fifth, background or ancillary theories (presuppositions) inevitably infuse and inform all four of the 'theory types' listed above (as they do all thinking; Achinstein, 2010). Picking up on comments in the Introduction it might be suggested that research narratives which coordinate explanation across these theoretic levels will – though 'coordination' is perhaps at best an ideal – honour the logical ties that, realists claim, bind ontology, epistemology and methodology together.

Realist research begins with the transcendental question: What must the world be like for this to be possible? Here 'this' refers both to empiric[2] occurrences and transitive or fallible theories about those occurrences, while 'the world' refers to postulated intransitive structures that generate empiric occurrences (i.e. the things or powers that 'really' exist – the things we want to understand and explain).

Morphogenesis involves the identification and temporal mapping of relations between social and cultural structures via or through descriptions of social and socio-cultural agential interaction (i.e. it involves establishing the complementary or contradictory situated social and cultural logics that pertain between agents). And, although Archer does not use the following Bhaskarian terms, it is henceforth assumed that in plotting these links between structure and agency, researchers using morphogenetic theory infer through processes of abduction (more specifically, retroduction and retrodiction) the generative causal mechanisms or objects (structures) that lie behind or produce empiric occurrences.

Data are therefore identified and 'read' within a complex system of theoretic presumptions and, for social realists; analysis does not await the completion of data collection. Analysis is or need not be distinct from data collection and, instead, inferential retroduction and/or retrodiction (*looking back* or *looking beyond*) accompanies and directs data collection. Theory is thus, to repeat, not separate from data collection or analysis and evidence cannot exist apart from theory.

The research process followed here, linking empiric events (the things we can see or the words people speak) with their generative causes (what lies behind

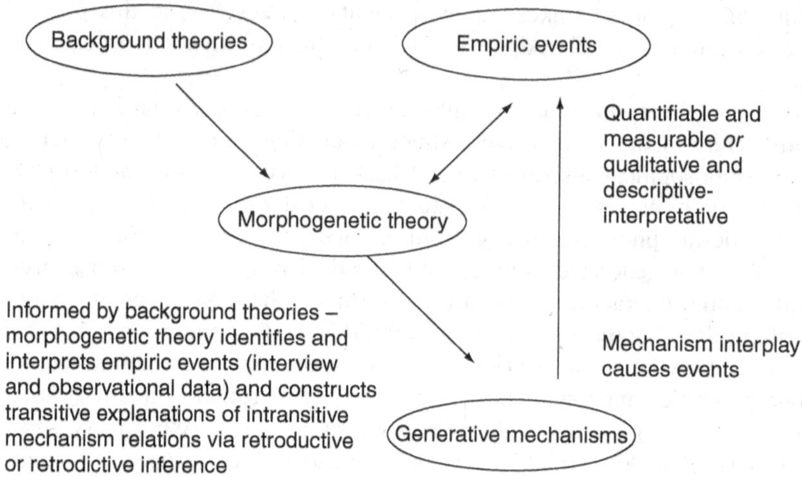

Diagram 3.1 Mechanisms, events and morphogenetic theory (from an idea by Mearman, 2008).

them) through morphogenetic modelling is pictorially represented above. In Diagram 3.1 "the empirical level is the access point to the transitive dimension" (Downward and Mearman, 2007, p. 88). Morphogenetic theory here leads the identification of data and its reconceptualization as evidence 'about' change at the study site. Empiric data-evidence thus acts as a "bridge" (ibid., p. 92) between transitive or theoretically informed and fallible understanding and intransitive generative causal mechanisms and, following Achinstein (2010) (a non-critical realist) the role and importance of background theories and assumptions is overtly acknowledged.

Although realists can and do advocate complex statistical and mathematical modelling (e.g. Pratschke, 2003; Williams and Dyer, 2004), this study is representative of realist research insofar as the data and evidence employed are predominantly qualitative in form. That said, realist qualitative inquiry differs in some respects from that undertaken by non-realists.

Qualitative research takes place across a wide and disputed theoretical spectrum (Creswell, 1998). It can therefore be misleading to describe qualitative research as a homogenous entity (Giddings, 2006). Nevertheless, Strauss's (1987) emphasis on the need to ground the theories (interpretations) generated by qualitative analysis *in* data (mostly but not exclusively textual) would be endorsed by many qualitative researchers albeit that terms such as 'ground', the nature of analysis and what counts as data, vary according to theoretic disposition. Realists likewise recognise the importance of empiric occurrence since without such occurrences generative mechanisms cannot be abducted. However, uncritically accenting the status of primary data is, as has been argued, mistaken since from a realist perspective this accenting ignores the directive role played by theory in data identification and analysis. Indeed realists must reject Polit and Beck's (2006) claim that qualitative findings emerge *bottom up* "from the data" (p. 404) if this suggests that analysis proceeds atheoretically.

In abstracting empirical data from interview transcripts realists seek to avoid the methodological or idealist individualism which, from their perspective, invests forms of transcript comparison (Downward and Mearman, 2007). Realists achieve this by recognising and building into analysis the *missing other* of social and cultural structure and, in this way, substance is given to the "context upon which the opinions of the interviewees, etc. were formed" (ibid., p. 95). That said and, as noted, realist explanation is transitive and provisional. Gorner (2000) suggests that, for Gadamerian hermeneutics, "understanding takes place within the happening of tradition" (p. 147) and realist investigators – from a very different standpoint – similarly recognise that theoretically informed explanation is necessarily limited by its reliance upon historically situated socio-cultural understanding and knowledge. Where this understanding and knowledge is considered developed, retrodiction rather than retroduction occurs (Lipscomb, 2012).

Procedural differences between realist and non-realist researchers should not, however, be overdrawn. Irrespective of avowed allegiances or stated assumptions, in practice, most qualitative researchers proceed realistically (if not critically) for, as Seale (1999) notes: "The attempt to use language to refer to, describe or explain aspects of the social world is a basic commitment [that] must ultimately depend on some modified form of realism" (p. 157) and even phenomenologists, whose focus upon unique individual perceptions and experience inevitably minimises the role played by external structural forces, generally produce research whose "concluding moment almost always makes implicit claims about reality" (Paley, 2005, p. 106). Indeed, often "without full awareness" (Miles and Huberman, 1994, p. 10) non-realist qualitative researchers impose top down ontologic and epistemologic frameworks onto the data when they situate or position that data within, for example, social or psychological understandings. (Hammersley (1990) makes a similar point regarding forms of ethnography.)

Realists thus deny that a datum can "speak for itself" (Strauss, 1987, p. 216) for, as Seale (1999) asserts: "No act of observation can be free from the underlying [interpretive] assumptions that guide it" (p. 148). Data do not exist outside of theoretical frameworks and realist researchers do not begin analysis (data reduction) as blank slates upon which data's meaning can be inscribed. Rather, realists approach their objects of study with developed ontic, epistemic and methodologic understandings that orientate and scaffold the interpretative process. And, one might add, who doesn't?

Recognising that the researcher cannot and should not be bracketed out from the analytic process goes beyond suggesting that data and evidence are theory laden, for, as Pawson (2006) states, realism allows that theory can legitimately *drive* data collection and interpretation. And, in consequence, the phenomenological insistence that data analysis must focus upon "lived interpretations and not interpretations of interpretations" (Levering, 2006, p. 451) is here rejected.

Acknowledging the underpinning role of critical realist philosophy (theory in the first sense) therefore permits Archer's morphogenetic methodology (theory in the second sense) to overtly steer middle range theory development regarding postulated generative mechanisms (third or middle range theory) as well as data collection, coding and ordering (e.g. transcript production and interpretation or theory in the fourth sense).

The danger here is that researcher prejudice (bias) prescriptively imposes, in theory, upon the study object whereas, ideally, theory, data and evidence should mutually or cyclically inform and support each other.[3] Reflexivity, reflection, transparency or 'openness' on the part of the researcher might ameliorate such prescription and Pellatt (2003) asserts that reflexivity, for example, allows researchers to recognise that they are an "integral part of the social world being studied" (p. 28). Moreover Murphy (2005), while gently parodying procedural attempts to demonstrate research goodness via reflexivity, likewise describes reflexivity as "vital" (p. 55), as one means by which the researcher can "acknowledge" (p. 55) their impact upon the study. Reflexivity cannot, of course, as hermeneutics attests (Gorner, 2000; Malpas, 2005), prevent the researcher's outlook and capability (or lack thereof) from influencing the interpretive and analytic process since reflexivity is itself informed by that outlook and capability. And, troublingly, the 'corrective' potential of self-knowing reflexivity is problematised by recent experimental work in philosophy and psychology that in important respects challenges both the limits and scope of reflexivity and reflection (e.g. Alexander, 2012; Kahneman, 2012; Roessler, 2013)

Reflexivity is not then a panacea. Attempting to combine a reflexive disposition towards data collection and interpretation, process transparency and overt theoretic positioning is useful insofar as it opens work up to critique and refutation. However, the utility and success (or otherwise) of this endeavour must be judged in relation to research 'as a whole'. Hopefully, a reflexive spirit informs the entirety of this work. Yet whether this is sufficient to meet charges that data collection and interpretative processes are overly directive remains a moot point.

As noted, in addition to interview data, observational data were collected by the researcher in his role as participant observer. Bernstein (1979) and Garfinkel (1984) suggest that participation brings investigative benefits and Simmons (2007) claims participant observation allows researchers to comprehend social environments in a manner that is denied to non-embedded researchers (albeit that the means by which 'embeddedness' privileges comprehension remains largely under-explored). As might be expected, the theoretical position here pursued inevitably influenced how the role of participant observer was interpreted and, for example, assumptions are made about the limits and function of description that non-realists might reject.

Thus, according to Hammersley and Atkinson (1995), naturalist ethnographers do not aim to explain or "go beyond" (p. 5) cultural description and their performance as participant observers therefore differs from realists who aim to get *behind* social description to reveal the structural and agential factors that reproduce or transform social life. That said, ethnographic approaches vary hugely (Murphy, 2005). Savage (2000) broadly defines ethnography as, in part, "any small scale social research that is carried out in everyday settings" (p. 1401) and Maggs-Rapport (2001, p. 376) cites Denscombe's (1998) distinction between (descriptive) naturalist and (generalising) reflexive forms to illustrate a major fault line among ethnographic approaches. Thus reflexive ethnographers such as Hammersley and Atkinson (1995) distance themselves from overly limiting interpretations of ethnography and, given such flexibility, realist and ethnographic approaches may successfully combine (see, e.g. Porter, 1993; Porter and Ryan, 1996). On balance, and bearing in mind the relative nature of descriptors, realists will probably generate more interpretive notes than naturalist ethnographers who will record proportionally more procedural and descriptive notes.

Data collection

Thirty-one semi-structured interviews were conducted with twenty-six clinical and administrative or managerial participants. Interviews lasted between fifty-five and eighty minutes. They generally took place in the interviewee's private office (for managerial and administrative staff) or in a comfortably furnished side room away from the ward (for clinical staff). Three off-site interviews occurred when workload pressures prevented on-site meetings. A second interview was arranged when interviewees appeared to require or requested more time to complete what they were saying (see Table 3.1).

Morphogenetic-morphostatic theory guided data collection and analysis. Data collection was informed by theory since morphogenesis established, a priori, the forms of structural and agential relations and the nature of interaction between those relations that might be encountered and thus, mindful of their position, role and interests within the hospice, interviewees were questioned with a view to revealing the situated nature of interaction and relations at the study site.

Interviewees were not of course expected to identify interactions or relations directly or in abstract (that would be preposterous) and, instead, an interview schedule or guide was used to flexibly steer conversations that, it was hoped, would allow structural-agential relations to be abductively recognised. Using guides in this way may appear prescriptive (and schedules can be used prescriptively). However, this tool was not formulaically 'worked through'. Rather, in use, it merely prompted or reminded the interviewer to bring forward topics for discussion and, moreover, interviewees frequently expanded upon or talked about other issues.

Initially the interview guide comprised four themes labelled: (i) change, (ii) admissions/discharges, (iii) consultant differences and (iv) treatment/interventions.

As a clinically situated participant-observer I was, in advance of the interviews, aware that 'change' within the hospice was viewed as significant by clinicians albeit that the form and implications of change were variously described and interpreted (indeed this 'recognition' formed the stimulus for the study). Familiarity and involvement in ongoing ward debates also permitted me to

Table 3.1 Interview list[4]

Role title or position	*1st interview plus interview code*	*1st interview duration (minutes)*	*2nd interview plus interview code*	*2nd interview duration (minutes)*
Nursing Assistant	A:a	70		
Nurse	B:a	60		
Charge Nurse (Sister)	C:a	55	C:b	65
Nursing Assistant	D:a	60		
Nurse	E:a	60		
Ward Manager	F:a	80		
Nursing Director	G:a	75	G:b	60
Doctor	H:a	70		
Educationalist	I:a	70	I:b	60
Day-hospice Manager (Nurse)	J:a	70		
Social Worker	K:a	80		
Doctor	L:a	75		
Special Minister of the Eucharist	M:a	70	M:b	80
General Manager	N:a*	60	N:b	55
Medical Consultant	O:a	75		
Full-time Chaplain	P:a	70		
Occupational Therapist	Q:a	65		
Fundraiser	R:a	55		
Physiotherapist	S:a	55		
Head of Administration	T:a	65		
Charge Nurse (Sister)	U:a	65		
Charge Nurse (Sister)	V:a	60		
Nurse	W:a*	65		
Assistant Chaplain	X:a	65		
Medical Registrar	Y:a	75		
Medical Consultant	Z:a*	60		

identify admission and discharge practice as, in some respects, contentious and, likewise, discussions about the evolving and contested nature of clinical treatments and interventions and variations in consultant attitudes and behaviours were widely seen as important.

Interviews were therefore guided by interviewer identified themes *and* the identification of themes was influenced by the researcher's interests and position within the organisation. By implication, alternatively positioned staff (e.g. non-clinical staff) might have identified other issues or themes as significant and awareness of this possibility encouraged a reflexively conversational approach to be adopted in interviews.[5] Reflexivity or, less grandly, thinking carefully about what participants said permitted fifth (v) 'spirituality/religion' and sixth (vi) 'external relations/consultant attitudes/care standards' themes to be added to the interview guide in response to unforeseen interviewee comments. The imprecision or clumsiness of this last descriptor reflected then unfamiliarity with the issues being raised (see Appendix A).

Insofar as pre-established background theories located within the palliative care literature and experientially derived ideas about hospice organisation, clinical care and agential relations informed the construction of the first four interview topics, it might be argued that inferential retrodiction best describes the process of morphogenetic modelling pictorially represented in Diagram 3.1 (p. 42). Alternatively, the fifth and sixth interview topics (labelled above) were not anticipated before interviews occurred and, to that extent, it would probably be more accurate to describe the process by which these themes were accommodated within the interview schedule (and developed in Chapter 4) as inferential retroduction. The role played by background theories in distinguishing retroduction from retrodiction is, however, 'relative' or, in this instance, subjective. The ability of the researcher to identify in initial interviews that the fifth and sixth interview topics were of interest and potential importance must rest on exposure to prior but hitherto unarticulated ideas and theories – while the understanding and knowledge that informed interview topics one to four was refined, amended or finessed by data collected in interviews.

Data analysis

In this study morphogenetic methodology leads or directs analysis by providing the conceptual framework through which data became evidence. Following the social conditioning–social interaction and cultural conditioning–socio-cultural interaction propositional models described in Chapter 2, it was assumed that internal and necessary relations exist (at least potentially) within and between social structures and that similar relationships pertain among components of the cultural system.

Data/evidence to identify these relationships came, as stated, predominantly from interview transcript analysis. Archer does not comment on or explain how researchers are in practice to move from data/evidence to explanation and it was therefore necessary to locate a suitable interpretive method. Template analysis (described below) is used in this study to code and order transcript data. However, before describing data coding, a few more words will be said about the manner in which interviewer-interviewee relationships affected analysis/interpretation.

In this study, interviewees, as work colleagues, were aware of the interviewer's opinion on a range of subjects and, although Hammersley and Atkinson (1995) dismiss too fastidious a preoccupation with "outsider and insider myths" (p. 109) as unhelpful, lacking the distancing formality that accompanies interview by an outsider, a noticeably unceremonious or relaxed atmosphere generally prevailed during interviews. As previously recognised, prior familiarity may prompt interviewees to limit or censure responses. Positively, prior familiarity can, as the example below demonstrates, also allow interviewers to discover in the mutual interchange of opinions, ideas and beliefs that the participant was not known to hold.

CHARGE NURSE – COLLOQUIALLY 'SISTER' (C:A): Well, you've got to, I remember you saying now, is it the system's organisational fault or is it an individual's fault. Is that what you said?

INTERVIEWER: Well.

CHARGE NURSE (C:A): You see I was listening.

INTERVIEWER: (Laughs) Well if a mistake happens once in a blue moon it seems reasonable to say an individual made a mistake. But if a consistent series of errors occur it seems to me that you're looking at a structural or organisational problem. To which, I presume, name bands etcetera are a response?

CHARGE NURSE (C:A): (Pause) Yea (pause). I'm just trying to think whether it's been the same person who did it or (pause) whether it's been different people.

INTERVIEWER: I thought it was a small group of people?

CHARGE NURSE (C:A): (Long pause) So you possibly think we should look at the small group of people and their practice?

INTERVIEWER: I don't know. I've changed my opinion a bit. But I can understand why it's been done.

CHARGE NURSE (C:A): But you still don't like it?

INTERVIEWER: I don't, no.

CHARGE NURSE (C:A): I don't like it. I don't like it but I quite like having them there. Probably because I'm part-time whereas you don't get as many days off as I do. But I know I can come back in and administer drugs, drugs safely to people that I don't know very well (pause). And know that I won't make a mistake. That I'll give them to the right person. And that makes me feel more comfortable.

In this excerpt the interviewee upturns interviewee-interviewer roles and questions the interviewer about pre-interview 'bed-side' conversations regarding the then contentious introduction of patient identity or name bands. A great deal of shared background knowledge is assumed in this passage. For example, identity bands were introduced largely at the interviewee's insistence and their introduction was strongly opposed by some staff.

Interviewer-interviewee familiarity greatly assists interpretation of this passage. Prior to the interview I believed identity bands were a response to a series of 'near miss' or potential and minor dosing errors by identified individuals (no harm to patients occurred). This was the advertised rationale for their introduction. These 'near misses' appeared to accompany a rise in high dependency admissions (i.e. patients with complex symptom control needs) and increases in the number and intricacy of prescribed treatments and interventions (described more generally by respondents as 'increasing busyness'). However, here it is apparent that the interviewee *also* sees them as a personal protective device.

From a realist perspective, for the interviewee 'actor', identity bands are, in part, a response to changes in risk perception that attend part-time status. They also physically highlight or make overt an aspect of symmetrical but unequal internal carer-patient socio-structural relations. Further, their introduction coincided with the placement of observation charts and care plans (kardexs) at the end of patient beds (kindred socio-structural changes) and, taken together, these developments challenged the deeply held (cultural system) values of some agents (mostly long-service nurses) regarding desirable forms of hospice care (i.e. values emphasising the importance of non-hierarchical relationships as well as the maintenance of a 'homelike' rather than 'ward-like' environment).

In socio-cultural interaction agents opposing the new developments were in a minority and their views were 'trumped' by rationales accenting the need to safeguard patients and staff (values universally supported). In addition, the socio-structural power inherent in this interviewee's role as senior nurse enabled enforcement of her will.

This description is out of place insofar as it runs ahead of the analysis of data and evidence that Chapter 4 presents. It is included here merely to illustrate the close connection between interpretation and theory that this study attempts. It also demonstrates how, by allowing opinions and beliefs to be easily exchanged, prior familiarity enabled the interviewer to rectify misconceptions. Ease of exchange is evidenced by the playful inversion of normal workplace etiquette and the teasing comment "You see I was listening" (usually the interviewer would *listen to* the Charge Nurse/Sister) as well as the interviewee's questioning of the interviewer ("Is that what you said?"). Of course an unfamiliar researcher would not have held preconceived ideas about the interviewee and, yet, given the decidedly back-stage (Goffman, 1990 [1959]) or non-public nature of disagreement about identity band introduction (and associated changes), a non-participant or unfamiliar researcher might easily have remained unaware of the existence of this controversy.

The example also illustrates that pre-interview discussion and reflection by the interviewee upon a topic subsequently raised in the interview had occurred. Here the interviewee uses what might be termed sociological concepts when she juxtaposes system organisational against individual 'fault' (see first line of dialogue). In this instance the interviewee attributes these concepts or ideas to the interviewer and, although the interviewee is here reinterpreting or translating earlier comments into a sociological idiom, rather than simply repeating them, kindred descriptors are thereafter employed by the interviewer to continue the conversation.

For Carr (2008): "Allowing people to tell their story is more than a semi-structured interview, it is also a conversation" (p. 121) and, as part of this conversation, researcher ideas about hospice activity developed over a considerable period of time. Thus, while the study primarily presents data from formal interviews, conversations and reflection on conversations were not limited to interview episodes. The themes developed in Chapter 4 often occupied part of the informal and everyday discourse of hospice employees and, for the researcher, discussion of such issues thus preceded and continued after 'official' interviews concluded.

No violence is done to critical realism or morphogenetic theory or the authenticity of interviewee comments by this. Critical realism and morphogenetic-morphostatic theory aim to reveal via retroduction or retrodiction the interplay of structural (social and cultural) and agential factors that influence change (genesis) or stability (stasis). Inference regarding the interplay of such factors – by an analysis of interview transcripts – is not compromised if the ideas informing inference are supported by concepts and understandings from without the interviews. Likewise, from a realist perspective, it cannot be assumed that the authenticity of participant responses is enhanced or degraded by prior sensitisation to and reflection on the issues discussed in interviews. (Archer appears to support this argument in *Culture and Agency*; see also Baert, 1998, p. 205, on 'second-order reflection'.)

Interviewee comments thus permitted the researcher to identify previously unknown or unrecognised events, perspectives and structures – and, as stated, prior familiarity played a beneficial part in this process. For example, the conflictual nature of certain forms of asymmetric socio-structural relations (e.g. relations exposed in or through interaction between the hospice and County Palliative Care Directorate) was not recognised in advance of interviews. Similarly, while the relationship between demographic change and evolving health needs is recognised in the literature (Fennell *et al.*, 1994; Allsop, 1995; Alcock, 1996), the possible significance of demographic change on admission and discharge practice at the study site was under-appreciated by this researcher before interviews took place. Further, hostility by some local NHS palliative care consultants towards hospices in general and the study site in particular would not have been realised without interviewing senior hospice staff. Clearly more detail is required to substantiate claims that these examples embody social-structural and socio-cultural structural level conflict and these 'assertions' are made here simply to illustrate that interviews provided or permitted insights that would not otherwise have been easily gained. Chapter 4, to repeat, fleshes out these examples.

Template analysis

Template analysis as described by Nigel King (2004, 2007) is used in this study to thematically order or code interview data. Templates describe the:

> themes identified in textual data. Some of these will be defined a priori, but they will be modified and added to as the researcher reads and interprets the texts. The template is organised in a way which represents the relationships between themes, as defined by the researcher, most commonly using a hierarchical structure.
>
> (King, 2004, p. 256)

Following King (ibid.), initial or primary template themes and codes were identical with a priori identified interview guide headings. Given that these headings formed the basis for each interview, it was, unsurprisingly, possible to locate a great deal of information within or against them (see Appendix A). However, as will be shown, interview codes were disaggregated and reordered in the process of analysis and new codes were also developed. To aid 'readability' a series of appendices are employed to illustrate the analytic process (see Table 3.2).

Appendices B and C present illustrative post-interview transcript summaries from the first two people interviewed (labelled A:a and B:a – see interviewee schedule, Table 3.1, p. 46). Summaries were compiled shortly after interviews concluded. They were constructed *before* template coding occurred and they form part of the process of pre-coding transcript familiarisation (described in Appendix D). Summaries contain interviewer comments (early and provisional interpretation or analysis) and they illustrate the distinctiveness of interviewee discursive or conversational forms. Thus interviewee A:a, a nursing assistant who had worked at the hospice almost from its inception, spoke in what might be described as a direct manner. She 'answered' questions and her comments are represented as a series of binary contrasts (Appendix B). Alternatively, interviewee B:a, a registered nurse with previous nursing home experience, spoke more fulsomely. Indeed significant transcript cuts had to be made to protect this interviewee from 'over-exposure' (Lipscomb, 2010b). Her effusive style is reflected in a summary that is less 'bulleted' than A:a's (Appendix C).

Table 3.2 List of appendices (B to H)

Appendix	
B	Pre-coding interview summary for interviewee A:a
C	Pre-coding interview summary for interviewee B:a
D	Interview coding process for A:a
E	Interview coding process for B:a
F	Template for A:a
G	Template for B:a
H	Master template (all interviews)

To illustrate the coding process transcript passages from both interviews are reproduced in appendices D and E together with a commentary. Appendix D outlines the importance of pre-coding transcript familiarisation. The procedure for applying coding labels to a short series of remarks from interviewee A:a is described. Appendix E interprets a longer passage of dialogue from respondent B:a. It carries forward themes raised in Appendix D by arguing for the importance of inter- and extra-transcript contextualisation in interpretation.

Appendices F and G present templates for interviewees A:a and B:a. Templates code and order data hierarchically. Different templates may have different numbers of hierarchical code ordering levels and, within the same template, different codes can be assigned different numbers of levels. Coding levels refer to degrees of abstraction.

Code levels: → Increasing detail and decreasing abstraction
1 2 3 4 5 6

Coding detail increases and abstraction decreases as code levels rise. However, codes with six levels (e.g. Appendix F – Change *to* financial crisis necessitated practice changes) and codes with two levels (e.g. Appendix F – Treament/interventions *to* rise in interventions linked to change from terminal to palliative care status) can share roughly similar degrees of detail and abstraction in final code levels – i.e. 'financial crisis necessitated practice changes' (level 6 code) and 'rise in interventions linked to change from terminal to palliative care status' (level 2 code) both contain the same *approximate* level of detail relative to the transcript source.

Coding exposes agreement and disagreement between respondents. For example, although interviewees A:a and B:a both talk about 'professionalism', interviewee A:a is saddened by a professionalism that, she believes, reduces the quality of staff-patient relationships whereas B:a welcomed professionalism as a means of, in part, reducing her emotional exposure to the high number of encountered deaths. Concepts such as professionalism are difficult to pin down and a variety of meanings are carried by this term. However, in this instance interviewees A:a and B:a affectively diverge and conceptually agree that professionalism, as they use the term, 'distances' staff-patient relations.

Appendix H presents the master template (adapted and abridged below – see Figure 3.1). This master template combines and further interprets or orders individual transcript templates. Combination was facilitated by the use of overlapping or complementary codes when coding individual transcripts. Yet interviewee comments varied in style (Appendices B and C) and content (Appendices F and G) and, in combining individual templates, considerable interpretative discretion is required. Thus every transcript contained unique data and every individual template contains specific codes. Template specific codes are excluded from the master template when, in the researcher's opinion, their content is irrelevant to those aspects of activity here under review.

For example, interviewee B:a juxtaposed nursing home against hospice care to illustrate, what to her, were deficiencies in hospice care (Appendix E). Other interviewees did not make similar allusions, however, and thus, while 'nursing home' appears as a code in B:a's individual template, it is not represented in the master template (Appendix H).

King (2004) supports this form of code or data winnowing. He also recognises that novice researchers find it difficult to balance the need for clarity and comprehension against the need to capture as much detail as possible. The need to 'collapse' data (now evidence) in this manner is difficult to avoid or argue against. However, significant and difficult epistemic questions are created by such practices for both novice and experienced researchers.

For example, it should perhaps be recognised that since template analysis does not assume "that the frequency of a code in a particular text corresponds to its salience" (ibid., p. 256), jettisoning superfluous codes and/or data for the sake of clarity is problematic. It is problematic because it is not necessarily clear how immateriality or redundancy can be established in advance of full analysis. Kindred issues are raised later (Chapter 5) in relation to this study's self-imposed limitation to 'aspects' of hospice practice.

In summary, template analysis advances through a number of stages. In the first instance and prior to coding the researcher reads interview transcripts mindful of the template that is being applied. Here theory's 'downwards' influence on data is most evident. Pre-coding familiarisation enables the researcher to form a mental picture of the relationships within and between interviews (discussed in Appendix D). Template coding then assigns labels (codes) to words, phrases and passages within each interview (see Appendices D and E). Labels identify ideas and events in accordance with template themes. However, by focusing on the detail of interviewee comments, labels also inform or 'clothe' template themes and in this way empiric data exerts what might be termed 'upwards' pressure on theory. Labels are then ordered and combined in individual transcript templates (Appendices F and G) and, at this point, original template themes re-emerge albeit that they are now 'fleshed out' and modified/developed. Individual templates are then combined in a master template (Appendix H) and the influence of morphogenetic theory again makes itself felt as, in this instance, data is coded and ordered to create (inductively colligate) evidence in support of the claim that understanding is best advanced by considering (in Chapter 4) 'Structures and institutions' and 'Relations within the hospice'.

Theoretical elaboration, abstraction and subjective researcher judgement is evident throughout this process. For example, although the master template (Appendix H), situates 'Professionalism' under the key heading 'Relations within the hospice', earlier versions of the master template used alternative codes and code ordering sequences (e.g. at one time 'Professionalism' was positioned under the heading 'Hospice – Internal Change') and, although alternative schemas – alternative hypotheses – did not diverge radically from that finally established (the schemas were 'more or less' commensurable), recognising that data and evidence can be variously ordered is important.

Structures and institutions

- State/NHS relations
  - Department of Health
    - Clinical Governance
    - Clinical Standards Act
  - Primary Care Trust
    - County Palliative Care Directorate
  - NHS Palliative Care Consultants
  - GPs
  - Macmillan Nurses

- Demographic relations
  - Admissions
  - Discharges

Relations within the hospice

- Organisational re-designation as a Specialist Palliative Care Unit (SPCU)
  - Hospice (historic)
  - SPCU
    - busier – less time for non-physical care
    - patients – 'sicker'
    - staffing – changes in numbers, ratios, roles and functions

- Consultant differences

- Treatment/interventions
  - Increasing use of treatment/interventions

- Admissions – Discharges
  - Admissions – 'sicker', more dependent
  - Discharges – conflict
    - end stage patients

- Professionalism
  - Bureaucratisation

- Medicalisation
  - Doctors more powerful/influential – nurses less powerful/influential

- Spiritual-religious issues
  - Religious withdrawal – spiritual claims made

Figure 3.1 Master list of codes – abridged from Appendix H.

It is important because minor variations in the coding and ordering of data or evidence potentially alters the conclusions or findings that are reached *and* this analytic difference may contribute to the generation of hypotheses (broadly defined) that fail to meet Hempel's (1945) equivalence condition (Lipscomb, 2008). (This is explored further in Chapter 5.) Here it is recognised that all description necessarily involves systematising narrative structures and tropes (Bruner, 1990) and a narrative's power or persuasiveness can rely upon plot coherence and plausibility rather than logical rigour or the truthfulness of claims made. (Bruner, ibid., labels this narrative's "indifference to extralinguistic reality", p. 44).

Thus, while both coding and sequential description meet a need for order that, in realism's case, rests on transcendental claims regarding the nature of reality, it is acknowledged that presentational forms may, in themselves, unwittingly distort or bolster the particular transitive description of intransitive reality that is proposed. For Fernandez:

> figurative devices lie at the very heart of discourse, defining situations and grounding our sense of what is to be taken as real and objective and, therefore, entitled (by means of the figurative elements we employ) to have real consequences.
>
> (Fernandez, 1991, p. 1)

In this study the master template outlined above links transcript analysis to morphogenetic theory by structuring the descriptive and interpretive statements of interviewees under headings that thereafter form the themes or topics explored in Chapter 4. As noted, not every identified code is utilised because not every code informs those aspects of hospice activity that are discussed. Thus in contrast to some varieties of ethnography, this study does not seek to develop a "holistic"[6] (Maggs-Rapport, 2001, p. 376; Simmons, 2007, p. 9) view of the organisation or its work (it has repeatedly been stated that this work looks at *aspects* of hospice activity). Realist theory asserts that mechanism interplay can and often does occur behind the backs of actors (mechanisms need not be actualised and actualisation need not be observed or identified as events) and it may therefore be unrealistic to assume that a totalising overview is ever possible. Nevertheless, not only does the choice and presentational ordering of codes inevitably influence the manner in which data and evidence thereafter inform – and is informed by – morphogenetic modelling, but, further, while it is legitimate to look at aspects rather than the totality of interactions within social settings, problematic questions remain regarding the coherence or delineation of 'aspects' under review. (The problem of event identity re-emerges in Chapter 5.)

Template analysis, aptness for realist research

Here a brief description of the aptness of template analysis for realist research is advanced. Template analysis has been employed in palliative care research (King *et al.*, 2003) and King (2004) argues that it might prove valuable where realist qualitative investigation seeks, contra idealism, to discover the hidden or underlying causes of action but where researchers do not wish to become locked into overly prescriptive frameworks.

King (ibid.) distinguishes template analysis from other forms of qualitative interpretation. He suggests, for example, that template analysis differs from phenomenological textual analysis in two respects. First, while phenomenologists often engage in detail with a small number of texts/transcripts, template analysts, on the other hand, organise data, perhaps more superficially, across larger numbers of texts/transcripts. Second, King (ibid.) argues that contrary to the stated practice of phenomenological researchers, template analysis generates coding templates, as stated, on an a priori basis and researcher interests thus overtly set the framework within which data collection and analysis occurs. Approaching both the interview process and subsequent data interpretation through the lens of pre-established themes (templates) is not unique to King (ibid.). However, King (ibid.) permits researchers to alter or develop codes as analysis progresses (as happened in this instance) and this flexibility is to be welcomed.

According to King (ibid.): "Template analysis works very well in studies which seek to examine the perspectives of different groups within an organisational context" (p. 268) and, as will be seen, retroducing and retrodicting the causes of group conflict and interaction form a major part of Chapter 4. King (ibid.) also argues (perhaps less plausibly) that template analysis's relative lack of a substantive literature is beneficial since it is, perforce, unencumbered by epistemological baggage. Attempts have been made to link template analysis with relativist-contextualism (e.g. Madill *et al.*, 2000). However, King (2004) suggests the method is incompatible with strong relativist positions that demand fine textual analysis as well as those forms of discourse analysis that dismiss coding as overly limiting. King (ibid.) also argues that template analysis is inappropriate for quantitative or qualitative research that seeks to code text as analytic units since, as stated, the frequency with which a unit of code is noted does not, in template analysis, correspond to the importance or significance of that code or theme. Template analysis thus appears to complement, in principle at least, morphogenetic methodology.

Situating the researcher in the research

The person and role of the researcher is overtly situated in this study at several points. The Introduction identified three personal factors or interests that direct the content and form of subsequent work. And I have, in this chapter, repeatedly argued that subjective criteria – criteria influenced by, for example, my position at the study site – are necessarily involved or implicated in the way morphogenetic constructs have been used. This does not mean that evidence is not objective and, although differing views on this topic exist, Achinstein's (2010) evidential criteria are not necessarily opposed here (I remain uncommitted on this subject). Nevertheless, the potential significance of prior socialisation into the role of nurse has been linked to research ethics and reflexivity – and the researcher's influence on data collection and analysis is noted.

Looking ahead to Chapter 4, where this study focuses on the hospice as a voluntary organisation, where it discusses treatment or intervention appropriateness and where spiritual matters are investigated, it is here acknowledged that extra-research factors may have and probably did influence the analysis offered. For example, earlier studies in social policy and a varied personal employment history presumably affect the way issues surrounding the hospice's voluntary status are approached. Further, D'Antonio (2006) argues that nurse researchers are socialised to ask questions that others may not. This may or may not be true. However, personal interest in treatment or intervention appropriateness at the end of life were I suspect encouraged, in part, by pre-hospice enculturation within 'high-tech' clinical environments (e.g. oncology and haematology – see Introduction) that allow and advance different values to those associated with palliative or end of life care. Moreover, discussions regarding the role and place of religious or spiritual values at the study site cannot but be influenced by a lack of personal religious belief and, following Paley (2008a, 2008b), doubts about the conceptual usefulness of the descriptor 'spirituality'.

Situating quantitative or qualitative researchers within their research continues to challenge traditional or deep rooted concerns regarding objectivity and bias minimisation (Drew, 2006). However, that said, while the prevalence of self-reflexivity varies markedly between disciplines and approaches (Pennycook, 2005), presenting personal narratives that acknowledge the influence of subjectivity within qualitative investigations is now something of a commonplace (Hammersley and Atkinson, 1995; Baert, 1998; Nelson, 2005; Holliday, 2005; Achinstein, 2010) and, moreover, Canagarajah (2005) states that: "Even quantitative studies now make a gesture toward acknowledging the personal" (p. 309).

Recognising the significance of researcher choices and decisions within this work it can be argued, following Ramanathan (2005a, 2005b), that the researcher must be, or inevitably is, part of the field of enquiry and Dean *et al.* (2006b) berate, from a realist perspective, researchers who lack an interest in the contribution of the pre-research self to study construction. For Nelson, positioning the self within research is:

> a means of expanding or enriching one's data sources; tracing one's complex and fraught positionings vis-à-vis the research participants or the subject matter; or recognizing one's own limitations as a researcher. Yet at the same time, texts in which the researcher's subjectivity is foregrounded can be perceived as irrelevant, self-indulgent, or insufficiently critical.
>
> (Nelson, 2005, p. 315)

Arguably, all three of Nelson's (ibid.) justificatory criteria are, to a limited extent, met in the above reflexive 'confessional'. However, again following

Nelson (ibid.), a criticism of this study is that the approach taken in this work is insufficient or underdeveloped and more attention should perhaps have been given to comprehending the extra-research components that the researcher brought to the study. It could of course be argued that this sort of analysis requires, among much else, that private or first-person thoughts be made public and the very nature and feasibility of such sharing remains disputed (Longworth, 2012). Nonetheless, rigorous exploration of the researcher's influence might focus on any number of overlapping factors including age, ethnicity, sex, gender, social and cultural positioning, role or workplace values and psychological outlook or temperament. Such an investigation would however be time-consuming, it assumes that the contribution of these factors is in some sense stable (i.e. it assumes that subjectivity is not in flux or ephemeral; Cihelkova, 2013) and, given the "complexifying" (Ramanathan, 2005a, p. 291) and contested nature of many of these variables (see, for example, Drevdahl *et al.*, 2006, on the conceptual misuse of race and ethnicity descriptors), it is likely that reflection upon these issues would inevitably remain ambling, speculative and partial. Therefore, while some combination of researcher social and cultural situatedness, psychological disposition(s) and, presumably, physical or biological attributes informs, at various levels, the identification and analysis of those aspects of hospice work hereafter discussed, these issues are now put aside. (Though some further comments are made in Chapter 5.)

Notes

1 This fourfold division differs from but has similarities with Cruickshank's (2003b, p. 114) "levels of realist theorising".

2 Empiric is used here to designate all occurrences and events that can be known or identified. This interpretation does not exclude qualitative or subjective occurrences from the category of events.

3 Where this ideal is realised – and from a very different perspective – analogies with Schleiermacherian hermeneutics may be made. Thus following Malpas (2005), Ramberg and Gjesdal (2005) and Habermas (2008), Schleiermacher [1768–1834] emphasised the interpreter's role in interpretation. He argued that textual analysis does not occur outside of an interpreter's psychological disposition and historical situation. Meaning is thus culturally and socially mediated. However, contra what would now be termed idealism or postmodernism, Schleiermacher allowed that interpretation occurs relative to an external world and that, while knowledge is perforce a product of experience, experience is informed by judgement and judgement, if theoretically sound, can provide knowledge of external reality.

4 Three interview recordings were in part or full corrupted due to technical errors or malfunctions. These recordings are identified with an * in the interview list.

5 Conversational is here used in its everyday or non-technical sense. The descriptor does not refer to forms of conversational or discourse analysis as described, for example, by Silverman (2005).

6 The terms 'holistic' and 'holism' are variously interpreted. Neural and psychological theorists counterpoise holistic or neural network theories against, for example, modular homuncular functionalism (Rose, 2006). Sociologists, on the other hand, use the descriptors to refer – as here – to the notion that: "The complex reality of society might

appear visible only in its entirety" (Trigg, 2001, p. 57). (Archer associates the term with the dissolution of personal identity – *RST*, p. 249.) Alternatively, in Chapter 4 the terms are employed in a third nursing or clinical context. There holism denotes an approach to healthcare that incorporates psychological, social, spiritual *and* physical dimensions or interests (Sarkis and Skoner, 1987; Jackson, 2007). Holism or holistic care in this sense seeks to distance or "move away from a biomedical model" of care (Earle, 2005, p. 61).

4 Study findings

This chapter begins with a brief scene setting description of the organisation and layout of the hospice or, as it officially wished to be known, a specialist palliative care unit. To aid clarity, throughout this chapter, the study site is generally described simply as a hospice. This might seem odd (is it a hospice or a specialist unit?). Nonetheless, as the Introduction records, the term hospice was colloquially used by all study site participants (even those who proclaimed the change in designation) and, in addition, and as will be seen, the nature and form of specialism remained a contested issue throughout the study period. Time frames (T^1–T^4) used in the study are then noted and problematised and – the main element of this chapter – findings are thereafter presented under two headings: 'Structures and institutions' and 'Relations within the hospice'.

To construct these findings, template analysis, informed and steered by morphogenetic-morphostatic methodology, identified ordered and coded data/evidence. Inferential abduction (retroduction and retrodiction) suggested social and cultural structural relations that, during the study period(s), underwent reproduction (stasis) and/or elaboration (genesis). Agential social and socio-cultural interactions are detailed that point towards the existence of contradictory and complementary situated logics. Differential morphogenesis is recognised.

The hospice

Unsurprisingly, aspects of the hospice's organisation varied over the study period (see Figure 4.1 below). For example, towards the end of T^3 a part-time chaplain retired and an additional part-time social work assistant was recruited. The following details are nonetheless substantively correct for the T^2–T^3 period (time frames are described shortly).

Situated a few miles outside the county capital and built on land originally provided at nominal cost by an adjacent but now closed nunnery, the hospice or specialist palliative care unit offers patients and visitors pleasing views over rolling farmland. Physically the building consists of or occupies three floors (first, ground and basement). The first floor contains office and managerial space. Storage, additional administrative space and hairdressing facilities are located in the basement. Clinical activity occurs on the ground floor. Attractive gardens surround the facility.

On the ground floor, a day-patient unit occupies one end of the building. This has its own entrance, seating areas, bath/shower, lymphodema-dressing and office spaces. A lounge area with dining tables, settees and television separates day- and in-patient spaces. Two family overnight suites and a compact self-service patient and family kitchen abut the lounge. The in-patient unit is approached through the lounge (from day-patients) or via a separate main reception and entrance. A chapel (God) and gift/sweet shop (Mammon) face each other across this space. The in-patient unit comprises three four-bedded bays and four single rooms (the hospice has sixteen beds in total). Staff dining, kitchen, clinical common room and office areas are situated at the far end of the building. A 'chapel of rest' is located within, but apart from, the main building. A small combined library and meeting room is sited within the grounds.

Hospice work structures reflect and are influenced by wider social/organisational norms, government policy and healthcare practice (McGuire *et al.*, 1991; Osborne and McLaughlin, 2004). A General Manager, appointed by the charity's trustees, provides day-to-day and long-term strategic leadership. Administratively, the General Manager oversees a team that includes secretarial, accounting and logistical support, a fundraising department, a part-time media unit, an estates department and a volunteer coordinator.

Expenditure on salaries and other variable and fixed costs is approximately two million pounds per annum. Less than 20 per cent of income comes from statutory sources of any sort and year-on-year statutory funding is declining relative to total expenditure. Throughout the study period bequests were a vital but erratic source of income. More consistently, revenue comes from eleven shops and a professional fundraising department of seven full-time equivalent staff generate income from the local community. Thirty-seven commissioned field canvassers promote a hospice lottery.

A full-time (registered) social worker and part-time (unregistered) social work assistant care for ongoing (e.g. bereavement follow-up) and specialist (e.g. child) emotional needs. Pastoral and religious or spiritual support is provided by a full-time clergyman and two part-time unpaid voluntary clergywomen. One and a half full-time equivalent educators run courses for external clients (e.g. nursing home personnel).

Clinical staff hierarchies mirror NHS medical and nursing establishments albeit that, importantly, staff-patient ratios are excellent compared with state sector provision. For example, during most of the study period in-patient morning shifts were covered by a mix of seven registered nursing and nursing auxiliary staff and afternoon shifts used in combination four registered nurses and nursing auxiliaries. Towards the end of the study period these a.m./p.m. ratios rose to eight : five. It was always possible to bring in additional staff if and when required.

The day unit has dedicated registrar medical cover (frequently augmented by a senior house officer or specialist registrar trainee) and the in-patient unit has a full-time consultant, a part-time consultant (shared with the local NHS county hospital) and two or more senior house officers or specialist registrar trainees.

Additional medical cover is provided as needed (e.g. over bank holidays) by general practitioners who are familiar with the hospice. Visits to outlying clinics are made by consultants and other medical staff on a rotational basis.

Nursing staff are headed by a nursing director and, for part of the study period; a nursing ward manager liaised between the nursing director, charge nurses – popularly known as 'sisters' – and staff (this person left during the study to become a Macmillan nurse). The in-patient unit had two charge nurses but this was upped to three following the departure of the ward manager. The day care unit has one charge nurse. More than forty nurses and auxiliary (assistant) nursing staff are employed in the day- and in-patient units and, of this number, at least 30 per cent work part-time.

The hospice also relies upon the goodwill and efforts of large numbers of volunteers. The trading wing uses more than two hundred volunteers to staff shops. Volunteers collect and deliver supplies, transport (some) patients and raise funds in innumerable ways. Within the hospice, voluntary (unpaid) nursing and auxiliary nursing support is informally available and non-nursing volunteers perform multiple roles. For example, the day unit uses four to six volunteers each morning. These people welcome patients and their carers, help make patients and visitors comfortable, prepare and serve refreshments and engage in friendly banter. They also provide entertainment and run activities on an ad-hoc basis. Likewise, the in-patient unit uses around six 'home-maker' volunteers each day. Home-makers circulate refreshments (including very good home-baked cake), talk with patients, assist at mealtimes in food distribution and collection, offer morning and afternoon drinks (alcoholic and non-alcoholic) and help tidy up. Volunteer receptionists greet visitors and answer incoming telephone calls during working hours.

Specifying and critiquing study time frames

The findings of this study are divided into two sections. The first section is titled 'Structures and institutions'. This section describes forms of social interaction that, it is argued, reveal structural relations that generated for the hospice a situated logic that contributed towards the decision to re-designate the organisation, in 2000, a specialist palliative care unit.

It is important to emphasise that many of the events described in this section – events which explain why re-designation occurred – took place *after* the event they describe happened. Re-designation is not then the T^4 outcome of the time frame specified in Figure 4.1 below. Rather, interviewee comments (obtained between T^2 and T^3) describe forms of pre- and post-2000 interaction (empiric events); these interactions permit contradictory structural relations to be abducted, and it is these relations, known by their effects on specific entities, that are inferred to have prompted organisational re-designation at T^1 (Figure 4.1). Hopefully, if this is not now clear, it will become so shortly.

In Figure 4.1, T^1 refers to the period prior to November 2001, T^4 is placed after September 2003 and T^2–T^3 occupies the intervening time. This study time frame captures events that are described under 'Relations within the hospice'

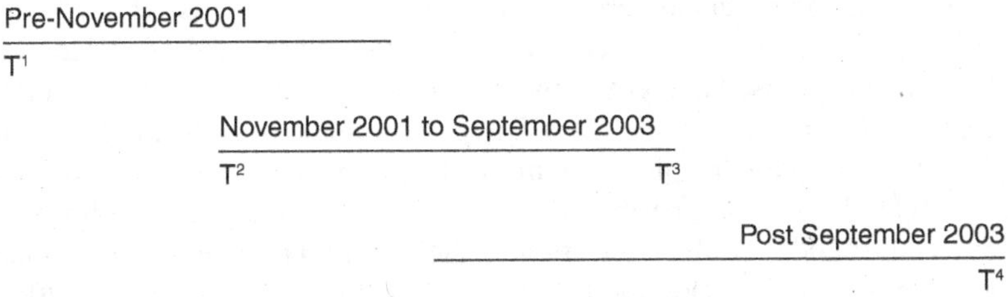

Figure 4.1 Study time frame.

(the second section of the findings). Here the meaning and consequents of re-designation and its correlates for hospice agents are explored.

This somewhat convoluted explanation highlights, among other things, the difficulty of establishing event identities and boundaries (i.e. the constituents and timings of events). To ease and aid the explanation of events described under 'Structures and institutions', Figure 4.2 on p. 80 presents the structural conditioning forces which led to organisational elaboration as a discrete yet partial analytic history. Figure 4.2 uses a different time frame (T^1–T^4) to that described in Figure 4.1 above. Re-designation is structurally elaborative insofar as it potentially alters relations with, for example, state and NHS institutions (though the structures precipitating re-designation existed before and remain after 2000). Re-designation also accelerated change in agential relations within the hospice.

The time frame outlined in Figure 4.1 accords with researcher study site access. Thus permission to proceed was granted in November 2001 and frequent contact between researcher and study site ceased in September 2003 when the last interview was conducted (I had by then taken up another post elsewhere). Establishing study periods according to access is not unusual. However, it is problematic. Researchers may wish to argue that their objects of study are in some sense 'stable' and it does not therefore matter when observation or investigation occurs. However, we might reasonably assume that this cannot or can only rarely be said of the social world where flux and change are commonplace. If this is accepted then 'good' or defendable reasons should generally exist, and be given, regarding why particular study time frames are chosen (decisions about when to conduct social research ought not to be made capriciously). Yet access and study periods were in this instance contingently set by the researcher according to personal rather than 'hospice/study' criteria.

Fortuitously three events occurred just prior to November 2001 that may, retrospectively, validate or 'make sense' of the time frame/study period employed. First, 2000 saw the passing of the Care Standards Act (Department of Health – DH, 2000). Implemented in England in 2001 (DH, 2005) this act is seen as a serious potential threat to organisational independence by some senior hospice staff. Second, around 2000 the hospice re-designated itself, as stated, a specialist palliative care unit and this change promotes, it will be argued, significant ideational dispute within the organisation. Third, 2001 saw the appointment of a new and, for some, controversial part-time medical consultant. This person introduced clinical practices at the hospice that were variously resisted or welcomed and, in this way, he exposed and challenged established shibboleths. This person also chaired the County Palliative Care Directorate and, as such, he played a major role in brokering the hospice's future relationship with external and potentially antagonistic local NHS 'partners'. Further, this consultant left the hospice towards the end of 2003. Draft publication of the County Directorate's plan also occurred at this time and T^4 (Figure 4.1) can reasonably be situated in late 2003 since this document heralds a new phase in hospice-Directorate relations.

Nevertheless, determining study periods according to access meant that, for example, it was not possible to fully evaluate the elaborative potential of organisational re-designation vis-à-vis state and NHS relations (since insufficient time elapsed in which transformation could be observed) and, moreover, despite retrospective justification, fixing time frames (temporal boundaries) at set points is problematic insofar as this disregards or hampers the investigation of alternative event or analytic histories. Indeed, it should be noted that, from the perspective of participant-interviewees, dating change proved to be largely a function of service duration.

Thus long service interviewees recognise that the pace of change increased post-2000. They also describe the impact that events such as organisational re-designation or the arrival of the then new part-time consultant had on clinical practice within their descriptions of change in the same way that colleagues with shorter service histories do. However, long service allows perspectives on change to be advanced that undercut explanations focused simply on recent events. For example, the interviewee identified as A:a held strong or developed normative views on what hospice care should be or encompass and these views informed her description of developments in staff-patient relations that had taken place over decades. As part of this narrative she outlined a movement away from overt religiosity or the easy expression of religious sentiment, something that had been permissible during the hospice's founding years, to the now present atmosphere in which religious succour has, in some key circumstances, to be offered covertly by clinical staff.

NURSING ASSISTANT A:a I find it very sad really. Because, well, it's not for me to say but, you know. It was nice for people who had sat with their relative dying for, you know, hours on end, and then they died, and then for somebody to say to them, would you like to say a little prayer? Would you like to say a little prayer? You know, would you like to say a little prayer, maybe not for the person who's died, but just for you, to shut your eyes and think, it's all over, you know.

INTERVIEWER: Would you feel comfortable saying that to anybody now?

NURSING ASSISTANT A:a (Pause) Not if anybody's looking, no (laughs).

INTERVIEWER: Would you say it if they weren't looking?

NURSING ASSISTANT A:a (Laughing) Probably.

Accounts such as this highlight the incremental or gradual character of some aspects of change and comments by long service staff force the researcher to acknowledge that dating and interpreting events or, when numerical modifiers apply, sortals, is often occurrence or topic specific. Recent change thus appears to have exacerbated the withdrawal by clinical staff from overt religious expression, an expression that some staff value; however, exacerbation advances trends that were already entrenched and this development is not in itself new. It is later argued that a consideration of evolving ideas about spirituality and religiosity at the study site, such as those described above, may helpfully aid or add to understanding in a variety of ways. However, the point being stressed here is that explaining spiritual/religious change requires longer time frames than 2001–2003 to be considered.

Questions about event identity and persistence are in some (possibly key) respects under-explored by Archer and Bhaskar. Both authors engage at length and in depth with these topics. However, they also overlook what might be termed 'traditional' treatments of event identity/persistence (see, e.g. Casati and Varzi, 2009). This issue is explored further in Chapter 5. Here it is simply noted that, negatively, the argument presented above opens up the possibility of unbounded regress and/or stultifying complication as individual participants (e.g. A:a) may reference – from their perspective – distinctive event sets (i.e. unique T^1–T^4 histories) *and*, if this line was pursued, each interpretation may require the recognition of alternative and potentially conflicting analytic histories. This would clearly be a recipe for muddle and, yet, positively, recognising the interlocking but distinctive nature of personal event histories (personal interpretations) extends the concept of differential morphogenesis outlined in Chapter 2 and, perhaps, reflects or captures important elements of real world complexity.

Structures and institutions

Structures and institutions are variously described in the sociological literature (López and Scott, 2000). Some realists (e.g. Elder-Vass, 2008) highlight integrative links between relational structures and institutions while others (e.g. Fleetwood, 2008) mark their difference. Following Fleetwood (ibid.), institutions are here defined as systems of coordinating rules and conventions. These rules and conventions are both external to agents *and* embodied by agents as habits and practices. Organisations such as the hospice under study represent a subset of institutions (Hodgson, 2006; Elder-Vass, 2007a). Structures, here synonymous with Archer's social and cultural structures, are internally emergent constraining and enabling "latticeworks" (Fleetwood, 2008, p. 29) of interest bearing relations. In this study, structures evidence causal influence when the interests they generate are taken up or mediated through the projects and actions of situated agents.

Organisationally the hospice is an independent third sector voluntary or charitable healthcare provider. Structurally it sits within systems of social and cultural system relations that are dominated by state run or sponsored forms of health and social care. Thus, on a daily basis the hospice cooperates with GPs (general medical practitioners), district nurses, local NHS trusts and social service departments. It also interacts with charitable non-governmental organisations such as Macmillan and Marie Curie nurses. However, these organisations are effectively integrated into NHS and other governmental-state infrastructures, and the hospice's focus is thus directed towards bodies that, from its perspective, can be classified as clinical and/or regulatory. (Though, to complicate matters: "there are different relationships with different parts of the same organisation", Nursing Director, G:b.).

The existence of structural relations between the hospice and socialised or state sponsored healthcare is here revealed through a description of interaction with (i) the County Palliative Care Directorate and (ii) Department of Health. The effects of (iii) demographic change on the hospice are also considered. It is argued that the structures revealed (mainly but not exclusively social structures) exerted and continue to exert pressures on the hospice that, in 2000, contributed to the creation of a situated logic favouring organisational re-designation. This was a significant event and the emergent consequents of organisational re-designation and its correlates for agents are, as stated, later described in 'Relations within the hospice'.

The County Palliative Care Directorate

The County Palliative Care Directorate (henceforth Directorate)[1] is a standing "strategic planning body for the creation, for the development of all palliative care services" (General Manager, N:b). Set up in the early 1990s "at our expense" (ibid., N:b) with the then Health Authority (now and henceforth Primary Care Trust or PCT) the Directorate was to be "a mechanism that would highlight the deficiencies in service and address those deficiencies and ensure that they somehow got the resources to be improved" (ibid., N:b).

Despite the small size of the hospice relative to the Primary Care Trust, the hospice need not be considered a micro referent if Archer's relational theory is accepted (Chapter 2) and, insofar as both bodies shared a common purpose (resource procurement) and both were mutually co-dependent (in establishing the Directorate) the relationship between hospice and Primary Care Trust could, initially at least, be described as symmetrically internal. However, once established, social and cultural structural contradictions emerged and, by 2000, the Directorate and hospice were related internally but asymmetrically. To describe the nature of asymmetry and explain how it came about (i.e. to retroduce from interview statements the factors defining and producing such relations) three *overlapping* topics or themes are considered. These are labelled (i) divergent interests, (ii) challenges to independence and (iii) NHS palliative consultant hostility.

Divergent interests

By and post-2000, divergent interests and powers characterised or underpinned the nature of relations between the hospice and the Directorate. Thus, while the hospice sees itself as a vital regional asset, from the Directorate's perspective it is of marginal concern. This was graphically conveyed by one non-hospice Directorate member who sketched the diagram reproduced below (Diagram 4.1).

The schema on the left places the hospice at the centre of activity and this, according to the Directorate member, is how the hospice presents and thinks about itself. Alternatively, the schema on the right illustrates the Directorate's viewpoint. Here the hospice is significantly less relevant for, in financial and other terms (i.e. annual countywide deaths), in-patient NHS acute and palliative care and community situated GP, district nurse, Macmillan, Marie Curie, supporting social and community services and nursing or rest homes, are simply more important. Asymmetrical relations are produced by divergent interests and an imbalance in power. For the hospice, the consequence of asymmetry stems from the unequal powers held by each organisation *and* the Directorate's willingness to wield its superior power in pursuing its own interests.[2]

Challenges to independence

The Directorate has been and is seeking to guide providers and, perhaps inevitably, this directive role is seen as a challenge to organisational independence.

NURSING DIRECTOR G:a I think you will find and, there're a lot of fights going on, that we are being pushed more and more towards, by the NHS. And I see that through the Directorate. I mean you only have to look at some of the stuff coming out of the Directorate and how they feel we shouldn't do 'x' unless the Directorate says so. Well, sorry, we will do 'x' whether the Directorate says so or not. Because, the hospice is here for the patients and if we wanted to spend 'x' million on upgrading the hospice it's got nothing to, to, for the Directorate to say whether we do it or not.

At a national level the main challenge to organisational independence comes, senior interviewees believe, from the Department of Health and Care Standards Act (DH, 2000) (described below). However, locally, as the above excerpt

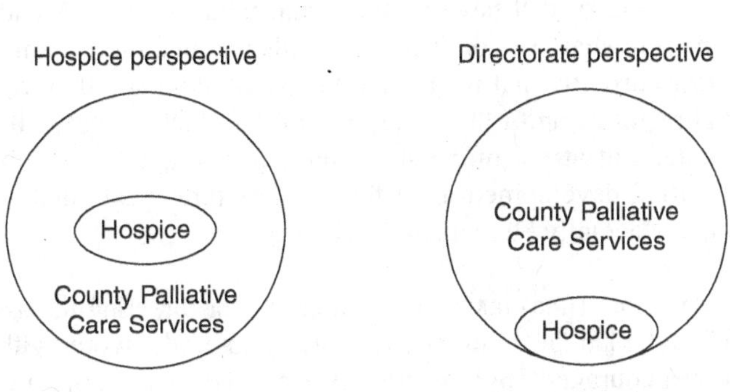

Diagram 4.1 Contrasting hospice and directorate perspectives.

indicates, the Directorate is viewed as the chief force *pushing* the hospice towards the NHS.

The Directorate's willingness and potential ability to "integrate" (Part-time Medical Consultant, O:a) the hospice into overall service provision was, initially, unforeseen. The Directorate's function is to plan, coordinate and resource palliative care. Originally, hospice personnel thought they would play a significant role in developing such plans and, to advance this process and in keeping with then recommended practice (e.g. Clark, 1994), it was decided that a needs assessment was required. However, despite "the longstanding duty placed on health authorities to develop strategic plans for palliative care" (Seymour *et al.*, 2002, p. 5) production of this document stalled during the 1990s and, much to the hospice's chagrin the Directorate became, in this period, little more than a "talking shop" (Nursing Director, G:b).

This changed when the new part-time Medical Consultant (O:a) arrived. This person works for both the NHS (three and a half days a week) and hospice (one and a half days a week). He also chairs the Directorate and in this capacity he expedited completion of the needs assessment. However, as the passage below makes clear, the assessment and its associated plan threatens to restructure the conditions under which palliative care is organised and delivered in a manner that runs counter to hospice interests. The significance of asymmetric hospice-Directorate relations is apparent in this excerpt.

MEDICAL CONSULTANT O:a [The needs assessment has] created a whole new model of delivery and care which I don't think will suit the hospice very well. And I think (name) and myself have been the driving forces in doing that. But we've been allowed to do that by the PCT and they've encouraged us.

INTERVIEWER: Can I ask you why you don't think it will suit (hospice)?

MEDICAL CONSULTANT O:a Well it means that (hospice) will be very much, well financially, will have to explain itself and its actions and its investments and what it does if it wants to get any money, then it's going to have to put forward a much better case than it does at the moment. If it wants to develop and change in its own particular ways then it's going to have to demonstrate that that fits in with the countywide needs rather than just (hospice) own perception. So it's got to, it'll have to show that what goes on outside its own walls fits in with what goes on inside its walls and that there's a mutual benefit there. Now currently that isn't what they want at all and they're very upset with the Directorate and I think they're going to make it very difficult for the Directorate. But at the moment we have got a fantastic, I think, a fantastic and exciting development plan for the next three years that's very workable and it will actually be financially viable.

Here the Medical Consultant (O:a) takes personal credit for directing the assessment and its associated plan in a direction unlikely to find favour with the hospice, a direction "encouraged" by the Primary Care Trust. Possible motivations for this actor's behaviour are explored later under 'Relations within the hospice'. Here it is merely noted that needs assessment is an "inexact [and] pragmatic" (Ingleton *et al.* 2001, p. 398) activity and the Consultant's "ambivalent" (see below) views regarding hospices match those of the corporate group (i.e. NHS palliative care consultants) to which he primarily belongs.

NHS palliative consultant hostility

Senior hospice interviewees claim the Directorate offers a platform to antipathetic local NHS palliative care consultants. Medical hostility to the hospice is not new. Conflict, reportedly centred on the development of in-patient facilities, erupted as early as 1979 when a hospice fundraising foundation was established.

FUNDRAISER R:a (Trustee) has said that when he and (Trustee) were looking to set up the hospice, there was immense opposition to it from the medical community.

This hostility may, in part, reflect divergent state-NHS and independent sector structural (social and cultural) interests. However, other influences were also evident insofar as some original Directorate members even queried the need for palliative care.

NURSING DIRECTOR G:b I remember going to a … meeting and hearing a very senior [edit] saying that she didn't believe in palliative care. And I thought then, what the hell are you doing sitting on a committee that's actually planning palliative care!

Nevertheless, although by 2000 the value of palliative care was recognised (it was at least not overtly challenged), NHS consultant antipathy towards the hospice and Directorate pressure appeared to coalesce. Asked what "we" now wanted from the Directorate the Nursing Director replied:

NURSING DIRECTOR G:b to say that we should exist. Why do I say it? Because, there is a, a national move afoot amongst some (pause) palliative care consultants to move palliative care beds into acute hospitals.

Confirmation of the existence of antipathy towards the hospice from local NHS palliative care consultants came from a number of sources including the new Consultant.

MEDICAL CONSULTANT O:a Well, and I'm sure I'd get absolutely shot down (pause). To be very controversial, there's probably something to be gained from looking at whether or not we need [independent non-NHS] hospices. And, and by having hospices we're creating an unequal service. So the minority can get excellent service and, you're absolutely right, they, they are NGOs [non-governmental organisations] and they have charitable status and the money the funding is from local people. Would we be better pumping some of that money if you like into services in a different way? It's just the model that we have certainly in the UK, and that has been rolled out worldwide, in many cases, is of fairly large in-patient units. Large not so much in the number of beds but large in the number of people involved with them. And should we be actually using that, that money that service in a completely different way to support people in hospitals, to support people primarily at home? So, I have a fairly sort of (pause) ambivalent attitude towards hospices.

In this excerpt the Consultant articulates two criticisms of the hospice movement that are here interpreted as being representative of those voiced within and without the Directorate by local NHS palliative care consultants pre- and post-2000. First, it is suggested that hospice resources could be used more effectively if channelled into the NHS. Second, questions concerning equity are raised.

Resources

Contra the views of Consultant O:a, the General Manager argued that redirecting resources would not improve utility. He claimed that such views were "narrow" (N:b) and he asserted that the hospice was more efficient and therefore more effective in deploying resources because, compared with the NHS, flattened management structures and the extensive use of unpaid volunteers allowed a greater percentage of funds to be spent on "the front line" (N:b).

That hospices direct a high proportion of income into clinical services may of course be true without undermining the claim that disproportionally elevated spending on independent sector patients occurs relative to NHS or state expenditure (though this simply begs further questions such as: What is adequate or appropriate expenditure? Who is to decide? Against what criteria should decisions be made?). More concretely, the General Manager challenged the feasibility of sequestrating hospice funds as well as the amount of money available.

GENERAL MANAGER N:b All they could have of the resource that we acquire is that bit of it that comes from the public purse. They couldn't have the rest of it because that is given to charity and it is given to a charity because it is *not* (emphasis) part of the NHS. That's why people give us money.

INTERVIEWER: Why wouldn't people give to a statutory body such as the NHS?

GENERAL MANAGER N:b Because they pay their taxes. It's as simple as that (emphasis).

The constellation of arguments suggesting that charitable donations fall, volunteers depart and organisational behaviour alters as state intervention and funding increases are well rehearsed (Prochaska, 1988; Powell, 1992; Leat, 1995; Lewis, 1996a, 1999; Seddon, 2007) though contested (for a historical perspective on the relationship of state-voluntary activity see Barry and Jones, 1991; for a discussion on volunteers in the public sector see Merrell, 2000).[3] The politicised nature of many of these arguments may in part indicate that structural tensions have and continue to adversely affect state-independent institutional relations. Nevertheless, if the feasibility of redirecting resources is open to question, it was also evident that other interviewees accepted aspects of Consultant O:a's second censure and the problem of inequity is more difficult to shrug off.

Equity

Discussion regarding the equity of hospice and palliative care provision takes many forms.[4] A consideration of the literature on this issue extends debate beyond local consultant rancour and, introducing the literature here (as elsewhere) illustrates, first, that many interviewee identified themes (Appendix H) have wide resonance, second, that these themes often pre- and post-date re-designation study time frames. Moreover, third, by informing the analysis offered here the literature highlights the catholic nature of data and evidence in realist theorising.

Arguments from the literature are therefore important. They often mirror interviewee insights and comments and they assist identification of the social and cultural structures which shape and reflect relations between the hospice and state-NHS institutions (here Consultant opinions on the equity question).[5]

Definitional problems notwithstanding it may be argued that patients with equal need should receive equal treatment or, given finite resources, at least an equal or 'fair' chance of treatment (Harris, 1985; Kukathas and Pettit, 1990; Tadd, 1998; Horner, 1998; Williams, 2003). Yet if hospices and palliative care services – independent *or* state-NHS – are in some respects superior to NHS non-palliative services, then the uneven distribution of hospice and palliative care provision throughout the country (St Christopher's Hospice and Help the Hospices, 2008) means that equal need (assuming demographically corrected geographic distributional parity) is being met unequally. Further, if independent non-state provision is partly responsible for a lack of NHS services (for example, Primary Care Trusts may be disinclined to invest in a service provided 'free' by others) then the independent sector should, perhaps, shoulder some responsibility for the ensuing inequity?

This last point implicitly informs statements by non-consultant medical staff at the hospice who note that, although new NHS consultant posts are being created, NHS palliative care and NHS medical palliative posts (their primary source of future employment) remain, allegedly, under-resourced (medical interviewees tended in conversation to conflate palliative care with palliative medicine). Local NHS palliative care consultants are keen to establish a palliative department so that they can "have their own beds in acute Trusts, so that they admit to their own beds" (Nursing Director, G:b). And, taken together, these perceived shortcomings in NHS provision might explain consultant antipathy *if* it is allowed that resources channelled to hospices prevent or handicap, directly or indirectly (as negative realities[6]) the development of NHS palliative services.

That the relative dearth of UK NHS palliative care units "may be the result of the large number of hospices that were built" (Abu-Saad and Courtens, 2001, p. 18) is noted in the literature and, as stated, local medical hostility to the prospect of a hospice focused, in 1979, on the creation of non-NHS in-patient beds. However, while resource covetousness may explain consultant antagonism at a corporate level, the assumption that the state is held back from investing in palliative services in those areas where the independent sector is inoperative or insufficient is hardly credible.

More damningly the literature recognises that, both within the UK and overseas, hospice services are not equitably available to all patients. Thus more services are provided to patients with cancer than, for example, degenerative disease, disablement or HIV/AIDS (SMAC/SNMAC, 1992; George and Sykes, 1997; Harding *et al.* 2005; Rucker, 2005; Ryan and McQuillan, 2005; Kristjanson *et al.*, 2006; Stienstra and Chochinov, 2006; Seymour, 2007). Hospices are exclusionary insofar as disadvantaged groups find access difficult (Ahmed *et al.*, 2004; Wood *et al.*, 2004). Where available, hospices predominantly evidence or cater to middle-class values and tastes (Walter, 1994; Sandman, 2005). Minority ethnic and racial groups are under-represented in hospice admission records (Corner and Dunlop, 1997; Fountain, 1999; Ahmed *et al.*, 2004) and, when seen, minority cultural needs can be poorly met (Dein, 2006). Out-patient and community palliative care may be under-funded because small in-patient units are resource hungry (Reynard, 1993). Focusing upon hospices might have hampered the development of alternative forms of palliative provision (Seymour, 2001) and, in synopsis, Douglas's (1992) longstanding and stinging accusation that hospices inequitably provide "de luxe dying" (p. 579) to a privileged minority may well still stand. Significantly, this conclusion was accepted by several interviewees and the genteel and exclusionary nature of provision appeared to be widely acknowledged at the study site.

WARD MANAGER F:a Where are the mentally handicapped people? [Also] the Chief Executive [General Manager] is very keen on small tidy chairs. I would like my house to be comfortable, where people can sit down. You don't get that here. It is, it is too neat and tidy.

DAY HOSPICE MANAGER (NURSE) J:a [Regarding volunteers] they are nearly all very well 'accessorised' [and] it's kind of excluding if you're sitting there feeling absolutely awful and you haven't had time to, I mean you haven't had the energy to iron your shirt and you don't possess any accessories anyway, and you're sick and you're, you're surrounded by people who have got very nice nails and perfect diction and a chic haircut.

MEDICAL REGISTER Y:a It's the same for all hospices you do only have a small number of beds and so it is a very exclusive group of patients that actually get the input from [hospice] palliative care. It's a problem with palliative medicine that we are not wholly inclusive; I think it is recognised that we don't properly address people from ethnic minority backgrounds or very

> low social classes. It's very much well you know, the people who have access to it are from a *very* (emphasis) closed (pause) community. Not everyone's going to feel happy here. I don't know if I would (laughs).

That said, every interviewee thought the standard of care provided by the hospice was generally superior to local NHS provision, every interviewee enjoyed working at the hospice and some, but not all interviewees, expressed views commensurate with apologists in the literature who assert that, for example, the creation of independent hospices spurred on the development of NHS services (Hockley, 1997) by generating interest in a hitherto underdeveloped branch of care (Costello, 2004; Bass, 2006). Those in receipt of hospice or palliative services benefit (Help the Hospices, 2008), unhelpful or unwarranted taboos about death are being demolished (Buckingham, 1996), total provision is increasing (Lawton, 2000) and, more broadly, charitable and voluntary organisations are valorised as vital components of civil society. For example, political support for third sector provision comes from the left (Deakin, 1994; Gamble, 1995; Field, 1997), centre-left (Deakin, 2000), neoliberal right (Marsland, 1996) and communitarian 'other' (Green, 1993, 1996; Etzioni, 1995; Whelan, 1996).

Alternatively, interviewees who highlight the advantages of NHS hospital care, that is, allowing that hospital care might be superior to hospice care in certain respects, present a different perspective to that outlined above. For example, palliative patients located in large acute settings are inequitably *advantaged* (compared with similar patient groups not so located) insofar as they can access more services more quickly than hospice patients in geographically isolated settings.

Until recently access to what would once have been described as complex or acute treatments and interventions was not a problem at the study site because, in the hospice's early years, care primarily involved non-interventionist support to patients at the end of their lives. However, as will be argued, changes in admission practice as well as new forms of treatment now necessitate that more patients make more frequent journeys to the County hospital. The significance and implications of physical "isolation" (Ward Manager, F:a) are therefore becoming increasingly important.[7]

> CHARGE NURSE (SISTER) C:b We are right out on a limb here and it's very difficult to get ill people to the County hospital. To hang around in an ambulance, wait for it to come back, whereas if we were attached to the County hospital in, in a unit, things would happen much easier.

The three factors outlined above (divergent interests, threats to hospice independence and medical or NHS palliative consultant antipathy or criticism) coalesced to create for the hospice, by 2000, asymmetric social structural relations and a situated logic of structurally emergent properties (SEP) that can be labelled 'necessary contradiction' (correction) (see Table 4.1).

Table 4.1 CEP (Cultural Emergent Properties) and SEP (Social Emergent Properties), logical relations and situational logics

	Contradictions		*Complementarities*	
	Necessary	*Contingent*	*Necessary*	*Contingent*
(Situational logic)	(Correction)	(Elimination)	(Protection)	(Opportunism)
CEP				
CS level	Syncretism	Pluralism	Systematisation	Specialisation
S-C level	Unification	Cleavage	Reproduction	Sectionalism
SEP				
SS level	Compromise	Competition	Integration	Differentiation
SI level	Containment	Polarisation	Solidarity	Diversification

(Source: adapted from RST, p. 303).

Relations between the Primary Care Trust and hospice are asymmetric because the Trust (speaking through the Directorate) no longer requires the hospice in the same way that the hospice requires the Trust. Moreover, the Primary Care Trust/Directorate's ability to set the structural environment in which the hospice functions and its power to direct finance and exert sanctions makes the hospice a minor and potentially dependent rather than major and leading element in service provision. Further, powerful antagonistic corporate agents (i.e. NHS palliative consultants) deploying forms of critique (e.g. regarding equity and the exclusiveness of provision) that find resonance at the study site, exacerbate the hospice's political remoteness and, perhaps, internal division.

Recognising that the Directorate is pursuing what to it are threatening policies (i.e. policies against its perceived interests) led senior hospice personnel to engage in social interactional (SI) strategies of containment and, at the socio-structural (SS) level, compromise (though alternative competitive responses were considered). Containment is evidenced insofar as the hospice deliberately and self-consciously attempts to assert its presence and interests beyond the Directorate by 'placing' staff wherever possible in positions that might influence national, regional and professional palliative care agendas. To this end hospice representatives have sought admittance to a wide range of organisations and bodies for, as the General Manager states, "If you're not in the ring you don't get heard" (N:b).

Compromise is evidenced, possibly, by organisational re-designation as a specialist palliative care unit. Re-designation is discussed under the heading 'Relations within the hospice'; however, occurring shortly before progression of the needs assessment, re-designation might reasonably be interpreted as a move towards meeting or heading off existing, foreseen and continuing Directorate (and other) pressures, since it promotes and positions the hospice as a necessary part of county palliative services. Politically deft, re-designation spikes, to some extent, calls by NHS palliative care consultants for the creation of a specialist palliative department within the local hospital. Indeed it might almost be described as 'integrationist' a term associated with protective necessary complementarities.

More 'competitively', a term connected with eliminative contingent contradictions, post-2000, the Chief Executive proposed at internal hospice meetings that, in the future, overt forms of spiritual and emotional care could be consciously and deliberately emphasised or marketed in order that the hospice might publically differentiate itself from competitor NHS provision. At face value this seems to be a form of cultural system positioning or pluralism.

> SPECIAL MINISTER OF THE EUCHARIST M:a (General Manager) was very worried if they have a palliative care department in the hospital. That then, well, (hospice) will become (pause) unnecessary. So our, if we 'up' (emphasis) our spirituality, then the people who want the spiritual side of it will come to (hospice).

That options such as 'spiritual branding' are being considered may be significant. It might indicate that the hospice remains pressured – so that pre-2000 social relations are reproduced and not elaborated by re-designation. It also raises questions about organisational decision making.

Awareness of the three topics described above (labelled: divergent interests, challenges to independence and NHS palliative consultant hostility) is widespread but not universal among interviewees. Senior staff such as the head fundraiser is party to such knowledge "because I'm a part of the management team" (R:a) and, unsurprisingly, non-consultant medical interviewees can comment on, for example, NHS consultant antipathy even if they know little about the Directorate. However, among interviewees, only one of four Charge Nurses (Sisters) was privy to such information and no nurse below the rank of charge nurse was cognisant of these issues. That such matters remain *sub rosa* may be important.

Although the situated logic generated for the hospice by structures such as the Directorate and agents such as NHS palliative consultants is primarily described here as a necessary contradiction, alternative and radical scenarios were aired that might, if enacted, be described using the situated logic of elimination. Given the contentious nature of such scenarios, senior staff let it be known that open discussion of these options would, at this stage, be 'unhelpful' and limited details are therefore given here.

Senior managers believe the organisation faces two interlinked problems. First, a future funding crisis is anticipated if rises in spending continue to outpace rises in income and, second, from the hospice's perspective, the Directorate is becoming unmanageably prescriptive. In response the hospice could withdraw from the Primary Care Trust/Directorate and accept direct user payment for services. The General Manager indicated that this option was under serious review and the new part-time Consultant described this as his (the General Manager's) "ultimate threat" (O:a). Further, the topic has been broached "within the management team, it has been discussed" (Fundraiser, R:a) and a small and discreet working group has been established to look at all fundraising options including direct payment.

However, if pursued, withdrawal from the Primary Care Trust/Directorate means withdrawal from meaningful engagement with the NHS and accepting payment would herald a revolution in structural relations. The move would create a situated logic of open competition with 'rival' NHS institutions and polarisation at the social interactional level could be expected between workforces.

> MEDICAL CONSULTANT O:a One of the things that it's capable of doing and might do it quite happily would be to opt out of primary or the primary care trust funding and direction and somebody mentioned that they might actually sort of start charging for their, for their (pause). So the rich can pay for it and the poor don't. But I think it would change the whole ethos of palliative care. It would completely disengage the hospice from the rest of palliative care.

Finance is crucial here. If statutory funding was cut or removed without warning the hospice would face immediate financial peril. The hospice also believes it is under-funded by the state for the work that it does and it initially anticipated that the Directorate would help remedy this situation. Yet, paradoxically, the option of absenting itself from the Primary Care Trust/Directorate can only be considered *because* statutory funding forms a relatively low proportion of overall income (hence the hospice has some latitude or freedom).

In reality it is unlikely that this course will be pursued. It is acknowledged that both developments would need to be introduced to staff sensitively, significant clinical and community resistance could be expected and "Once you've moved the goalposts you can never move them back. My great fear as a fundraiser is if you, in effect, became private, you would get another organisation, a charity, coming and doing what we did" (Fundraiser, R:a).

Morphogenetic-morphostatic modelling here steers, permits and encourages distinctions to be made regarding social interaction (SI). That is, morphogenetic methodology licenses the consideration of varied explanations involving, in this instance, actual and potential necessary and contingent contradictions. Archer's realist social theory prompts researchers to describe and advance graded or alternative hypotheses (loosely defined) and this is, I suggest, a major strength of her approach.

The Department of Health

The main legislative threat to hospice independence comes, it is believed, from the Department of Health in the guise of the Care Standards Act (DH, 2000) and its method of implementation. Part II, Section 11(1) of this Act requires that non-NHS healthcare providers such as the hospice register with the National

Care Standards Commission (after 2004, the Healthcare Commission, 2008). Registration depends upon certain standards or procedures being demonstrated (Campbell, 2005) and it was anticipated by several interviewees that new regulatory frameworks associated with devising and monitoring these standards will, if not resisted, align hospice and NHS practices.

NURSING DIRECTOR G:b Basically, I think, they're doing a 1948 on hospices.
INTERVIEWER: What do you mean by 'a 1948'?
NURSING DIRECTOR G:b Well that was when the National Health came into being.
INTERVIEWER: Yes.
NURSING DIRECTOR G:b And they grabbed all the local little community hospitals and things and cottage hospitals and dragged them all into the NHS.
INTERVIEWER: And [they] lost their voluntary status.
NURSING DIRECTOR G:b Yes.
INTERVIEWER: But they can't grab us.
NURSING DIRECTOR G:b They're trying; they're trying to grab us through the inspectorates.
INTERVIEWER: So they can force us to comply, or rather, the things they measure can force us to comply and change our behaviour?
NURSING DIRECTOR G:b They might think so. Because we have to, here, comply with what they're going to say.

Consequent to the Care Standards Act (DH, 2000), Section 11 (Hospice Standards H1 to H15) of the Department of Health's Independent Health Care National Minimum Standards Regulations (DH, 2001) generates significant bureaucratic burdens for small organisations not previously used to detailed record keeping or audit functions.

Putting to one side the merits or otherwise of this sort of record keeping, senior interviewees believe these demands threaten to compromise current clinical and administrative expenditure ratios. And, for the hospice, such regulations are indicative of the Department of Health's disobliging nature – "they wouldn't understand the, this organisation" (Nursing Director, G:b). Section 11 (DH, 2001) prescribes and regulates almost every aspect of care and insofar as "standards will be closely linked with the development of NICE [National Institute of Clinical Excellence] guidelines" (ibid., p. 126) prescription is only likely to increase.

The reality of this threat remained untested during the study albeit that, perceptually, it presents a clear and imminent danger to senior hospice personnel. It also continues and entrenches negative trends and relations established in earlier encounters between the hospice and Department of Health (e.g. surrounding Clinical Governance, DH, 1997, 1998, 1999). The Care Standards Act (DH, 2000) again illustrates the asymmetric nature of socio-structural hospice and state-NHS relations and, as before, the hospice's reaction at the level of social interaction involves attempting to work with similarly placed institutions to exert influence on those national, regional and professional bodies and organisations that it has access to in an attempt to head off or mitigate future clashes. However, this approach has recognised limitations and regarding, for example, NICE guidance "I think there is, or might become, the seeds of conflict as to whether we should comply" (Nursing Director, G:b).

Demographic change

Interviewees suggested that changing family relations and work practices (e.g. more divorce and remarriage, greater geographic mobility and increasing female labour market participation) mean that fewer "good families" (Nursing Director, G:a) are available to fulfil supportive domestic healthcare roles. 'Good families' here indicates families in which a competent and available adult child – almost always a daughter – is on hand to provide personal and sustained intimate homecare to parents and/or in-laws.

Evidence for the existence of changing demographic structures occurs widely throughout the literature (Field and James, 1993; Lawton, 2000; Hirst, 2001; Arksey, 2002). However, the politicised nature of commentaries on family and gendered roles, values and responsibilities in health and social care complicates discussion of such factors (see, for example, Davies *et al.*, 1993, or Morgan, 1999, for a neo-liberal free market perspective; or Finch and Mason, 1993, or Graham, 1993, for a feminist left of centre viewpoint). Curiously, although reduced domestic support could only be experienced by the hospice at an aggregate level, 'rest-room' conversations readily linked non-traditional family structures with premature admission and delayed discharge in particular instances.

Several respondents also stated (and it is generally assumed) that, at admission, patient symptom severity or dependency had been and is rising. Assessing patient dependency is difficult (Quinn *et al.*, 2004) and respondents could be mistaken in their observations. Nevertheless, if correct, demographic factors might, in combination with other changes, be *partially* responsible for altered admission patterns.[8] For example, longer life expectancy in the general population (Hirst, 2001) and treatment survival advances among cancer patients (Doll and Boreham, 2005; Griffiths *et al.*, 2007) as well as, paradoxically given the above noted changes in family structure, "re-domestication" (Exley and Allen, 2007, p. 2317) of end of life care and improved home and community support, could all produce worsening dependency or symptom severity for those requiring admission.

However, the evidence here is confusing and, in consequence, caveats must be placed against interviewee comments. Thus significant numbers of subsidiary assumptions must be made about the nature of older and later referrals if rising dependency is to be associated with changed demographic factors. Indeed, while improved post-diagnosis cancer survival is linked with heightened dependency levels in hospice admissions (Bruera *et al.*, 2000), palliative symptoms are often diagnostically specific for cancer patients (Guest *et al.*,

2006), and minor and possibly contingent fluctuations in referral and admission patterns could account for the changes perceived by study interviewees. Further, variables other than those noted above could produce similar results. For example, it is suggested that the rise in hospice treatments and interventions results, in part, from growing and occasionally unrealistic public pressure: "we've raised the expectations of the general public" (Nursing Director G:a – see also Connor, 1998 or Elsayem *et al.*, 2004). Moreover, in addition, it is recognised that within a largely agricultural catchment area, seasonal influxes of migrant foreign workers may be producing or placing new demands upon the hospice (the need to engage with under-served migrant and diverse populations is acknowledged, e.g. Morris, 2005; BEN PCT, 2007). Alternatively, conflated influences can and possibly should be disaggregated and, for example, increased female labour market penetration and greater general population mobility might more profitably be treated separately.

To compound the difficulty inherent in linking changes in aggregate demographic influences on patient referral and admission patterns at the local level, it will be argued that organisational re-designation publically signalled and permitted a change in admission practice. Further, improved general palliative and end of life care in the community might reduce the number of non-complex or non-dependent patients available for admission while clinical success might raise the profile and reputation of the organisation among referring GPs who would then, in turn, submit sicker patients. Moreover, actors such as the new part-time Medical Consultant deliberately sought, not always successfully, to open up access to previously excluded groups (discussed below).

Whatever the mix of causes involved, changing demographic social structures probably contribute in part – though this cannot easily be quantified – to changes in referral and admission practices as well as discharge difficulties. Indeed, while the scale and extent of these changes may be over-emphasised by interviewees, the need to accelerate stalled discharges that, in some instances, are associated with non-supportive and non-traditional family structures was frequently commented on by study participants.

It is thus suggested that, insofar as they contribute to the rise in patient dependency (symptom complexity) and discharge difficulties (as home support diminishes), social structural demographic change exerts causal influence on social interaction at the hospice. It is not possible to measure or be specific about these developments and, given the lack of conceptual clarity, the role played by these factors must be treated with caution. Nonetheless, demographic social structural relations prompting elaboration at or within social interaction are, if they exist, internally asymmetric.

Conclusion to 'structures and institutions'

Figure 4.2 (below) models or describes in summary form the relations outlined above (note comments on p. 80 regarding the use of T^1–T^4 descriptors in this model). Social structural rather than cultural structural factors are emphasised here since although, for example, NHS consultant hostility was influenced by or represents/involves social *and* cultural mechanisms, overall, social structural tendencies that might be labelled 'threats to hospice' appear to dominate relations between the hospice and both the Directorate and Department of Health. Further, all three of the topics outlined above are pushing the organisation through their influence on senior staff perceptions/beliefs in ways that, ideally, would be resisted or tamed by those staff. Finally, since in realist theory "the actual outcome of a tendency will generally be co-determined by the activity of other mechanisms" (Porter, 1993, p. 604), the consistency or synergy between tendencies is or appears to be important.

Two forms of social structural conditioning influence are identified in Figure 4.2. First, demographic change is (with caveats) associated with worsening patient admission severity and discharge delays at the hospice. Room for manoeuvre in the face of demographic pressure is limited. Second, structural relations between the hospice (as an independent healthcare provider organisation)

Social structural (SS) conditioning

T^1

Demographic
- Affects (perhaps) admission dependency and ease of discharge

State-NHS
- County Palliative Care Directorate
  - Seeks to direct hospice activity – threatens hospice independence
  - Hostile NHS palliative Consultants challenge hospice
- Department of health
  - Presents regulatory threat to hospice independence

Social interaction (SI)

T^2 — T^3

Response *Containment* – hospice actively and deliberately engages with institutions producing (or that might affect) T^1 pressures
Response *Competition* – hospice considers alternatives to current SS relations
- Increasing focus on discharge planning
- Increasing numbers of treatment/interventions

Social elaboration – relative to T^1

Organisational re-designation (2000)

T^4

Structural reproduction – relative to T^1

Conditioning T^1 SS remain unchanged

Figure 4.2 Social structural factors acting upon the hospice at T^1, their T^2–T^3 SI consequents and T^4 outcomes.

and state-NHS (in the guise of the local Primary Care Trust/Directorate and Department of Health) are evidenced by perceived 'threats' to hospice independence. Policies of 'containment' are pursued ('competition' is considered) and structural elaboration *and* reproduction occurs.

Morphogenetic modelling here describes processes of morphogenesis and morphostasis. These processes are identified from interviewee comments made after 2000. With regard to morphogenesis, interviewees provided data/evidence from which 'reasons for' organisational re-designation are abducted. Descriptions of events occurring after 2000 (e.g. completion of the needs assessment and implementation of the Care Standards Act, 2000) here explain and justify an interpretation of relations that are inferred to have existed between the hospice and external institutions/organisations before 2000. Morphostasis is apparent insofar as relations evident between the hospice and external institutions/organisations at T^1 remain, at T^4, essentially unchanged albeit that, in time, (i) re-designation may alter relations between the hospice and state-NHS *or* (ii) existing state-NHS structures may exact further relational change from the hospice. Forms of socio-interaction identified in Figure 4.2 continue to be reproduced post-2000.

Because exact time frames cannot be generated for pre-2000 relations (i.e. available evidence does not with any specificity indicate when these relations came into being) precise dates are not ascribed to T^1, T^2 or T^3. T^4 is placed at 2000. However, as stated, 'pressures' or mechanisms prompting hospice re-designation continue after that time. Re-designation may have dampened some of these 'felt' pressures. It did not eradicate them. The effect of re-designation on agential interaction is hereafter described in 'Relations within the hospice'.

Relations within the hospice

Following the T^1–T^4 time frame detailed in Figure 4.1 (p. 63) it is argued that socio-structural developments – notably organisational re-designation – promoted changes within the hospice at the level of social interaction that expose socio-cultural dispute and cultural system contradiction. Relations within the hospice are here explored under five sub-headings labelled (i) Organisational re-designation, (ii) Agents, actors, persons, (iii) Increasing medical engagement, (iv) Treatments and interventions and (v) Spirituality/religion. Sub-headings differentiate only loosely between themes and overlap between descriptions occurs.

Organisational re-designation

Although the General Manager, senior management and medical teams were all involved, it proved strangely difficult to pinpoint when the decision to re-designate the hospice a specialist palliative care unit was taken (re-designation or re-description occurred 'around' 2000). Less ambiguously, it is apparent that some agents hold dramatically opposing views about organisational identity (where identity defines the apposite role or function of the organisation). These beliefs – beliefs about the 'correct' or 'proper' function of the organisation – directly impact upon or influence clinical practice. Interviewee reactions against or acceptance of re-designation and its correlates proved to be a tangential referent or talisman in disputes about appropriate organisational identity and clinical activity.

Evidence highlighting the importance of organisational re-designation appears in most interview transcripts and short illustrative quotations struggle to convey the richness of discussions from whence they come. Here, the Ward Manager (F:a) specifies what, to her, specialist palliative care entails:

> WARD MANAGER F:a Our hospice 'deems' (emphasis) itself to be a place where we offer specialist palliative care. So it's largely for those patients who have complex needs. [However] there are not enough specialist palliative care patients for us to fill our beds with. And I, I see that as meaning patients where they have complex symptoms for me it's [specialist palliative care] the complexity of the symptoms. Terminal is for someone who is very soon to die (pause). And what do I mean by very soon to die? Someone who comes in for terminal care I would expect to die within (pause) three or four weeks perhaps. Terminal to me means that you're at the end-stage. Specialist palliative care or palliative care could be much further down the line.

Before proceeding it is, given these comments, important to note at least some of the difficulties that surround definitions of the descriptors terminal care, end of life care, hospice care, palliative care and specialist palliative care.

Unsurprisingly terminal or end of life care describes care offered to patients towards the end of life. Yet the duration and/or time at which these descriptors start or begin to apply – and the 'intensity' and objectives of interventions offered – remain a matter of conjecture or negotiation. Here I simply focus on when descriptors apply.

It might be argued that end of life care can commence days or even weeks before death. Terminal care, on the other hand, can designate care given in the terminal phase – often the last hours or days of life. However, as the above quotation illustrates, these terms are easily conflated and consensus on how descriptors should be used remains elusive. More confusingly still, the terms 'hospice' and 'palliative care' are often used interchangeably within the literature (Bass, 2006) and study site participants also tended to elide these descriptors.

If a distinction between these terms is to be drawn then, whereas palliative care can be offered in a variety of settings (including non-hospice settings), hospice care must presumably take place within a hospice or, if one is an outpatient, within settings staffed by hospice personnel. (Alternatively, if hospice care is taken to designate an approach or orientation to care then this distinction need not apply.) In contrast to end of life or terminal care, both hospice and palliative care can begin at any time following diagnosis and, in theory at least, this 'beginning' can occur months or even years before death.

The Ward Manager thus notes in the above quotation that palliative care may be appropriate in advance of the terminal or end phases of life and neither hospice nor palliative care need necessarily be associated with the death event (though they often are). Hospice and/or palliative care might therefore focus on or prioritise symptom control in the 'run up' to death rather than care of the actively dying. That said, these definitions remain as noted fluid, and it is this fluidity that proved to be contentious at the study site. It will be argued that some study participants want to position hospice care much closer to end of life/terminal care than palliative care *if* palliative care means long-term physical symptom control.

Moreover, interviewees almost universally associated *specialist* palliative care with complex physical symptom control. 'Complex' is of course another woolly term. However, this descriptor was widely used to distinguish or describe a particular form of care. Thus the overwhelming majority of interviewees linked specialist palliative care, in both the pre-terminal and terminal phases, with complex physical symptom control. Interviewees did not necessarily agree that this conflation should occur. They did not necessarily think that specialist palliative care must or should be associated with complex physical symptom control. Yet this is what appeared to be happening. (And, as an aside – while terminal care can be complex, proximity to death does not in itself automatically signal the presence of complex needs physical or otherwise. Indeed, many or even most deaths are not complex insofar as they do not necessitate complex physical or other forms of care.)

Terminal, end of life, hospice, palliative and specialist palliative care are thus opaque descriptors. These terms describe overlapping but also, perhaps, distinct forms of care. Ideally, all of these 'cares' will involve cross- or multi-disciplinary physical, social, psychological and spiritual inputs.[9] However, uniquely, *specialist* palliative care, when associated with complex *physical* symptom control, is predominantly viewed by interviewees as a medical speciality – i.e. care in which medical direction and biomedical discourse predominately frames activity.

Within this study the beliefs or assumptions made by study participants about the meanings attaching to the various descriptors 'in play' are in measure reflected in the hospice and palliative care literature where, for example, specialist palliative care is associated with the care of patients with complex symptoms (Woods, 2007). And, moreover, when "palliative medicine and the palliative *approach*" are not delineated (Doyle, 1993, p. 253 – italicisation in original), complex and physical symptoms can be conflated (see, for example, Randall and Downie, 1999).

That said, to repeat, terminological classifications are contested and, as the Nursing Director (G:a) noted, defining specialist palliative care in juxtaposition with or against terminal care is problematic since, first, this approach makes implicit but possibly unfounded assumptions about traditional forms of hospice activity. It thus assumes that hospices historically focused primarily on end of life or terminal care. However, given the variation and diversity in hospice activity, this assumption may be overly simplistic. Second – a related point – it is uncertain what hospice practice actually entails or should be. Indeed, "the problem with defining hospice care is that there are three hundred and something hospices around the country" (Nursing Director G:a) and considerable difference continues to exist between organisations and the activities undertaken by or within those organisations (Lawton, 2000).

Thus irrespective of the production of authoritative and widely cited taxonomies (see e.g. Saunders, 1996; Stjernsward, 1997; WHO, 2002, 2008), the difficulty in delineating between hospice, terminal, end-stage, symptom control, complex symptom control, palliative and specialist palliative care remains and, as the literature attests, this issue is well documented (Connor, 1998; Clark and Seymour, 1999; Clark *et al.*, 2002; Doyle, 2003).

Despite these terminological riddles, at the study site, a variety of patient groups are admitted. Terminal or end-stage patients and those designated as having symptom control needs (complex or otherwise) form the bulk of admissions. A limited number of social admissions occur when symptom control and family support needs coincide and a very small number of short-stay respite patients are also taken. Excepting respite patients (a few respondents expressed strongly held opinions that this group should be excluded) interviewees accept that each patient group has a legitimate place within the organisation.

That said, respondents who define specialist palliative care in opposition to terminal or end of life care also tend to articulate firm preferences for terminal/end of life patient care and, where this occurs, interviewees disagree on normative grounds with organisational re-designation and its correlates. Indeed, descriptions of the form in which organisational re-designation occurred and explanations regarding the implications of re-designation made by those favouring terminal admissions highlight, it is argued, forms of T^2–T^3 change at the level of social and cultural interaction that retrodictively point towards T^1 socio-structural and cultural structural conditioning. Evidence supporting this claim is presented throughout this section. (Developments in identity and practice took many forms and these forms are not easily disambiguated.) Here it is merely noted that re-designation recognised and catalysed several existing pre-2000 T^1 trends.

If it is granted that specialist palliative care unit status is associated with complex physical symptom control, then claiming special unit status publicly signalled that the hospice's focus is directed or is at least potentially being directed towards complex physical symptom control and this formally alters the social structural relations of the organisation relative to other institutions and agents. (However, see caveats to this statement in conclusion to 'Structures and institutions'.)

Within the hospice re-designation affected social interaction by promoting and entrenching pre-established shifts in, for example, the balance between patient groups admitted (e.g. it increased the number of admissions for complex physical symptom control at the expense of non-complex end of life/terminal patients). Admitting a larger number of patients with complex physical needs produced a busier environment and this busier environment led to alterations in staff-staff and staff-patient relations. Further, meeting heightened physical needs encouraged 'clinical innovation' by sanctioning the use of different and more numerous treatments and interventions. It also necessitated staffing changes. For example, in-patient nursing numbers rose, as stated, from seven:four to eight:five during the study period – the proportion of nurses employed increased relative to auxiliary nurses – auxiliary (assistant) nurses were invited to expand their roles (i.e. retrain) – and more doctors were taken on.

Where these developments produce discord (described hereafter) emergent containment or polarisation may be operative at the level of social interaction and contradictory socio-structural level compromise or competition may be evidenced. Alternatively, re-designation affects socio-cultural interaction because clinical change (sketched above and developed later) is promoted by and exacerbates ideational conflict among staff holding *pre-established* and divergent views about the proper purpose of organisational activity. (For disaffected staff both the "regulative and constitutive" rules of institutional activity are broached, Fleetwood, 2008, p. 15.) The suitability or otherwise of practice change is thus assessed by agents according to their 'fit' with ideas concerning appropriate organisational activity and, insofar as socio-cultural interaction or interplay between T^2–T^3 suggests the presence of individuals and groups within the organisation who hold competing views about such activity, re-designation can be linked at T^1 to cultural structural conditioning and a situated logic of contingent contradiction.

Thus virtually every interviewee stated that having time to engage personally and emotionally with patients and families distinguished hospice and palliative care from NHS non-hospice and non-palliative care. However, re-designation and its correlates are associated with increasing clinical activity and those opposed to re-designation and the changes it wrought lament the distancing in staff-patient relations that busyness forces or threatens. Personal experience verifies that activity is increasing. In 2000 and the earliest part of 2001 time was occasionally available to sit with patients and engage in extensive 'social' non-clinical activity. By the end of 2002 workload pressures meant this was increasingly difficult and attention shifted to the performance of clinical 'skills'. (Though it is important to note that, compared with NHS/state organisations, considerably more opportunities for supportive and relaxed staff-patient social interactions continued.)

Socio-structural changes in the in-patient unit (e.g. the introduction of patient name bands and the transfer of kardex notes to patient bedsides – described in Chapter 3) are, in part, responses to the consequences of rising activity. And several established traditions, such as leaving the bed space of a deceased patient empty for twenty-four hours as a mark of 'respect', were abandoned in the T^2–T^3 study period as busyness rose.

CHARGE NURSE (SISTER) V:a Some of the things which I'm sure people have said [*referring to the researcher*] are things like, Oh patient dies and the room

> was left for twenty four hours before another patient comes in and that just doesn't really happen now and it can't with the fast turnover of patients that we've got. When we've got five patients [now] on the waiting list to come in.

In contrast to the position of interviewee V:a, who favoured the changes described, these and other events were interpreted negatively by other interviewees. Those opposed to change suggest the in-patient unit now appears more 'ward-like' (i.e. it now more closely resembles an NHS ward), busyness limits opportunities to form emotionally intimate or therapeutic relationships with patients and their families and the cessation of traditional post-mortem practices (now seen as resource wasteful) offend those for whom relationships with the living include implicit promises of particular forms of after-death care. Indeed, long service interviewee A:a's comments in Appendix D such as "just let's sit" and "that isn't part of it any more" articulate a sense of sadness and loss at change that may be associated with re-designation *and* point towards cultural system level ideational contradiction.

Disagreement with the manner in which organisational re-designation occurred comes predominantly from long service clinicians. For example, depreciatory sentiments are lodged in the term "deems" (Ward Manager F:a – p. 82) and phrase "gradually one discovers" (Nurse E:a – p. 87). Criticism of this sort ultimately reflects full or partial rejection of the implications of change. However, re-designation occurred without widespread discussion or consultation and in so doing it possibly also contradicts important cultural precepts regarding what might be termed the ownership of organisational identity. Thus, although "most charities were never intended to be democratic institutions" (Kirkland, 1996, p. 107) the legitimacy of decision makers is on occasion openly challenged.

> SOCIAL WORKER K:a There are a lot of [junior] doctors and they're all leaving. Do you remember that meeting? I said, I pointed out you're all leaving. You'll, every doctor around the table will be gone within a year. And what are we doing forcing our (pause). Or planning our (pause). That's what really bugs me [medical staff] around here are very short term. They're actually paid a lot as doctors. And actually have a big impact on what happens.

Here, the Social Worker (K:a) questions whether relatively junior medical staff who are working at the organisation for short periods and those who are about to leave should be involved in policy decisions (broadly defined). It should be noted that transient medical staff were automatically involved in 'policy type' discussions whereas long service nurses and other employees where not necessarily included.

Following Rochester (1995) on "internal accountability" (p. 193), if long service employees (here nurses and nursing assistants) believe they might legitimately contribute to decisions about organisational identity (i.e. the role and function of the organisation), then it is not unreasonable to assume that they will react against the denial of such input. This negative reaction will be particularly strong when the change envisaged contradicts firmly held ideas about what hospice care should be. Support for this interpretation comes from several sources.

The hospice and palliative care literature thus records that early pioneers valued collegiate or multidisciplinary decision making (see comments on holistic care below) (Lawton, 2000; Parker-Oliver *et al.*, 2005). Non-hospice third sector/charitable literature notes that while definitional problems abound (Kendall and Knapp, 1995), in the start-up period, decision making and role boundaries are frequently fluid within charitable organisations (Gann, 1996). Post start-up, however, mature organisations can display managerial and bureaucratic tendencies and, if this occurs, roles may be formalised (Kirkland, 1996; Lewis, 1996b; Smith, 1996); a process that can encounter or generate internal resistance (Flynn, 1996; Merrell, 2000) – resistance similar to that demonstrated explicitly by K:a (above citation) or implicitly by A:a (Appendix D).

Long service clinicians also suggest that professional and role boundaries are becoming more prescribed. This theme reappears later under the heading 'Increasing medical engagement'. However, the Social Worker notes that "people who choose to work in an organisation that's small and struggling are perhaps people who are prepared to give it a little bit more" (K:a) and, in recounting how she and other clinicians took the lead in seeking community support during a period of financial turmoil (mid/late 1980s), nursing auxiliary A:a contrasts contemporary role rigidity with historic role elasticity. (See also Clark and Seymour (1999) on re-professionalisation.)

In addition to role prescription, organisational re-designation is, as previously stated, associated by some interviewees with changes in staffing numbers, ratios and role remits. Rising total numbers of rostered nurses have already been commented upon and the expansion in medical numbers is discussed more fully later. However, during the T^2–T^3 study period ratios of auxiliary (assistant) nurses fell relative to registered nurses as, it was believed, technical demands increased and, towards the end of the study period, Charge Nurse C:b stated that nursing auxiliaries still in post would be invited to expand their roles to meet the new demands that an influx of "sicker" patients created.[10] Nurse interviewee E:a (below) plainly links re-designation to concrete changes in nurse ratios when she states that acute or specialist palliative care needs: "So many trained and untrained".[11]

NURSE E:a Gradually one discovers, that we are going to be an acute palliative care unit and therefore we need 'x' number of people at our end. So many trained [registered nurses] and untrained [assistants] to do this and that (pause). I don't particularly feel that's how it should be done. I don't say the wrong decision's been made. But I do think we need to know and decide what we are so that we can be that, instead of being, a bit of each (pause). When I came back (pause – sighs) my, my gut feeling was that the hospice is now not really a hospice. And we actually need another hospice now. To do what we were doing before. Because everything we are doing here is valid and useful and (pause) all those sorts of things but we, we lost a lot of what we had when we first opened, it was sort of, we'll love you, you know, you come here we'll look after you and we will see it through. And, we, we'll always be there for you. And that's gone. And I feel we need a sister unit where people (pause) can be, if they're going to be here for longer. There are very few people here who were here when it opened. There are very few people who could relate to that feeling. When you walked in through the door (pause) the feeling was (pause) it was a feeling of love, and I don't, I make no apology for using that word for that's how you felt. Now when you walk in, it's different. It was (pause). It's lost something. It's gained a lot of other things and I'm not saying those things are unimportant. A lot, a lot of them are important. But it has lost the essence of being a hospice.

This extract (and the wider discussion in which it took place) acknowledges that formal change in organisational identity continued pre-established trends (see earlier commentary on T^1–T^4 time frames) and, in suggesting that the organisation is now "a bit of each" (i.e. a hospice associated with "loving" care *and* a specialist palliative care unit focusing upon complex physical symptom control) participant nurse E:a allows that the process of change is incomplete or under way. Reservations about the success of re-designation are likewise voiced by the Nursing Director who responded to an interviewer statement about the organisation's specialist status with an acerbic "Are we?" (G:a) and the Ward Manager's statement (p. 82) that "not enough" (F:a) patients with complex symptoms exist to fill the beds. This last comment in particular implies, perhaps, that a percentage of beds must continue to be occupied by patients with non-specialist needs (i.e. non-complex terminal patients). However, the idea that not enough palliative patients with complex physical needs exist appears intuitively erroneous and, in the passage below, the new Medical Consultant expresses frustration with T^2–T^3 admission practice. Here, attempts to admit a patient apparently meeting specialist palliative but not traditional study site admission criteria are initially rebutted. This suggests that re-designation is a process rather than event. At a minimum it again indicates that re-designation is not perhaps universally or consistently understood or accepted.

MEDICAL CONSULTANT O:a I've just recently tried to get somebody in and was not allowed to bring them in. And (pause).

INTERVIEWER: Well you're only the consultant.

MEDICAL CONSULTANT O:a (Laughs) Yes, well, exactly, too right! So it was then taken, having rejected me I had a massive strop about it. It was then taken back to the Chief Executive [General Manager], the lead nurse and the educationalist and then finally the patient's GP to see if it was appropriate for this patient to come in and once everyone had been consulted the decision for him to come in was finally agreed upon. He was allowed to come in. Having actually been turned down.

INTERVIEWER: May I ask, vaguely, what were the criteria for turning him down?

MEDICAL CONSULTANT O:a They didn't have any, apart from being [*edit to ensure anonymity*]. He didn't fulfil the life-limiting illness criteria. (*Said with strong irony – the patient had numerous complex physical needs – the patient died following admission.*)

This extract illustrates that admission criteria were at this time confused, contested or undecided. Dissonance is evident between what might be termed traditional hospice admission practices and specialist palliative care's more expansive remit which, for example, appears more willing to 'take' non-cancer patients and patients with compound problems.

The key point here however is that whereas Nurse E:a (p. 88) conveys, through strong emotional affect, sadness at the changes she witnesses, the new Medical Consultant is seeking to expedite such changes. Nurse E:a claims that change has now advanced so far that another "sister" organisation is needed to fulfil the function originally performed by the hospice and, invoking the concept "love", she suggests that the non-physical and spiritual components of care have been devalued. Interestingly, this last point was mirrored by the long service outpatient doctor who concludes comments remarkably similar to those presented above by E:a with the statement: "I'm quite convinced that in ten years' time somebody will reinvent the hospice" (H:a).

Practice changes associated with re-designation are later explored further. Here it is noted that accentuating forms of care prioritising physical symptom relief may contribute to both medicalisation, *if* this term implies increasing biomedical activity and a concomitant diminution in non-medical aspects of care and secularisation, *if* this means that the "secularizing impacts of a process of cultural and social rationalization" (Habermas, 2008, p. 2) produce disengagement or disenchantment with spiritual interests. In both instances it is assumed that an increase in one form of care (here complex physical symptom control) leads to the withdrawal of other forms of care. If this is permitted then shifting the balance in care delivery towards complex physical symptom control inevitably undercuts forms of working and holistic or spiritual care that have (despite the Nursing Director's comments regarding organisational difference) traditionally or popularly been associated with hospice care. Thus it can be argued that, at its inception, the modern hospice movement placed great store in what is now termed holistic care and multi- or interdisciplinary working[12] (West, 1990). Cicely Saunders's earliest writings stress the importance of multi-disciplinary care (2006d [1959]) or "casework" (2006c [1958], p. 4) as well as non-physical social, psychological and spiritual care (2006e [1961]).[13] References to God's love and care's spiritual dimension infuse these publications (e.g. see Saunders, 1990, 2002a, 2003, 2006b) and, contra those who would now prioritise physical symptom control, she asserted that: "if we do not look beyond these things [physical needs] to see a person of eternal value, then our work is no more than the use of techniques of relief" (Saunders, 2006a [1961], p. 37). Contemporary challenges to naive or unreflective holism come from a variety of sources. Reference texts such as Portenoy and Bruera's (2003) *Issues in Palliative Care Research* are overwhelmingly medical or physiological in content. Lawton's (2000) influential description of the difficulties of administering to physically disintegrating or "unbounded" (p. 128) bodies emphasises the dominance in practice of physical care needs. And Randell and Downie (2006) forcefully critique overly ambitious palliative psychological and spiritual claims in their reassertion of traditional medical views regarding priorities and prioritisation.

Nonetheless, as works by Sheldon (1997), Kearney (2000), Cobb (2001), Rumbold (2002b), Jewell (2004) and Stanworth (2004) attest, interest in palliative non-physical and spiritual end of life care continues and, mirroring these contradictory perspectives within the literature, at the hospice, while the benefits provided by improved techniques of, for example, pain relief, are welcomed by all, some interviewees challenge physical care's ascendant pre-eminence. Moreover, where organisational re-designation appears to undermine certain forms of holistic care, it must also be acknowledged that multi-disciplinary decision making (or decision blocking) continues – as is evidenced in the requirement that the new Medical Consultant speak with the General Manager, educationalist and lead nurse before a "non-standard" (O:a) patient was admitted.[14]

These issues are developed further below; here it is noted that social structural change (i.e. organisational re-designation) formalises and accelerates pre-established practice changes within the hospice at the level of social interaction and two socio-cultural "networks" (Cruickshank, 2003b, p. 122) or groups are identified whose constitution reflects cultural system ideational divergence. Thus, some individuals, loosely constitutive of a group, oppose organisational re-designation and the changes this encourages (changes that are "diluting the non-physical components of care", Educationalist, I:a) while other recognisable individuals, similarly constitutive of a group, actively support such changes (for example, Medical Registrar Y:a suggested that change offers the welcome opportunity to "concentrate on physical symptom control").

Assuming the reality of what might crudely be termed 'pro-' and 'anti-change' groups, it is here suggested that socio-cultural (S-C) interaction or interplay points towards cultural system (CS) contradiction *and* social interaction (SI) points towards socio-structural (SS) tensions *and* insofar as socio-structural change precedes and prompts cultural system contradiction, a form of differential morphogenesis may be indicated (i.e. socio-structural change has, for the anti-change group at least, outpaced cultural acceptance). The major social and cultural structural premises identified in this section are outlined below.

Social structural organisation re-designation at T^1 altered social interaction between T^2–T^3 insofar as:

1 Organisational re-designation caused the number of patients admitted for terminal end-stage care to decrease relative to patients admitted for non-terminal specialist symptom control.

2 Patients admitted for specialist symptom control generally have complex physical needs.
3 Focusing on physical care reduces the time and resource available for non-physical care.
4 Patient groups with complex physical symptom control needs necessitate and legitimate the use of more treatments and interventions.
5 Clinical staff numbers, ratios and roles altered in response to changing needs and pressures.

Organisational re-designation and the changes in social interaction noted above altered T^2–T^3 socio-cultural interaction by exposing and invigorating already established T^1 cultural system ideational contradictions. Following Archer, socio-cultural agential positions are stated propositionally (below). Propositions may focus upon detail (e.g. concerning 'time' or 'post-mortem practices of respect') or, as occurs here, they can seek to capture more general perspectives. In this study it is suggested that pro- and anti-change groups can broadly be differentiated according to two criteria. First, whether holistic *or* physical care is prioritised and, second, whether terminal *and* complex (physical) symptom control *or* complex (physical) symptom control patients are prioritised. It is not claimed that these groups meet List and Pettit's (2011) exacting criteria for group agency (nor need they) and it is not suggested that these groups have corporate status. It is claimed that the two key T^1 cultural system/structural differences or distinctions between groups exposed in T^2–T^3 S-C interplay are or can be propositionally expressed as:

> Hospice/palliative care involves physical, social, psychological and spiritual components – in practice no one aspect of care will or should be prioritised.
> vs
> Hospice/palliative care involves physical, social, psychological and spiritual components – in practice physical care will and should be prioritised.
> *and*
> Hospice/palliative care should primarily focus upon end-stage terminal rather than pre-terminal complex (physical) symptom control care.
> vs
> Hospice/palliative care should primarily focus upon complex (physical) symptom control irrespective of whether this occurs in end-stage terminal or pre-terminal stage patients.

Agents, actors, persons

The following extended extract from interviewee I:a (Educationalist) supports the idea that escalating busyness and heightened patient symptom acuteness stimulates practice level changes. It also exemplifies the cultural system/socio-cultural position of the group of hospice employees that is resistant to socio-structural level change.

EDUCATIONALIST I:a [When I first came here] (Pause) It was lovely. In the sense that you could focus very definitely on individual patients. There were lots of staff for the numbers of patients. And so it was possible to give a lot of time to each individual patient and family surrounding the patient. A lot of the time the patients were poorly (pause). But they weren't as acutely poorly as they now are. They were generally poorly in a weak, cachexic, reaching the end of their days sort of way. And so there was lots of need for hands-on nursing care. But there was also the time to spend talking with people in a way that's not now possible. There was time to, for example, there was time to sit and *be* (emphasis) with someone through the experience of a breathless panic attack. Where now, probably, you might spend a minute or a minute and quarter and have to make the decision that you're not going to be able to spend three quarters of an hour getting that person through that. So you would then go to the drugs trolley. Or you would use oxygen to try and ameliorate that, or placate it (pause).

INTERVIEWER: Has patient dependency changed as well then?

EDUCATIONALIST I:a Patient dependency has changed because of acuteness (pause). Yes, I think it has because actually if, if the majority of people who are with you are there for the last phase of life, you know, less than 10 per cent went home, so we were talking about the last couple of weeks of life. And because we saw people with what would now be called general palliative care needs as well as the one or two who really had very complicated difficult problems, palliative care symptom wise they (pause) needed a lot of general nursing care. And they needed (pause) what probably we would now see as fairly basic symptom control. But that meant that because we had the staffing numbers, we did have the time to put into the sorts of psychosocial and spiritual explorations with them that may or may not have been helpful but certainly that, that was what we perceived we were there for. [Now however] I think what we haven't quite lost, but run the risk of losing is, is the vision of, that roundedness, that for me palliative care is about. That we run the risk of (pause), because as we do more and more interventions, inevitably we will attract into the team people who are comfortable and competent undertaking those interventions. And although we haven't lost it yet, I do have a fear that in ten or fifteen years down the line, when the old codgers like me go, that actually there will be much more, there will be many more of the technical-rational people in post in all different sorts of things here. And that we might then lose, that horrid word 'holistic', but that we might then lose that real rounded approach that palliative care is.

Here participant I:a states that change risks "losing" what "palliative care is about". She proposes that new hospice recruits undervalue non-physical care because they have undergone prior socialisation in acute care environments *and* change within the hospice now allows and fosters an acute or interventionist approach. It is suggested that change has produced an environment conducive to the recruitment of "technical-rational people". By definition such people are disinclined to prioritise emotional non-physical care and it is noted that as "old codgers" like the speaker retire, fewer people remain to protect "holistic" hospice principles. This perspective differs from the bleaker outlook of Registered Nurse E:a (p. 87) since for E:a the hospice's "essence" is already "lost". Nevertheless, I:a's position is compatible with E:a's and others similarly disposed insofar as she explicitly values holistic or palliative care (the terms are here elided) as something *more than* physical care and she distances herself from technical-rational care which she equates with specialist palliative biomedical care. Further, I:a implicitly presents herself as part of a conscious rearguard action against emerging practices (associated with organisational re-designation) and, it is argued, such evidence supports the claim that at least some staff (mostly but not always long service nurses) champion the first of each of the two cultural system propositional statements stated above (p. 91).

Interviewees like the Educationalist I:a who are critical of emergent trends tend to emphasise their distinctive outlook by highlighting, as binary opposites, alleged differences between the personalities and behaviours of early "old codgers" and modern "technical-rational" hospice recruits. For example, interviewee J:a (Day-hospice Manager (Nurse)) stresses past collegiality and the relegation of routine physical to emotional care when, to the detriment of current study site practice, she favourably recounts previous experience at another hospice.

DAY-HOSPICE MANAGER (NURSE) J:a We were a very homogenous group of nurses, we were all, you know, members of Greenpeace and Amnesty and (pause) often people were Quakers for some reason. You know, you could come and hand over and say you hadn't washed him and that was okay. And it really was okay I think, I mean early hospice nurses were, were a type, because things in the health service were not that bad. And, but my sensing of it was that they were more humane.

Strong normative assumptions and judgements are contained in these and similar statements. However, rather than focusing on individual morality or responsibility, interviewees stress the more abstract role played by pre-hospice socialisation in explaining why early and modern recruits differ: "I mean it's all to do with our backgrounds isn't it, it has to be?" (J:a). Hospice clinicians always came from the NHS. However, as noted, new recruits are now seen, by those antagonistic to change, as being acutely rather than hospice orientated – i.e. new recruits are more willing to treat and intervene physically and they are more willing to accept the second of each cultural system propositional statement presented on p. 91.

Clark and Seymour (1999) offer putative support for this argument or possibility and, further, as new staff are engaged, the percentage of those holding "old codgers'" views inevitably declines. Socio-structural change (i.e. via recruitment) thus exposes and exacerbates cultural system discord regarding appropriate forms of hospice care/behaviour for the group antagonistic to new developments. Importantly, those indifferent or predisposed to accept change need not be aware of cultural system discord to the same extent and, therefore, while the relationship between groups (crudely those pro- and anti-change) is internally symmetric, their influence differs since those in favour of change are less vocal but 'politically' ascendant.

Most interviewees, but invariably those hostile to change, comment upon contrasting Medical Consultant behaviours at the hospice and, given the importance of these particular agents within the organisation, addressing differences in the way Consultants embody their roles advances discussion of the variation between new and old recruits by focusing attention upon distinctions between agency (interest laden positions and roles), actors (how positions and roles are filled) and persons (the self who is an actor).

As noted the organisation employed two Medical Consultants. One was full time and the other, the new Consultant, was part-time. As agents both Consultants occupy similar positions and roles. However, the senior long service and full-time Consultant was generally believed to be disposed towards the organisation differently to the new Consultant who remained engaged with and orientated towards NHS work. Thus, the new Consultant had, as he described, an "ambivalent attitude towards hospices" (O:a) and only visited the study site for a day and a half each week. Significantly, virtually every interviewee, including the Consultants themselves, suggested that differences in pre-hospice socialisation and personality-psychology contributed to the way they embody, as actors, their agential roles (though they did not use these specific terms).

Thus, the full-time Consultant like the other senior doctor (H:a) came to the hospice from a rural county hospital or GP background while the new Consultant came from an acute metropolitan setting. The full-time Consultant readily acknowledged that GP experience sensitised him to local limitations in community and familial support for patients (see earlier comments regarding demography) and this stays his hand, he suggests, when considering options (e.g. surrounding discharge planning). Alternatively, the part-time Consultant, having spent most of his career in large urban teaching hospitals, enjoys trying new procedures, is more willing to admit and discharge patients following short stays and, a particular bone of contention, he has been and remains keen to help patient groups not usually seen at the hospice.

> MEDICAL CONSULTANT O:a [I seek to care for and admit patients who are] high immigrant, high sort of deprivational indices, the under-resourced, the marginalised groups in society and patients who were, you know, prisoners, HIV, refugees and, you know, sort of people who were, that weren't particularly pretty and didn't fit into the nice sort of cancer model that we've built up [here].[15]

Interviewees were anxious to stress that they personally 'like' both Consultants. However, whereas the full-time Consultant is "conservative" (Ward Manager,

F:a) in his medical practice, non-interventionist and disinclined to hurry patient discharges – the part-time man is, by hospice standards, radically innovative and interventionist, inclusionary rather than exclusionary (see above) and active in promoting swift discharge. Thus, despite occupying analogous positions or roles, contrasting (actor) styles (role embodiments) concretely affect practice and occasionally produce sharp differences in professional opinion.

For example, somewhat extraordinarily, meetings have been held to discuss and diffuse tension among junior medical staff when overt disagreement about clinical decisions and practice threatened to compromise activity. And, similarly, conciliatory meetings have been required to appease nurses who queried and/or challenged divergent or novel clinical decisions. Both Consultants have thus attended formal and informal debriefing sessions to talk through and explain or justify their respective actions. Specifically, meetings were required to allay concerns about innovations in analgesic dosing, the use of blood products and antibiotic administration in terminal/end stage patients.

Interviewees who defend what they see as traditional hospice practice favour, unsurprisingly, the full-time Consultant's approach. They also criticise the product of Consultant tension: "So you've got people in [one] team whose discharge is totally different from, to the [other] team" (Charge Nurse, C:a) and they challenge medical decisions made by the new part-time Consultant and/or junior medical staff who follow his lead:

EDUCATIONALIST I:b I mean I guess I am trying to do what I can. So when I appear at multidisciplinary meetings and I hear that patient 'x' has had his hypercalcaemia[16] treated I think [*expletive*]! What are we doing here? What are we doing here? I raise the question by saying when this happens again, in the next week or two's time, would it be your plan to retreat this? Because that's my gentle way of saying to [full-time Consultant], for God's sake sort your medical staff out. Okay!

Conversely, tension between Consultant (actor) styles is described as "healthy for the organisation" (Ward Manager, F:a) when it promotes modernisation or debate. And, in this vein, the new Consultant's arrival challenged the "inward looking [and] precious" (Ward Manager, F:a) nature of some hospice practices. Moreover, interviewees not antagonistic to change (or all aspects of change) suggest that the new forms of care are gaining acceptance.

CHARGE NURSE V:a You still get some (pause) grumblings that should, should we really be doing this. But I think that that has changed over the last few years. That it's not new. That we're doing more to patients. That's been happening since you've come really, since you've been here [referring to researcher]. You know, hasn't it? So it's not a new thing. So if someone turned up with an epidural for pain control or a (pause) were giving antibiotics for symptom control even though they're dying, I think people are getting to grips with that a little bit now.

More provocatively those favouring change propose that hostility results from limited 'wider world' experience.

NURSING ASSISTANT D:a A lot of people who have been here a long time have only ever worked here and never worked elsewhere (pause). They haven't seen this [treatment or intervention]. So it's all new to them and they can't adjust to new things. Because it wasn't a hospice thing. They'd never had anything like that in a hospice. It was just basic nursing care and the patient died pain free without interventions. So they see these as unnecessary interventions.

And even those hesitant about change recognise that limited non-hospice experience plays some part in generating reticence.

DOCTOR H:a Very few people here have worked in other palliative care institutions and so we just assume this is how it's meant to be.

Suggesting that prior socialisation, specifically past employment experience, influences attitudes (psychological dispositions) to current change seems plausible and evidence for the exertion of 'downwards' social structural mechanism pressure on individual personhood (psychology) surfaced, in this study, when some clinical interviewees made unrequested disclosures about the emotionally disturbing nature of witnessed violent deaths. Details of these disclosures are not described here because they are deemed overly exposing (Lipscomb, 2010b). Nevertheless, where altered social structures (e.g. demographic change or organisational re-designation) contributed to a rise in acutely ill admissions (patients requiring specialist physical symptom control) – and assuming that (on aggregate) the deaths of these patients are more traumatic for staff than those historically witnessed – it might be argued that new forms of social interaction between staff and patients (involving staff exposure to what might be described as more 'violent' deaths) led some clinical personnel to experience psychologically negative or adverse reactions. And, in consequence, the ability of actors to fulfil agential role expectations (e.g. offering emotional support to patients) may be compromised if or when personhood (here psychological 'resilience') is damaged by, in this instance, contact with multiple violent or traumatic deaths. (See also comments by Registered Nurse interviewee B:a Appendix E on professionalism and emotional disengagement.)[17]

Alternatively, the 'upwards' influence of individual psychology on social interaction may be evident where personality (definitional problems notwithstanding) affects the manner in which actors such as the full- and part-time Consultants embody or experience agential roles. However, linking psychological attitudes or dispositions to experience and social explanation in the manner outlined above is problematic insofar as this can allow or imply reductive individualism or social determinism.

To avoid both over-socialised and over-rationalised concepts of humanity, critical realist theorists such as Archer (2000, 2002, 2003a, 2003b, 2007) are exploring the place of extra-social personal psychology or "selfhood" (Gronow, 2008, p. 243) in mediating or interpreting social and cultural conditioning structural interests.[18] Archer's taxonomy of persons, actors and agents provides a way into discussing the "projects" (Mutch, 2004, p. 384) that agents involve themselves in. And, in such discussions, geological and/or directional metaphors usefully suggest forms of causal influence. However, the mechanisms of interaction between psychological and social strata remain under-theorised[19] and, while individual psychology (personhood) and prior (agential) socialisation contribute to and must be acknowledged in any description of actor difference, categorical statements about their interaction would require clarification of the mechanism(s) of interplay between, for example, genetic, mental-psychic and environmental or social factors as well as conjecture regarding the nature of consciousness and free will. Such explanation is beyond the purview of this work and, as the Introduction asserts, the version of free will apparently lodged in critical realist and morphogenetic theory is perhaps open to query. At a minimum, as Rose (2006) makes clear, discussions involving or invoking the concepts of selfhood and consciousness are complex and undecided.

At the level of cultural emergent properties, the situational logic operative between Consultants and the pro- and anti-change groups that may loosely be associated with their respective behaviours is one of necessary contradiction *and* compromise. Those opposed to or hesitant about new forms of treatments and interventions and the prioritisation of physical care nonetheless recognise that patients benefit from some new practices. Those promoting or acquiescing in change often acknowledge the importance of 'older' hospice values. Indeed, although the social structural mechanisms promoting change and cultural system values linked with that change are ascendant, neither pro- nor anti-change group can or wants to ignore the other. (Though, as noted, those antagonistic to change *must* engage in social and socio-cultural interactions that they find irksome whereas the reverse is not always or necessarily the case.)

Over time (T^2–T^3) both positions showed signs of compromise albeit that greater movement was required of those antagonistic to change. Thus in speaking about the relationship between the Medical Consultants the Ward Manager noted that "we are inevitably (pause) changed by our environment. And those with whom we work. We can't not be" (F:a). And, towards the end of the study period, while the full-time Consultant had, it was widely thought, become more like the part-time man in his behaviour, even the part-time Consultant evidenced, on occasion, a slightly less interventionist approach.

WARD MANAGER F:a (Laughs) "Is chemotherapy appropriate for this patient?" (laughs). Were you here? (laughs) I've never heard him [part-time Consultant] say it before! I couldn't believe it!

Albeit that, at T^3, significant differences remain between Consultants and pro- and anti-change individuals and groups.

CHARGE NURSE C:a This is just an example, because [Charge Nurse] was going to do one of my team meetings the other day and she said "Oh, oh what's the plan for this lady". And I said "Oh I expect [full-time Consultant] will just say, oh we'll just keep her for another two weeks before we do anything" and [Charge Nurse] was tutting saying "Oh we need to do this and that". And I said later, "Oh what did [full-time Consultant] say about this lady", and she said "Oh we are to keep her for another two weeks." And I knew that's exactly what he'd say and I was happy with that.

Increasing medical engagement

The number of medical staff engaged at the hospice rose dramatically during the study period. Short-term fluctuations preclude overly declarative statements. However, while the hospice engaged just two doctors in its early years, upwards of six and seven (part and full time) medical staff were engaged at any one time between T^2 and T^3. Rising numbers of medical staff can be interpreted, in part, as an outcome or effect of organisational re-designation. Put simply, re-designation caused doctor numbers to increase at the hospice.

NURSING DIRECTOR G:a We have a phenomenal amount of doctors at the moment. I mean that's, this last twelve months, isn't it, really, if you look at it.

For nurses, engaging more medical staff produced two forms of contradictory situational logic. First, insofar as the presence of more medical staff contributes to the development or focus upon physical care, it exposes, in socio-cultural interaction, those cultural system structural contradictions previously described. For most agents (medical and nursing) these contradictions remain necessary and corrective. However, in relation to medical engagement, nurses strongly antagonistic to the second of each of the propositional statements detailed on p. 91, describe forms of social and socio-cultural interaction (SI and S-C) that might, in the forcefulness of their presentation, suggest commensurability with eliminatory contingent logics.

Second, increased medical engagement is itself a socio-structural development since it alters the dynamic of doctor-nurse corporate or professional relations within the hospice. In disturbing the respective authority, power or 'territorial mandate' (Taube *et al.*, 2003) of medical and nursing positions and roles within the organisation, raised medical engagement provoked contradictory forms of social interaction among doctors and nurses that appeared to exist irrespective of previously described pro- and anti-change perspectives. Thus, even nurse interviewees not antagonistic to other changes critically note the consequences of the expansion in medical input.

Doctor–nurse relations have long attracted professional and sociological interest (e.g. Warelow, 1996; Oughtibridge, 1998; Porter, 1998: Ashworth, 2000; Manias and Street, 2001; Coombs and Ersser, 2004; Fitzsimmons *et al.*, 2005). Attention has focused, among other things, on gender (Jones, 1994; Gjerberg and Kjølsrød, 2001; Davies, 2003), conflict (Mackay, 1993) and the effect that changing doctor–nurse relations have on other professional groups (Jones, 2003). In discussing positions and roles, sociological texts tend to link commentaries regarding medical power to descriptions of the medicalisation thesis (e.g. see Armstrong, 1994, or Nettleton, 1995)[20] and, while these issues are not overtly explored in this study, the palliative literature recognises their potential significance (see, for example, Biswas, 1993; Field, 1994; Corner and Dunlop, 1997; Mola, 1997; Clark and Seymour, 1999; Cobb, 2001; Hockey, 2001; Seymour, 2001; Janssens *et al.*, 2002; Woods, 2002, 2007; Sandman, 2005). Here it is merely noted that, first, the descriptors 'medicalised' and 'medicalisation' are often used loosely and without clarification.[21] Second, it has been claimed that medical training in the UK and elsewhere is, with regard to palliative care, erratic, sparse and biomedically focused and, in consequence, non-specialist medical staff may lack a holistic or social perspective (what Macleod, 2003, p. 123, terms the "art" of palliative care) (Schulman-Green, 2003; Oneschuk *et al.*, 2004; Löfmark *et al.*, 2006). Third, not only do nurses associated with the anti-change group believe there are now "far too many" (Educationalist, I:a) doctors at the hospice, others, less hostile to developments, record a shift in "intimacy" (Ward Manager, F:a) and role or professional boundaries as more medical staff appear. Indeed, for nurses, rising medical numbers equate with diminished "power" (Educationalist, I:a).

WARD MANAGER F:a It was more intimate many years ago. Because it's a changing period now, I think that has perhaps caused some distancing between the doctors and the nurses, seeing themselves as different groups. By intimate I mean that I think that (long pause) they felt more a part of the, of the nursing team. There, there didn't seem a difference. That's from a nursing perspective. I think the doctors relied more on the nurses. And I think that where you've got more doctors they don't have to rely so much on the nursing staff they can (pause). Because, there are enough of them to do what they're wanting to do and they'll do more of the doctoring. And therefore the nurses may tend to do more of the nursing.

EDUCATIONALIST I:a As you get more doctors involved you get more doctors doing doctor stuff. And [the organisation is now] much more medicalised. There's no doubt about that. We were much more, in the early days, we were extremely informal and there was a huge amount of overlap in our roles and (pause) certainly in professional terms nursing staff had far more decision making power.

Medical staff concurred with this analysis.

MEDICAL REGISTRAR Y:a I suspect people have got used to having more doctors around and people then change their roles .. when there aren't so many doctors around nurses, you know, quite, you know, more than capable of getting on with things on their own. But when there are more doctors around to ask you just sort of ask for their, and, and it can be a little bit more support.

In response, self-conscious efforts are being made to recapture nursing's lost authority. For example, the Nursing Director and other senior nursing personnel have suggested to the Consultants that medical staff are now "duplicating" (Nursing Director, G:a) or taking over what had previously been nursing duties. Furthermore, it is claimed that the present situation causes communication difficulties.

CHARGE NURSE V:a I suppose communication is sometimes less good because there's more people to go round. There used to be just, like, two of them and now, you know, but when you're trying to liaise between them you just spoke to (doctor) or (doctor). And you knew that the information was getting along. But now, you've got two Consultants who are very busy, and then you're like pressing on their time. And you've got junior doctors who, perhaps, are just here a year, and how much do they know? You know. They come in to do just their bit and so communication is sometimes perhaps a bit harder.

The transient nature of some medical staff has been noted (e.g. the Social Worker K:a challenged the authority of short-term doctors to make policy decisions – see p. 86) and junior medical staff (e.g. Doctor, L:a) agree that, despite the organisation's small size, lack of professional doctor–nurse familiarity hampers communication. For nurses/nursing assistants, the loss of collegiate intimacy and trust, evidenced by deteriorating communication and reduced autonomy, negatively impacts on patient care.

NURSING ASSISTANT A:a I think the doctors have tied the nurses' hands behind their backs in some cases [*referring to analgesic use at night when medical staff are not present*] whereas before if somebody was in pain, the nurses that we had were (pause) so experienced (long pause) that the doctors then (pause) trusted them, trusted them to do their job and not, and they felt that if anything did go wrong, well they knew they didn't feel they knew, that if anything did go wrong, they would have total support of the doctors behind them (*emphatic*). And I don't think people feel that now.

If more doctors are equated with heightened levels of treatment-interventions *and* changed professional boundaries reduce nursing role remits, then even those nurses who are not against all forms of change now face new challenges in promoting or protecting non-medical (non-interventionist) care.

WARD MANAGER F:a It's a danger, perhaps, with having more doctors. They're terribly keen to do things where they, sometimes you can get carried along. You want to be active when you really need to step back and think, do we really need to be intervening now and is this for the benefit of the patient? And I think that's when nurses actually have a very important role to play in encouraging doctors to stop. The interventions are a changing thing. And the number of doctors are a new and changing thing. And I think it's for us to say, you know, "hang on a minute, is this appropriate?"

More dramatically nurses associated here with the anti-change group were, when faced with instances of what to them were unwarranted interventions, able to cite examples of overt nurse–doctor confrontation (e.g. surrounding the blank refusal to comply with instructions to undertake formal observations on a patient undergoing blood transfusion) and, in this vein, Educationalist I:b argues (below) that significant numbers of senior nurses should continue to attend weekly multidisciplinary meetings in order that they might deliberately and overtly form a counterweight to medical numerical superiority.

EDUCATIONALIST I:b I was having a conversation yesterday with [Charge Nurse] and [Charge Nurse] and they were saying, [Charge Nurse] particularly, that she feels that for an E grade,[22] plus (Nursing Director), plus herself to be in a multidisciplinary meeting is a waste. And I said: "well hang on a minute" if you want to make an impact, if you want to turn things round, if you want to regain some ground, you need a presence there. And you need a presence that's senior enough and confident enough to say: "hang on a minute, what is this about." (Pause) But I'm not sure that, I'm not sure that she really took on board what I was getting at. Anyway, I think it's quite difficult. It's quite difficult to say. What the hell were we doing? What were the issues there? Who made the decision? How was the decision made? And would we do that again?

The multidisciplinary team meeting is intended to structure and organise patient care for that week and, in view of the above commentary it is or can be, unsurprisingly, a site of inter-professional confrontation. From the perspective of the part-time Medical Consultant, extended discussions about the nature and direction of organisational development – discussions of the sort Educationalist I:b seeks to initiate – are "pathenomonic [*indicative of*] of people having a process that [they] don't understand" (O:a). For the part-time Consultant the multidisciplinary team meeting is a medically led, medical decision making meeting and not a policy debating forum. From this perspective it should ideally and correctly follow the "medical model" (O:a) of problem identification and solution seeking (a model that clearly fits with previous statements about this Consultant's preferred way of working) and this view is supported by some junior doctors for whom ill-focused multidisciplinary discussions and timing overruns are an "irritating grievance" (L:a).

Both the part-time Consultant and junior doctor perspectives conflict with those mostly long service nurses who maintain (what they term) 'holistic' ideals that extend the legitimate boundaries of discourse beyond a rationalised (unemotional) approach to non-physical care.[23] Indeed the loudest voices against increasing medical engagement come from nurses antipathetic to change in general (i.e. the group most likely to subscribe to the first of each T^1 cultural system propositional statement described on p. 91) albeit that, as stated, almost every nurse interviewed, even those inclined to support other developments, problematised rising numbers of medical staff at the organisation.

Nurses as a corporate entity thus appear to be threatened (their power to direct patient care is limited) by increasing medical engagement. A situated social emergent property logic of contradiction at the level of social interaction is therefore evidenced between medical and nursing professional groups (T^2–T^3). Recognising this contradiction, or rather the manner of its expression suggests that, at T^1, the balance of power between medical and nursing staff was, if not equal, then (i) more favourable inclined to nurses or (ii) qualitatively different to that which it subsequently became. However, ‘power’ is a difficult concept; it is used here simply to refer to nurse perceptions regarding their ability to make or block decisions.

Retrodiction is, perforce, tentative. Nonetheless, this analysis is consistent both with previous ‘readings’ of the data/evidence and literature. It supports earlier suggestions regarding differential social and cultural system (SS-CS) morphogenesis since, again, social interaction (SI) change (between doctor–nurse relations) brought about by social structural (SS) amendment (rising medical engagement) precedes and ferments socio-cultural and cultural system (S-C and CS) contradiction.

Treatments and interventions

Numerous references have been made in this chapter to increasing levels of treatments and interventions. Virtually every clinical interviewee said that, compared with T^1, more and more complex treatments and interventions were being performed in the T^2–T^3 period. Specifically, interviewees say that more IVIs,[24] antibiotics, blood and blood products are being administered (necessitating staff re-training and the procurement of new machinery for storage, preparation, agitation and delivery). More DXT[25] and chemotherapy is being given (for palliative purposes). Long duration epidural infusions are becoming commonplace. Stents[26] are inserted more frequently, SpO_2[27] and blood gas monitoring is now routine. Indeed, many forms of observations previously not undertaken or recorded at T^2 were habitually being performed by T^3.

Various factors might account for this increase. For example, and as suggested, raised physical patient dependency on admission if genuine (it is important to stress that this is a perception and not a proven given) means ‘need’ has increased. Emphasising physical care consequent to organisational re-designation as a specialist unit suggests (caveats aside) that new needs are organisationally welcomed and recognised. Acutely orientated staff supply the means by which treatments and interventions can be ordered and delivered (needs are met). Increasing medical engagement (more doctors) may in itself act to raise intervention levels and the absence of blocks to change from acutely recruited nurses (but not resisting “old codgers”) could all be involved in this development.

Unsurprisingly, interviewees hostile to change deplore the rise in treatments and interventions albeit that they acknowledge some limited patient good ensues. Alternatively, those favouring change accentuate the benefits new procedures allegedly bring. Here, rather than simply reiterating the now well-rehearsed dichotomy between pro- and anti-change groups the position of treatments and interventions within the palliative care literature are discussed. As will be seen, identified tensions within the hospice mirror those in the wider palliative community.[28]

The decision making processes involved in determining treatment and the legitimacy or appropriateness of specific palliative interventions are both contested. Glaser and Strauss (1968) argue in relation to non-hospice care that staff attitudes towards and decisions about the treatment of dying patients vary according to staff perceptions of the position of patients on dying trajectories. Staff perceptions are therefore important and yet, as this study attests, staff perspectives can differ markedly. Further, in the absence of agreed criteria regarding appropriateness and given that concord need not exist between staff or staff and patients it has, in the modern hospice and palliative care context, been suggested that – although patients have always, to some extent, been involved in decision making – greater input into decisions about their own care should be encouraged (Walter, 1994; Núñez Olarte, 2003; Small, 2003; Oliver *et al.*, 2005; Sargeant *et al.*, 2007). The intentions 'behind' these sorts of move can be applauded. Substantive patient involvement in care decision making (when desired by patients) is a laudable aspiration. However, where patient ideas about treatment appropriateness conflict with the views of hospice and palliative clinicians and commentators who hold and express firm opinions regarding good or fitting treatment and good or fitting ways to die (e.g. Stoddard, 1979; Kastenbaum, 2000; Roy, 2004; McKechnie, 2006), questions about how disagreement should be resolved remain unanswered.[29]

At issue in such disputes is the idea, implicitly evidenced by some interviewees, that there exists a good, appropriate or "thanatologically correct" way to die (Núñez Olarte, 2003, p. 76 – see also Sandman, 2005). Assumptions bundled into the concept of 'a good death' are rarely made explicit. Nonetheless, like many palliative scholars, Connor (1998) suggests that "death is a natural part of life" (p. 79). Natural here suggests something uncontrived, non-technological, traditional (see also Kearney, 2000) and, in the hospice context, peaceful, accepted, unhurried and unmedicalised (Parkes, 1986; Walter, 1994; Seale, 1998).[30] Someone experiencing a natural death is not over-treated and the "amateur dramatics" (E:a) of last ditch rescue and curative medicine have been laid aside.

Because the good or natural death excludes interventionist "depersonalised science" (Kübler-Ross, 1973, p. 10), Connor (1998) is able to state that: "Hospice has been set up in such a way that patients must renounce further attempts at curative treatment" (p. 123). This setting up occurred when hospices supposedly dealt primarily with end-stage terminal patients and yet, today, the requirement that patients *must* relinquish curative aspirations or hopes appears somewhat imperious. It is a demand that may be resisted by those admitted or seen significantly in advance of the terminal stage. Indeed, as medicine successfully extends and alters disease trajectories, patients might reasonably want to receive radical interventions for symptom and disease control even at a 'late stage' in illness and, in these circumstances, patient wants can run counter to clinician assumptions about good or appropriate care.

Thus, not only can the naturalness of traditional or idealised hospice deaths be queried (even non-complex deaths typically involve the use of Graseby pumps,[31] elaborate drug cocktails, pressure relieving mattresses, catheterisation, monitoring and support by highly trained personnel), it is also recognised that some patients (e.g. end-stage AIDs patients) simultaneously seek to access curative and palliative services (Buckingham, 1996; Connor, 1998). Further, as medical 'ability' and public expectations evolve, patients might be expected to increasingly request what are, by 'assumed' hospice and palliative standards, "high-technology interventions" (Clark and Seymour 1999, p. 102).[32] Indeed even:

> patients who are terminally ill are prepared to accept invasive procedures and treatments more readily than are their nurses. Care must be taken to ensure that the judgements and attitudes of staff are not denying patients the opportunity of simple tests and therapeutic interventions from which they may obtain clinical benefit.
>
> (Meystre *et al.*, 1997, p. 1202)

Meystre *et al.* (ibid.) do not explain why *elaborate* as opposed to *simple* tests and interventions should be denied if these procedures deliver patient sought clinical benefit. Nevertheless, this finding challenges the position of study site interviewees who seek to resist the expansion in treatments and interventions. Patients and staff can differ about the appropriateness of curative and palliative goals (Dekkers *et al.*, 2002) and, it is here suggested that, in the literature *and* at the study site, at least three problems invest treatment-intervention or technology use. First, as interviewee G:a points out, hospice activity varies markedly between institutions and this might indicate that consensus regarding appropriate treatment limits or boundaries is absent. Second, if consensus does not exist because it is illogical or meaningless to construct or insist upon restrictions in treatments, then those wishing to maintain or create non-interventionist forms of care must perhaps resort to or rely upon normative exhortation in making their case and, third, if the focus of hospice or palliative care moves away from terminal care towards symptom control (as evidenced at the study site) then the rationale for non-interventionism collapses.

> The hospice community varies considerably in its medical sophistication. On one extreme are programs that refuse to do any "intrusive" interventions. On the other extreme are hospices that set no limits on the types of treatment administered. Arrogance comes into play when hospice thinks it

> knows what is best for the patient. [However] removing all limitations to treatment in hospice leads to hospice care that is indistinguishable from care provided in the rest of the health care system.
>
> (Connor, 1998, pp. 113–114)

Fears that external pressures are propelling the study site towards a close and perhaps indistinguishable relationship with the NHS were outlined earlier. Within the literature Foggo (2006) suggests that palliative patients not in the terminal phase could profit from the dismantling of barriers between categories of care (e.g. hospice patients may at times beneficially transfer into and out of specialised NHS acute settings) and, in extending the range of treatments available to patients, interviewees such as the 'new' Consultant appear ready to blur the distinctiveness or difference separating hospice and palliative from mainstream care. Moreover, in a move that further authorises the use of interventionist treatments, Randall and Downie (2006) attack what might be seen as core traditional hospice values when, contra accepted wisdom and WHO (2002, 2008) definitions, they suggest that life prolongation should and can be a justifiable aim for palliative clinicians.

As stated, those hostile to change at the study site tend to conflate terminal with non-specialist (non-complex) hospice and palliative care and, within the literature, similar conjunctions abound (e.g. Lishman, 2003; Roy, 2004). Such linkages privilege terminal care. Yet *specialist* palliative care introduces non-terminal patients into the clinical environment.

Cicely Saunders (2002b [1959]) noted that problems ensue for end-stage care when terminal and non-terminal patients are mixed since: "The latter are often in a younger age group and their problems are not by any means the same" (p. 14).[33] James and Field (1992) link the expansion of organisational roles (e.g. extending care beyond terminal support) and the influx of new or later generation staff (i.e. staff inattentive to early hospice ideals) to "goal displacement" (p. 1372). And Gracia (2002) argues that hospice care historically represented the antithesis or "corollary of intensive care" (p. 30). Thus, what is displaced for these authors and the anti-change group at the study site is a conception of hospice activity that primarily involves holistic low-intervention or non-intensive end-stage care. Clearly, "removing all limitations to treatment" (Connor, 1998, p. 114) violates this conception and, to resolve ambiguity, Webb (2000) suggests – probably unrealistically – that clinical, palliative and experimental treatment or technologies should be delineated.

The desire to draw boundaries around what is permissible and what is taboo litter the literature. Roy (2004), for example, regrets that end of life palliative care is now delivered "in a technological age" (p. 267). This presumes that past ages (decades?) were less technological and, as so often, end-stage and palliative or hospice care are here conflated. Roy (ibid.) goes on to claim that technology and the treatments it describes are part of ascendant "mechanical or instrumental reason" (p. 267) and that this is both "monstrous" (p. 267) and immoral. It is likely that such sentiments would resonate favourably with those at the study site who wished to limit or draw back from the new procedures and interventions.

Less emotively, philosophers of technology such as Dusek (2006) distinguish between hardware, rule and system technologies. Under this schema treatment interventions (e.g. inserting a stent) involve hardware (the artefact itself and the accompanying tools for placement and patient monitoring), rules (e.g. norms determining who decides upon recipients) and systems (e.g. healthcare systems or social and cultural assemblages of people and knowledge that enable processes to occur). For Timmermans and Berg (2003), three sociological perspectives interpret these technologies. Technological determinism describes the political force of technology's existence to shape social relations and behaviours.[34] Essentialism, on the other hand, situates technology as "neutral tools to be interpreted in social interactions"[35] (ibid., p. 97) and technology-in-practice highlights the "relationship between technology and its users in health care" (ibid., p. 97). However, it is here asserted that judgements about the appropriateness of technology use (i.e. treatments and intervention) are, contra essentialism, ultimately and necessarily evaluative, normative and political rather than objective (Kleinman, 2005; Dusek, 2006).[36]

Preliminary conclusion to 'relations within the hospice'

Organisational re-designation produced socio-structural (SS) morphogenesis *and* stasis within the hospice (see Figure 4.3 below). Re-designation reproduced existing relational trends *and* elaborated new staff–staff and staff–patient relations. Morphogenetically, organisational re-designation was, in part, responsible for the engagement of more medical staff and, in consequence, during T^2–T^3 and at T^4, nurses as a collective group have lost power (loosely defined) relative to doctors (compared with T^1).

Re-designation and the engagement of more medical staff also encouraged the deployment or use of treatments and interventions previously unseen at the hospice (or seen infrequently). It also enabled changes in admission practice (allowing the intake of more physically dependent patients) and this, at T^4, contributes to changed staff–staff and staff–patient interaction. Staff–staff relations are altered as professional role remits and organisational focus shifts in response to increased treatments and interventions. A growing emphasis on physical care is noted. Staff–patient relations alter insofar as rising busyness and more treatment-interventions are indicative of a heightened interest in physical care and this reduces the time and emotional 'space' available for non-physical emotional care.

Significantly, socio-structural change, exemplified or captured in the process of organisational re-designation, causes, in social interaction, competitive groups to emerge within the hospice *and*, in socio-cultural interaction, competition based around the ideational cultural system positions described on p. 91 apprehends key relations between these groups. The reproduction or transformation of group and primary agency within the organisation can be modelled apart from cultural system morphostasis or genesis (see Figure 4.4). However, excepting changes in doctor-nurse power relations (here associated with socio-structural/

Social structural (SS) conditioning

T^1
Organisational re-designation (hospice becomes specialist palliative care unit)

Social interaction (SI)

T^2 T^3

Changes balance between patient groups admitted
    More patients admitted with complex physical care needs
Creates busier environment
    Less time available to engage in non-physical care
More registered nursing staff engaged
    Changes ratio of auxiliary and registered nursing staff
    Auxiliary nurse remit expanded
More medical staff engaged
    Power balance between medical and nursing staff alters
More treatments and interventions performed

Social elaboration – relative to T^1

Relations between professional staff groupings altered
Relations between professional staff and patients altered

T^4

Social reproduction – relative to T^1
Continuation and entrenchment of existing
(pre-organisational re-designation) trends

Figure 4.3 Socio-structural factors acting within the hospice at T^1, their T^2–T^3 SI consequents and projected T^4 outcomes.

Socio-cultural conditioning of groups

T^1
(Group agency and Primary agency)

Group interaction

T^2 T^3
(Between group agents and primary agents)

Group elaboration

T^4

(Increase of group agents)

Figure 4.4 Group and primary agency in the morphogenetic sequence (source: adapted from *RTS*, p. 264).

social interactional change), agential elaboration or reproduction is closely intertwined with cultural system ideational positioning and the description of group (not group agents) and primary agency is here conjoined or subsumed within a diagrammatic representation (Figure 4.5) of cultural system transformation and reproduction.

In Figure 4.5 competitive contradictions are identified at T^1. Following Archer, cultural system (CS) logical relations (ideational sets) have ontological existence within the literature but, to exert causal effect, they must be taken up and concretely embodied in socio-cultural agential habits and practices. It is here asserted that groups holding contrasting ideational sets evidence disputation in socio-cultural interaction between T^2–T^3 and it is this disputation that allows cultural system structures and groups at T^1 to be retroduced/retrodicted.

Cultural elaboration is not identified. The ideational sets described by the propositional statements on p. 91 are not amended at T^4 relative to T^1. Cultural

Cultural System (CS) conditioning

T^1

Contradictory ideational structures exposed. Competition revealed between groups favouring:

1. Holistic vs. less-holistic approach and
2. End-stage/terminal vs. specialist palliative (biomedical physical) focus

Socio-Cultural interaction (S-C)

T^2 T^3

Pro-change group (focus less on end-stage care and holistic practice) appear ascendant and confront anti-change group (focus more on end-stage care and holistic practice). Anti change group lack exchange power but present 'rearguard' resistance to change

Dispute evident in, for example, MDM, the refusal to perform certain observations etc., and verbalised reactions to increasing treatment-interventions and (for nurses) medical engagement

Cultural elaboration – relative to T^1

Significant CS elaboration *not* evident

Pro- and anti-change groups and primary agents (most nurses and doctors) indicate at least some acceptance of aspects of change

T^4

Cultural reproduction – relative to T^1

CS reproduction evident – ideational fault lines apparent at T^1 remain in place and intact at T^4

Pro- and anti-change groups and primary agents maintain CS allegiances (pro-change group appear ascendant while anti-change rump remain)

Figure 4.5 Cultural system (CS) factors acting within the hospice at T^1, their T^2–T^3 socio-cultural (S-C) consequents and projected T^4 outcomes.

system reproduction or morphostasis therefore occurs. No evidence was uncovered to suggest that primary (indifferent or unaligned) agents had, between T^2 and T^3, been recruited to either the pro- and anti-change groups. Limited socio-cultural compromise did occur (e.g. see comments by participant V:a p. 95 or F:a p. 97). However, the groups identified here remained essentially intact between T^1 and T^4. As stated, since socio-structural/socio-interactional developments precede and expose and exacerbate cultural system/socio-cultural dispute, differential morphogenesis is, again, claimed vis-à-vis those opposed to change.

Spirituality/religion

Spiritual and religious discourse is important at the study site for three reasons. First, an exercise in what might be termed 'spiritual branding' has been proposed (see p. 75). Second, nurses may use spiritual talk to advance professional interests. Third, and contentiously, it is here suggested that a consideration of the concept of spiritual suffering and the location of meaning in suffering may help retroduce part of the motivation or interests of the anti-change group (i.e. consideration of these issues might in part explain *why* beliefs are held). Comments regarding this third theme are especially tentative and for that reason a discussion of spirituality/religion within the organisation is considered apart from the rest of this chapter.

Study site trends

As previously noted, the hospice stands on land donated by a religious order. Key founding trustees were, to some extent, religiously motivated. Prayers were once said before multidisciplinary team meetings and, historically, long service interviewees (see p. 64) recall staff praying openly with the relatives of deceased patients. Sunday services were once held in the chapel and a hand bell was irregularly rung during weekdays to invite attendance at a semi-formal reflective prayer meeting during which staff and patients would "think about hospices all around the world and patients suffering" (J:a). These practices had ceased by T^1 and following T^2–T^3 changes in busyness (p. 85), post-mortem procedures (p. 86), staff ratios (p. 87) and the influx of acutely orientated staff (p. 92) their resurrection would now be incongruent.

NURSING ASSISTANT A:a As more and more trained staff came in it became (pause) less sympathetic to religion.

Contradictory impulses are however also evident. Upon appointment, the General Manager funded a full-time clergyman (replacing the organised but informal visits of local clergy) and non-denominational services continue on alternate weekdays. However, religious influence is now reduced, albeit that spiritual themes have, to some extent, emerged in religion's place. Thus, moves are afoot to relocate and develop the chapel into a less formal 'sacred space' and the General Manager, recognising that spiritual care is currently (T^2–T^3) side-lined relative to physical care, now believes it was a mistake to appoint a "dog-collar" (N:a) wearing Anglican, since the conflation of religion with spirituality that this represents might be considered exclusionary.

Most interviewees are interested in the spiritual component of care (fewer spoke about religious matters). Interest cut across professional position and role boundaries and this could appear to challenge previous claims regarding those, often medical staff, who support and actively advance change within the hospice since, as suggested, change appears to emphasise physical rather than holistic and spiritual care. No anomaly obtains, however. Interest reflects the sustained attention given to such issues in the professional and palliative literature (Coyle, 2002). Further, doctors and nurses in their professional (corporate) capacities may be interested in spirituality for different reasons *and* those associated here with the anti-change group (irrespective of professional position or role) are employing spiritual language and symbolism in, I suggest, a distinctive way.

Thus although most interviewees discussed spiritual issues, medical staff tend to be more reticent than nurses in claiming jurisdiction or competence in such matters (a few nurse exceptions to this trend were identified). For example, while doctor Y:a thought spiritual care important, she did not think it part of her remit because she lacked "training" in such matters and, professionally, such training would be inappropriate.

MEDICAL REGISTRAR Y:a You can't have doctors training about spirituality you have to have (pause) kind of, people who are, who know what they're talking about (laughs).

Alternatively nurse interviewees are, on aggregate, more willing to accept responsibility for spiritual and even, in some instances, religious care. This acceptance mirrors proclamation and discussion within the UK and international nursing (e.g. Tanyi, 2002; Henery, 2003; Theis *et al.*, 2003; Callister *et al.*, 2004; Cavendish *et al.*, 2006) and palliative literature (e.g. Nelson *et al.*, 2002; Hermsen and ten Have, 2004; Narayanasamy, 2007). It may indicate that nurse interviewees define spiritual care more broadly than their medical colleagues (e.g. as ordinary kindness, in which case 'training' is not needed). And it should be noted that claiming spiritual competence also serves to advance nursing's professional interest. "The extension of spirituality into secular domains is part of a professionalization project in nursing, a claim to jurisdiction over a newly invented sphere of work" (Paley, 2008c, p. 175). As discussed, increased medical engagement produces, it is believed, a diminution in nursing socio-structural (SS) power relative to historic levels. However, serendipitously, nurses who – in socio-cultural interaction (S-C) – profess an interest in spiritual matters tap into and reproduce established cultural system (CS) precepts located in the palliative literature *and* meet the contingent need to protect and develop, in social interaction (SI), professional (SS) interests. Situated logics of complementary necessity are here demonstrated and this interpretation – claiming that spiritual competence serves nurse structural interests – is recognised in the (non-realist) palliative literature. Specifically, spiritual discourse is seen to offer nurses:

> a means for challenging the authority of medical science and of regaining some agency, some autonomy, in situations that otherwise would be defined as scientifically determined [it is or can be] a tool for preserving or enhancing the status of a particular discipline or distinguishing it from another.
>
> (Rumbold, 2002a, p. 8)

The importance of spiritual discourse in advancing professional interests at the hospice should not be over-emphasised. However, study site trends resonate closely with the wider palliative literature and the relationship between societal modernisation-secularisation and spiritual influence may therefore be significant.

Spirituality/religion and secularisation

Spirituality and religion are difficult concepts to pin down (Coleman, 2004). Spirituality has been linked to a personal search for meaning or value (van Hooft, 2002; Stanworth, 2004; Pesut, 2008a). However, Paley (2008b) skilfully deconstructs the coherence of these asserted linkages. Religion on the other hand is, among much else, associated with creedal theology, ritual, deity and organised or socially positioned faith communities (Seale, 1998; Dein, 2006). Gunn (2003) however argues that religion escapes definition and, from a historic and philosophic vantage, Sell (1996) catalogues the descriptor's dynamic and mutable nature. To further complicate matters, while spirituality and religion may depict discrete concepts (Mohan, 2004), this is contested (Cobb, 2001) and in use the descriptors are often collapsed (see, e.g. Bouchal, 2007).

Nonetheless, definitional problems aside, many early hospice pioneers were religiously motivated (Clark and Seymour, 1999) and religious conviction continues to propel new hospice and palliative care developments in Eastern Europe and Asia (Clark and Wright, 2003). Within the literature, however, an interest in spirituality rather than religion emerged among commentators in the 1970s as secularisation produced or accompanied a decline in formal religious observance (Rumbold, 2002a).[37] Secularisation is, of course, as difficult to classify and characterise as that which it opposes and Cupitt (1984), for example, chronicles the evolving and dynamic nature of secularisation in Christian Europe from the twelfth century onwards. On the other hand and more contemporaneously (more assertively), Habermas (2008) states: "During the period since the end of World War II all European countries, with the exception of Ireland and Poland, have been gripped by a wave of secularization that goes hand in hand with modernization" (Habermas, ibid., p. 116).

Linking secularisation with modernisation is important *if* modernisation is associated with biomedical advance and technological ascendency. Cobb (2001), who accepts this conflation, suggests that palliative clinicians' interest in spirituality and holism arose as a counterpoint to secularising and modernising tendencies and the biography and writings of Cicely Saunders (e.g. Saunders 2002a, 2006b) could be said to evidence kindred themes. Significantly, the language of spirituality offers a non-sectarian alternative to reductive rational and bureaucratic medical discourse (Bradshaw, 1996) and, thus, those who want to engage with forms of holistic care that prioritise emotions, values and existential meaning may find in spiritual talk a more inclusive and acceptable vehicle than what many perceive as 'narrow' religious dialogue (Confoy, 2002; Lavoie *et al.*, 2008). For Bergman (2006), spirituality provides a "non-contentious term somewhere in between religion and scientific psychology" (p. 5) for those interested in the existential or humanitarian dimensions of extra- or non-physical care.

Meaning in suffering – one reason why the anti-change group may resist change

From a nursing perspective Henery (2003) claims that the "literature on spirituality tends to agree that modern science is relatively powerless to address the loss of personal meaning experienced by people facing death, suffering and loss" (p. 550).[38] However, irrespective of professional allegiance, antipathy to change at the hospice is, in large measure, a reaction against changing forms of staff-patient relations. Idealised and preferred relations are variously described. Yet a recurrent and apparently significant aspect of such relations involved, for the anti-change group, 'being with' patients who were suffering emotionally or spiritually *and* 'being with' appeared to require that suffering's potential meaningfulness be valued.

Thus, while good technical and clinical skills are necessary attributes for hospice carers they are not, for the anti-change group, sufficient. Interviewee J:a emphasised that a willingness to "be with people who are suffering" is also required. However, organisational re-designation threatens this capacity, since, for example, the increased busyness that it produces reduces the time available for non-physical care and acutely orientated recruits are now less inclined to value non-physical care.

DAY-HOSPICE MANAGER (NURSE) J:a I would like us to be much more freer as professionals to say okay, you don't want a shave, you don't want a bath, you don't want to whatever, but you'd like me to sit with you under that tree at the bottom of the garden and talk about the pain in your past life, or whatever. I would like us to be much freer to do that. But I think, I think if I did that, that it would raise a few eyebrows.

'Being with' a patient was also linked with a particular view of holistic care.

EDUCATIONALIST I:a I think holistic care is about trying to attend in your heart and in your head to not only the physical elements of the things that you can 'do' for the people in your care, but also how you can 'be' (emphasis) with them.

And it was recognised that staff exposure to patient suffering incurs personal costs.

NURSING ASSISTANT A:a I, I never turned away; I never turned away, ever. I never tried to escape it. You didn't. It was, you know, what you were all there for.

Appendix D describes how, for participant A:a, this aspect of care was now in decline or abeyance and Appendix E notes that conscious or deliberate emotional withdrawal in the face of repeated traumatic death was an option for some healthcare professionals. Nevertheless, for participants A:a and E:a 'being with' remained a vital component of care. It was also described as an act of love.

NURSE E:a ...we'll love you, you know, you come here we'll look after you and we will see it through. And, we, we'll always be there for you. And that's gone.

Most nurses here associated with the anti-change group appeared to link the object of care with 'love' and/or 'suffering'. Moreover, notes made as a participant observer record that members of this group talked in everyday conversation in a manner that might easily hold or connote a spiritual interpretation (e.g. patients were now 'at peace' or their 'souls' were still 'troubled'). As Chapter 2 makes clear, the researcher's own position and views cannot be extracted from either data collection or data/evidence interpretation and, in this instance, personal non-belief and a disinclination to value spiritual talk presumably influences the analysis presented here. Nonetheless, it is tentatively suggested that, wittingly or unwittingly, interviewees associated with the anti-change group (doctors and nurses), who described patient suffering using what are here termed spiritual concepts, also believe that certain forms of suffering might feasibly serve some beneficial or redemptive purpose. For these staff, suffering was not something that should necessarily be obliterated or avoided and, to assist or facilitate patients in their experience, it was claimed that staff had a duty to 'be' or 'stay with' sufferers. Needless to say, the developing emphasis on physical care and expansion in treatment-interventions marginalised this discourse.

There is of course nothing new in positively evaluating suffering (or at least allowing that suffering has a positive potential). Western Christianity traditionally valued some forms of suffering as a route to Christ (e.g. Julian of Norwich, 1998 [1388]). And, from a non-Church or non-religious vantage, many nineteenth and early twentieth century European existential and phenomenological thinkers favourably embraced dolorist themes (Lipscomb, 2003). The supposed redemptive value of suffering is also deeply lodged in the palliative and end of life literature (e.g. Kearney, 2000; Jewell, 2004; Johnson and Scholler-Jaquish, 2007) and elements of this perspective or way of thinking may (or may not) intuitively appeal to people who have experienced personal trauma or witnessed the loss/trauma of loved ones.

From within the realist fold, Bhaskar has undergone or experienced something of a "spiritual turn" in his more recent work (Collier, 2004, p. 168), Archer evidences strong religious convictions (Archer, 2004a, 2004b in Archer *et al.*, 2004), and Collier (1999) develops a line of reasoning through St Augustine, Spinoza and Heidegger to argue that all being (human and natural) has intrinsic and objective (i.e. non-subjective) value or worth. If, for the sake of argument, the validity of Collier's (ibid.) proposition is accepted (and importantly this does *not* require agreement with the premises or conclusion of his argument) then being has worth and worth is good (since being is good) and thus, suffering can be good (it has a good potential) insofar as it, suffering, reaffirms or constitutes being in its most authentic or fullest sense.

Essential to this argument is the idea that in the act of suffering it is possible – but not determined – that some utility, growth or blossoming (to invoke horticultural metaphors) might occur in some but not all sufferers and, where or if this benefit occurs, it is a good (albeit an unrequested one). Further, it is assumed that this good will not/cannot find form or occur in those whose suffering (experience) is taken away (e.g. by chemical or other means) or devalued by carers. Therefore, by implication, carers are required to recognise and valorise this good.

Some readers may find these ideas 'odd'. And, yet, curiously, although the difficulty and appropriateness of engaging in conversation about such matters with patients was fully acknowledged, every member of the hospice clergy accepted that suffering might bring spiritual, religious or psychological gains. These were not then ridiculed ideas at the study site.

SPECIAL MINISTER OF THE EUCHARIST M:b If you are a Christian and have a faith [then] if you suffer, you automatically draw closer to Christ because you are, you would call upon him and you would unite yourself more with Christ to help you through this suffering.

FULL-TIME CHAPLAIN P:a People often speak to me of, when the suffering is at its worst, that's when they sense a presence of God most they quite often speak of that presence of God 'in' the suffering and they, they value that. They don't necessarily value the suffering because that's obviously not very pleasant. But what, what the suffering has brought to them in the sense of spiritual experience is immensely valuable.

ASSISTANT CHAPLAIN X:a [Can suffering bring benefit?]. Yes, I think it is a valid notion and it is within Anglicanism.

The strength or importance of the argument being proposed here should not be over-egged. However, it is suggested that socio-structural (SS) change (organisational re-designation and its correlates) altered doctor-nurse relations in social interaction (SI). Interest in spiritual matters is expressed by doctors and nurses. However, the nature of expressed interest differs by profession in socio-cultural (S-C) interaction. Nurses find, in the cultural system (CS) register (i.e. the 'library' of ideas available to them) concepts or ways of thinking about spirituality that potentially offer a means of protecting or advancing lost professional privilege. (Though this remains an aspiration – it may not happen.)

Further, staff identified here with the anti-change group (all professions) appear to use spiritual or religious metaphors – spiritual and religious language – to describe forms of care that are threatened by the consequents of re-designation. Ideas about spirituality that are lodged in the cultural system register are thus available and, if taken up and deployed successfully, these ideas might help protect those forms of care that are perceived as threatened. Moreover, as stated, the potential redemptive dimension of suffering (Pesut, 2008b) is accepted by all members of the study site clergy (albeit that the acceptability of such ideas to non-spiritually inclined staff must be doubted).

Despite these possibilities, cultural system and group reproduction rather than elaboration is evident at T^4 (relative to T^1). The ideas outlined above – if correctly interpreted – did not undergo transformation between T^2 and T^3 and, as previously noted, pro- and anti-change groups remain substantively unaltered. The cultural system logical propositions here associated with the pro- and anti-change groups are stated below. However, these propositions can be described in a variety of ways and the problem of expositional clarity is particularly pertinent here. In defence of the claims being advanced, the propositional statements presented below do not contradict those described on p. 91 and the schema outlined could easily be overlain on Figure 4.5 on p. 108 (CS factors acting within the hospice) without compromise to arguments presented earlier in this section.

> Certain forms of suffering experienced by hospice patients may be linked with spiritual benefit *and* hospice staff should support patients in achieving this benefit through the provision of holistic spiritual care.
>
> vs
>
> No benefit accrues from the experience of suffering *and* hospice staff should seek to obliterate or remove suffering.

Notes

1 Frequent service reorganisation led to this group being variously reconstituted and titled. Here, to aid clarity, the term Directorate is consistently applied.

2 Unequal power is here synonymous with size-importance and, contra Archer, by T^1 micro-macro differences of bulk also exemplify institutional relations.

3 It might be objected that voluntary or charitable and non-state independent sector provision are not necessarily coterminous. However, in the interests of expositional clarity the descriptors are here conflated.

4 Space precludes engagement with the full range of equity debates. For example, the International Association for Hospice and Palliative Care's promotion of equitable provision within a socially contextualised framework (Bruera *et al.*, 2004) and Aoun and Kristjanson's (2005) discussion of discipline specific research equity are not progressed here.

5 It might be objected that NHS palliative care consultant antipathy instances professional medical rather than state-NHS-hospice relational structures. However, this view is rejected since it appears to be the location of consultants within the NHS that is significant.

6 Negative realities may make themselves felt insofar as the presence of one form of service organisation (independent hospices) forecloses on the possibility of alternative provision (e.g. creating 'in-house' NHS palliative beds at the County hospital).

7 Ward based clinicians are also aware of cultural isolation. For example, interviewee F:a stated that: "I think (pause) isolationism, does (pause) encourage us to think that we are 'pretty good' and that we know lots. But we don't. We only know a bit about this aspect of care and we should recognise in other [non-hospice] professionals what they know."

8 A 'stretched' definition of demographic factors is admittedly used here.

9 This widely made claim (e.g. Callahan, 2005; Mino and Lert, 2005) is explored further later.

10 No contradiction exists between role prescription (the idea that remits are tightly defined and enforced) and an expansion in role remit (the specific tasks or functions to be performed).

11 'Untrained' here refers to auxiliary nurses. More correctly auxiliaries are trained but not registered with the Nursing and Midwifery Council.

12 While multi- and interdisciplinary work may designate different entities the terms are often conflated, e.g. see West (1990).

13 Although Saunders's ideas about religion and spirituality's relation to care evolved, the emphasis she placed upon the importance of Christian values in caring for the dying is apparent in statements made about wanting St Christopher's to be a 'really Christian foundation' (Saunders, 2002c [1959], p. 16). As such, Saunders initially considered establishing a Trust specifically 'so that it didn't get into the hands of cranks or non-Christians in years to come' (ibid., p. 16).

14 Griffiths (2001) discusses (from a mental health perspective) the relation between appropriate referrals and exclusion or service rationing.

15 Towards the end of 2003 the 'new' part-time Consultant left the hospice and county, returning to work in metropolitan palliative care with the "marginalised groups" that, in his opinion, the study site ignored.

16 Elevated levels of blood calcium (Hope *et al.*, 1993).

17 Self and society interact, Archer claims (2003a), when agents activate or encounter "causal powers of constraint and enablement" (p. 131). The impact of structures and powers is mediated by agents who consider and interpret options via internal reflective conversations and, in this respect, agents are free to act *within limits* (Archer, 2003b). Insofar as interviewee B:a (Appendix E) claims that, in response to numerous witnessed violent deaths, she self-consciously ascribes to a version of professionalism that distances her from patient emotional suffering (she states that she does not "allow myself to feel a great deal here"), it might be suggested that B:a sidesteps the otherwise disturbing (constraining) power of structure to cause her psychological harm. She is enabled to do this by SS/SI changes between T^2 and T^3. See also Abendroth and Flannery (2006) or, more recently, Ballatt and Campling (2011) for a discussion of similar themes.

18 Gronow (2008) argues that Archer presents an "*undersocialized* picture of selfhood and agency" (p. 244 – italicisation in original). Similar themes are being pursued in non-realist literature. For example, from an allegedly constructionist perspective and to avoid social determinism, Clouder (2003) examines "the scope for individuals to exercise personal agency within the professional socialization process" (p. 213) of health and social care workers.

19 This is particularly the case vis-à-vis brain function (body) and experience or mind (Rose, 2006).

20 Sociologically, the medicalisation thesis connotes a critical stance taken by social theorists to medicine's ideological and control functions. In this sense medicalisation is associated with "the disempowerment of individuals [and] an increasing tendency to define 'normal' aspects of life as medical problems" (Clark and Seymour, 1999, p. 113). More loosely, medicalisation describes the unwarranted usurping of power or authority by members of the medical profession, extensions in the use of clinical technologies and an emphasis upon biophysical care.
21 For example, without further explanation McKechnie (2006, p. 255) states that designating palliative care: "a medical speciality has influenced the way in which end-of-life care is provided and [it] has become routine and medicalised" (p. 255).
22 Hierarchically, during the study, 'E' grade nurses outrank 'D' grade nurses but are junior to 'F' or 'G' grade nurses. Post T^4 this grading system changed.
23 The descriptors 'rationalised' and 'unemotional' are used because, while medical staff do discuss psycho-social and even spiritual care, their approach differs in tone and content from nurses holding views here associated with the anti-change group. These nurses, in contrast to their medical colleagues, are noticeably effusive and expressive in discussing non-physical needs and they readily make evaluative or normative judgements about patients and patient care.
24 Intravenous infusion.
25 Deep x-ray treatment or radiotherapy.
26 A lattice-shaped metal tube inserted into an artery or body conduit to maintain function. Used to support end-stage palliative patients with, for example, gastrointestinal cancer (Bowles and Benjamin, 2001). For a critical perspective on stent use in palliative care see Neale *et al.* (2004).
27 Optical pulse oximetry measures blood oxygen (SpO_2) by passing red light through (normally) a finger. Algorithms derived from applied plethysmography and spectrophotometry allow light absorption and thereby oxygen concentration to be calculated (Smiths Medical, 2008).
28 Several old references are cited here. It may be that the contradictions now being experienced at the hospice are long recognised within the wider hospice and palliative community and literature.
29 See, for example, Hoefler (2000) on artificial feeding at the end of life.
30 While Hinton's (1967) *Dying* does not specifically address hospice deaths (the book was written before St Christopher's opened) it is tempting to add his name here because, as is clear, Hinton (ibid.) validates this list.
31 Proprietary name for a make of, in this context, portable slow release syringe driver – used to deliver continuous medication including, normally, opiates.
32 Tong *et al.* (2003) provide an alternative perspective.
33 The presence of younger patient groups also affects staff. At the study site it was proposed that old (80 years plus) and young (30–50-year-old) patients now present with complex conditions and co-morbidities that, until recently, would already have caused death. Further, when "average age goes down psychological dependency goes up" (G:a). Within the context of G:a's transcript it is clear that psychological dependency has two meanings. It refers to heightened emotional tension among clinical staff who care for those dying "at the wrong age", those in "our age group" (G:a) and it refers to the increased workload that accompanies the care of "three generations" when "you've got parents losing children" who themselves have children (G:a). See also Alexander (2004).
34 Technological determinism may be evidenced at the study site when interviewees linked the availability of equipment (e.g. SpO_2 monitors) with the perceived need or imperative to use that equipment.
35 This position was perhaps taken by those favouring change when they emphasised the patient benefits that accrued, for example, from new treatment-interventions. This is not to say that the interventions are value neutral.

36 More could be said about the relationship between technology and treatment-intervention use. For example, gender may have been a factor when male medical staff promoted technical or rational solutions to problems against female nurse resistance (Kleinman, 2005; Dusek, 2006; see also Davies, 2003). See Heath *et al.* (2003) for a review of technology and medical practice.

37 Paley (2008c) highlights differences between UK-European and US religious and spiritual beliefs and practices. Rumbold's (2002a) observations describe secularisation in a Western European and Christian context.

38 Davis *et al.* (2000), however, suggest that clinicians can enable meaning identification.

5 Conclusion

Social realists emphasise – correctly in my opinion – the closely interwoven nature of research activity and theory (broadly defined). Research practice and theory can be considered separately. However, researchers who undervalue or ignore theoretical and indeed philosophic engagement are, according to realist precepts, likely to generate impoverished findings and, contrariwise, theorists who distance themselves from the real-world applicability of their ruminations may produce work of limited use value. It can therefore be a mistake to disaggregate or pull apart research practice from theoretical considerations.

Of course it is possible to admit the general tenor of these propositions without accepting that social realism offers a suitable vehicle for understanding – i.e. a vehicle capable of effectively integrating theory with research practice. Nevertheless, that said, hopefully the nature and utility of realism's offering has, to some extent at least, been demonstrated by the study described in this book. And, if this is the case, if the study presented in Chapter 4 does indeed illustrate the value of social realism then, as the Introduction suggests, critical realism and more specifically the realist social theory of Margaret Archer – morphogenetic methodology – beneficially contributes to understanding in health and social care, or, as in this instance, palliative and hospice care (at least in one location at one time).

Social realism's contribution stems from its insistence on making overt key theoretical issues that are of concrete importance to researchers involved in social investigation. The guidance offered by Margaret Archer to practicing researchers as regards these issues remains at a high level of abstraction. However, it is nonetheless extremely helpful. That said, rather than simply beating the drum for social realism and morphogenesis, in conclusion, a brief and partial critical evaluation of this approach is outlined.

Unsurprisingly, reflection on the study presented in this book suggests that some elements of research practice 'performance' could have been improved and, further, a number of difficult questions remain concerning social realism. These two critiques – a critique of research practice and a critique of realist social theory – deserve recognition since they together undercut or problematise the analysis offered in Chapter 4. To discuss these issues Chapter 5 is structured using the following headings: (i) Morphogeneis applied, (ii) Critical realism, (iii) Morphogenetic theory and (iv) Summation.

Morphogenesis applied

As noted, critical realists assert that, put crudely, more robust or 'better' understandings of social reality may be generated (though this is not guaranteed) when realist philosophic insights and theory inform research activity. The different levels or forms of theory that appear in this study were described in Chapter 3 (p. 41) and Figure 5.1 (below) illustrates how, in Chapter 4, philosophy, theory and research were combined.

In Figure 5.1 two oft-repeated claims are cashed. First, realists assert that logical ties bind together ontic, epistemic and methodological understandings and, second, it is proposed that these ties must be respected if argumentative coherence is to be preserved. Figure 5.1 restates how metaphysical philosophy (critical realism) and meta-theoretical methodology (morphogenesis) together steered the development of study site or domain specific theories as well as, via template analysis, the identification of empiric data/evidence. As will be recalled, Archer pragmatically stresses that the ultimate measure of any theory lies in its use value and I would suggest that morphogenetic methodology does, despite caveats, demonstrate great usefulness.

Specifically, considering those aspects of hospice work detailed in Chapter 4, morphogenetic modelling permits social and cultural structures operating upon and within the organisation under investigation to be distinguished. The mediating responses of agents to structural influences are described and, in reaction to external pressures and internal change, forms of relations that indicate situated logics of contradiction and compromise are identified. Notably the hospice re-designated itself a specialist palliative care unit in response to external pressures and, internally, pro and oppositional groups emerged in response to the clinical impact of re-designation and its correlates. Differential morphogenesis is observed insofar as, for the anti-change group, evolving forms of social interaction (SI) outpaced socio-cultural (S-C) acceptance (for this group) and this indicates at least partial disjuncture in the temporal development of social structural (SS) and cultural system (CS) logical relations.

Metaphysical realism
(Bhaskar's claim that a reality exists beyond our representations of it, that this reality can be understood, but with no substantive claims about that reality beyond its general form)

↓

Realist meta-theory
(Archer's emergentist and relational social morphogenetic theory)

↓(↑)[1]

Domain-specific meta-theory
(Specific theories regarding the study site – described here under the headings 'Structures and institutions' and 'Relations within the hospice')

↓↑

Empirical research and the development of specific theories
(Data collection/analysis using Template Analysis)

Figure 5.1 Levels of realist theorising (source: adapted from Cruickshank, 2003b, p. 114).

We can therefore claim that morphogenetic modelling 'works'. And, yet, some of the findings presented in Chapter 4 closely match ideas already found within the literature and, if this is so, we must be wary of over-egging the revelatory ability or potential of morphogenesis. On the other hand, not only would it be surprising if this was not the case but concordance itself lends credence to the conclusions offered here.[2] Further, if it is granted that the explanation detailed in Chapter 4 is in some measure 'genuine' – i.e. if it is granted that Chapter 4 does capture important elements or aspects of hospice activity at the study site – then it might also be conceded that morphogenesis offers social researchers advantages in explanatory power over perspectives grounded in the literal application of alternative epiphenomenal and elisionary metaphysics.

This is a significant achievement and, mindful of the synopsis of Archer's theoretical position outlined in Chapter 2, we could note that, for example, since elisionists must refuse to delineate structural from agential interaction they cannot in consequence identify differential morphogenesis. Or, alternatively, epiphenomenalists who by definition over-emphasise the significance of agential *or* structural influence (depending on orientation) must omit in explanation any substantive reference to their interplay.

It might of course be that non-realist researchers do not adhere stereotypically, strictly or unbendingly to either elisionism or epiphenomenalism. (We do not need to demonise 'the other'.) Nonetheless, by correctly identifying and acting to circumvent alternative and flawed positions/explanatory forms, social realist researchers obtain significant positive benefits.

Despite these 'goods' it might however, self-critically and with hindsight, be argued that important aspects of pro- and anti-change group allegiance remain undeveloped in this work. Underdevelopment takes at least two forms. First, identified positions (the pro- and anti-change groups) may be insufficiently resolved and, second, their demonstration should perhaps have been more forcefully pursued. Thus, no attempt was made to quantify aspects of individual engagement with the positions identified and the degree or level of commitment to pro- and anti-change groupings remains undecided. This is of course a failing of the study rather than the theory underpinning it and yet many realists – perhaps mindful of the proposed link between quantification and crude empiricism – do appear reticent in pursuing the quantification of data/evidence (Willmott, 2003).

Another way of phrasing this would be to say that since data/evidence are, in this study, predominantly qualitative in form, then the extent and forcefulness with which pro- and anti-change group opinions are held remain indistinct. Further, given the qualitative nature of data/evidence, it cannot but be granted that another researcher may have reached different conclusions from the same materials. Indeed, the subjective nature of analysis in qualitative study (even when performed from within a realist frame) means that other interpretations of the data not only *could* but generally *must* be possible. (Conceptual relativism can but need not challenge ontological realism.) Consequently, the findings presented in Chapter 4 remain somewhat tentative and it may be the case that, for example, the cultural system propositional statements presented on p. 91 fail to capture the full complexity of positions held by or within pro- and anti-change groups at the hospice. Again this is a critique of the study rather than morphogenesis and, yet, by relying on abduction (retroduction or retrodiction), social realists may underplay 'issues' surrounding the inferential form they ostensively valorise and, when qualitative analysis is undertaken, these issues may prove to be especially problematic (Lipscomb, 2012).

Alternatively, a longer study period might and maybe should have been employed. An extended time frame would have permitted developing emergent structural and agential processes to be more clearly identified. Indeed, had the study been extended then the effect of, for example, the pro-change Consultant's departure could have been plotted onto the development of relations within the hospice (to further illustrate the significance of agential mediation on structural influence). This is important. It highlights the way in which researcher decisions impact on the findings that become possible (i.e. possible to conclude). And, for example, it is conceivable that had a longer period of study been undertaken, then a very different interpretation of events/social causation might have been produced. Moreover, crucially, this different interpretation could even apply to the time frame (T^1–T^4 – see Figure 4.1, p. 63) here examined (Lipscomb, 2010a). This aspect of event identity clearly requires greater consideration and I return, albeit briefly, to this subject in 'Morphogenetic theory'.

Critical realism

At a general level it can be argued that critical realist philosophy beneficially informs social theory and research in at least three ways. First, Roy Bhaskar (the 'founding father' of modern critical realism – see Chapter 2) provides, in *A Realist Theory of Science* and *The Possibility of Naturalism*, a powerful critique of what he terms the epistemic and linguistic fallacies in positivistic Humean-empirical and Kantian or idealist phenomenological and hermeneutic inquiry.

Bhaskar's work is vulnerable to challenge (see below). However, he nonetheless advances a compelling if idealised vision of scientific practice that both undercuts alternative theoretical assumptions and provides the philosophic underpinning for Archer's methodology. Bhaskar's conception of science is interesting enough to command the attention of social researchers and theorists. And, even those who discard critical realist claims will, in reading Bhaskar, be prompted to consider and perhaps refine their grounding beliefs, argumentative forms and investigative procedures. Engaging with Bhaskar therefore has value *even if* his metaphysical claims are rejected.

Second, critical realism emphasises the importance and central role of ontological presumptions in understanding and reasoning and, as the Introduction claims, the implicit links binding ontology, epistemology and methodology in natural and social scientific explanation are thereby highlighted. This emphasis provides a corrective to perspectives that underplay or ignore these linkages and, as stated and at the risk of dull repetition, studies that respect these logical ties or chains are more likely to generate coherent and robust explanations than those that do not.

Third, if Bhaskar's arguments are accepted, critical realist theory redefines and clarifies the problem field and goals of scientific endeavour. In the social field this involves delineating emergent agential from structural (social and cultural) relations, abjuring prediction in favour of explanation and re-describing, as nomic, causality and the nature of law-like statements.

On the other hand, Bhaskarian argument and philosophy is susceptible to criticism and flaws perforce detract from realism's allure. It would be inadvisable in a concluding chapter such as this to begin to explore potential weaknesses in great detail and readers are instead directed toward the wider literature (e.g. see McLennan, 2009). However, that said, one important challenge will be noted and, if this challenge 'holds', then key concepts scaffolding Margaret Archer's methodological claims are damaged.

Bhaskar constructs his philosophy on what might be termed 'oppositional readings' of Hume and Kant and, if these readings are seriously misjudged then, since so much rests upon them, realist philosophy is compromised. This need not be fatal to critical realist prescriptions as regards scientific practice and/or the work of authors such as Archer who use Bhaskar's philosophy as a grounding base. However, unfortunately, Bhaskar's reading of Hume and Kant can be questioned and this does somewhat tarnish or remove the shine from his work.

For example, in *A Realist Theory of Science* (1997) Bhaskar positions Hume as a representative of or for orthodox empiricism and all its ills. Bhaskar charges Hume with misunderstanding the place and meaning of experience in scientific theory/experimentation and, in consequence, explanatory criteria, ideas concerning confirmation, falsification and notions of rationality become confused (*explanandum* becomes conflated with *explanans*). Supposedly these failings derive from Hume's description of causality and scientific law.

At the risk of oversimplification – and oversimplification may be the problem here – Hume's *An Inquiry Concerning Human Understanding* (1955 [1748]) distinguishes between knowledge derived from "Relations of Ideas" (e.g. Euclidian geometry, p. 40) and "Matters of Fact" (e.g. that the sun has risen, p. 40). Relational knowledge can be discovered "by the mere operation of thought" (ibid., p. 40). However, observation rather than a priori reasoning (mere thought) is necessary to determine factual/causal understanding since, to quote from Book One of *A Treatise of Human Nature* (Hume, 2004 [1739], emphasis in original) it is "by EXPERIENCE only, that we can infer the existence of one object from that of another." Experience is, importantly, *of* an event and a constant conjunction of events are required to "make us pronounce any two objects to be cause and effect" (ibid.), that is, establish the relationship as law-like. Indeed, Hume's argument within the three books of *A Treatise of Human Nature* might be summarised in the phrase: "No matter of fact can be proved but from its cause or effect. Nothing can be known to be the cause of another but by experience" (Hume, 1955 [1740], p. 191).

Bhaskar argues that Hume's focus on the significance of objective event regularities in law determination and the investigator's attempt to *abstract* him or herself from the process of understanding leaves experimental science as a "kind of automatic and behavioural response to the stimulus of given facts and their conjunctions" (*RTS*, p. 25). Indeed Humean empiricism fails, according to Bhaskar, to acknowledge the perceiver's role in understanding or defining experience (other than to see 'it' – the perceiver's presence – as a nuisance to be eradicated or overcome). Further, the pre-eminence afforded to observable event conjunctions cannot but problematise the role and function of theory (remainder) in explanations of what is observed. That is, although theory is necessary to realise and order experience, theory is itself unobservable and therefore (and quite absurdly) theory is *un*-real according to Humean standards. However, problematically for Bhaskar, Hume's developed concept of causal relations involves:

> three elements: ideas of spatial contingency, temporal succession, and necessary connection. Whereas in the case of the first two the matching of these ideas to experiences is unproblematic, there is, Hume presumes, no perceptual warrant for the idea of a necessary connection between events, such that given the first the second had to follow, and that had not the first occurred the second would not have happened. This being the case he offers a *psychological substitute*, namely that succession and contiguity of types of objects found conjoined in our experience are such as to determine the mind to *form the idea* of one object or event upon the occasion of observing (or forming the idea of) the other object or event.
>
> (Haldane, 2002, p. 100 – italicisation in original)

Given Haldane's (ibid.) account it might reasonably be argued that Bhaskar's interpretation of Humean empiricism as *negating the perceiver's role in experience* is misguided or at least 'short' insofar as Bhaskar appears to overlook readings of Hume – and therefore Humean empiricism – that emphasise or situate causation "in the mind (imagination)" (Salmon, 2002, p. 26) as well as those that focus on Hume's wider sceptical challenge (e.g. Fogelin, 2009).

Bhaskar is, it must be acknowledged, persuasive in his attack upon naive empiricism and its consequents. However, noted Humean scholars such as Kail (2010), explore the extent to which Hume thought of mind as interpreting, creating or projecting outwards a version of a putative external reality and these sorts of investigation are markedly at odds with Bhaskar's interpretation of Hume's writings. To maintain the disputational high ground Bhaskar should perhaps have focused his attack simply upon specific examples of the misuse of empiricism rather than individuals associated with empiric philosophy. He probably does not adequately do justice to Hume or Humean philosophy.[3]

Likewise, Groff (2004) maintains that Bhaskar misconstrues Kant on a number of vital issues including empirical realism (as defined by Kant) which, she alleges, Bhaskar wrongly equates with subjective idealism (Lipscomb,

2006a). Bhaskar may also be mistaken in associating transcendental idealism with relativist idealism since Kant's Categories of the Understanding (*Critique of Pure Reason*) allow that while causality is a necessary part of human cognitive reasoning, causality is not necessarily a required element of the external world.[4] However, most damningly of all, Groff (2004) notes that, contra Bhaskar, Kant fully accepted the existence of an external world (albeit that this world can only be known via mind mediated experience)[5] and she cites the *Prolegomena* to demonstrate the energy or passion with which Kant sought to distance himself from critics who might claim otherwise.[6]

> I say, that things as objects of our senses existing outside us are given, but we know nothing of what they may be in themselves, knowing only their appearances, i.e. the representations which they cause in us by affecting our senses. Consequently I grant by all means that there are bodies without us, that is, things which, though quite unknown to us as to what they are in themselves, we yet know by their influence on our sensibility. Can this be called idealism? It is the very contrary.
>
> (Hatfield, 1997, p. 36 – Kant [1783] *Prolegomena to Any Future Metaphysics*)[7]

The charge against Bhaskar is that, as with Hume, he conflates an attack upon a generalised tradition or perspective, in this case idealism, with a philosopher whose contribution, while seminal within that tradition, is not necessarily coterminous with it in all its forms. And, given the notorious ability of Hume and Kant's writings to carry multiple interpretations, these types of criticism should perhaps have been anticipated by Bhaskar (albeit that the views he expresses are those which were influential when he wrote – i.e. 1975 for *RTS*).

Morphogenetic theory

Margaret Archer's specialist nomenclature and the extended employment of acronyms (e.g. SS, SI, CS, S-C, etc.) can be both cumbersome and confusing. Nevertheless, building on Bhaskarian philosophy, morphogenetic theory provides the outline of a realist conceptual methodology that potentially allows researchers to achieve significant degrees of expositional clarity. In particular, the integral nature of temporality in morphogenetic modelling forces researchers to consider not only the time frames involved in description but also the wider history and nature of events being described. Moreover, this focus on temporality, when conjoined with analytic dualism and a theory of situated logics, allows structures (social and cultural) and agents (corporate and primary) to be identified and analysed discretely but relationally. Hopefully, the study outlined in Chapter 4 illustrates how this approach equips researchers with evaluative tools that, in important respects, are denied to non-emergentists. And, importantly, it must be stressed that the benefits of this approach stand *even if* the study presented here fails adequately to exemplify them. (That at least is my assertion.)

Alternatively – and negatively – while researchers anxious to describe or resolve 'real world' problems may consider it diversionary, it can be argued that anyone wishing to exploit morphogenesis also needs to engage with Bhaskarian philosophy. This engagement is necessary since many of Archer's underlying concepts, premises and assumptions, ideas needed to understand her work, are lodged in Bhaskar's texts. And, as noted above, problems with this underpinning exist.

Further, Archer's methodology must be considered somewhat rarefied insofar as it provides little prescriptive direction to researchers. It is therefore necessary to locate intermediary or bridging ideas/methods (e.g. Template Analysis) when using morphogenesis and, again, this can slow or disrupt the use or implementation of realist social theory.

More importantly, if Bhaskar can be accused of misrepresenting the arguments of Hume and Kant (and one could add Berger and Winch), it could be suggested that Archer is perhaps overly enthusiastic in assaulting Giddens's (1976) Structuration Theory. Thus, despite demonstrating, in places, clear elisionist sentiments, sections of Giddens's *New Rules of Sociological Method* (ibid.) can support alternative interpretations to that offered by Archer.

New Rules (ibid.) does therefore, as Archer argues, downplay the idea that structure pre-exists agency ("*Sociology is not concerned with a 'pre-given' universe of objects, but one which is constituted or produced by the active doings of subjects*", p. 160 – italicisation in original). However, while this assertion places enormous burdens upon subjects who now must continually constitute society (no doubt a tiring process), other statements fully acknowledge the significance of context or situation. For example, Giddens claims that: "*The realm of human agency is bounded. Men produce society, but they do so as historically located actors, and not under conditions of their choosing*" (p. 160 – italicisation in original) and this could easily carry an emergentist, Durkheimian or, most obviously, a Marxist spin.

Cherry picking quotations can unfairly misrepresent texts. Yet passages such as: "The production of society is brought about by the active constituting skills of its members, but draws upon resources, and depends upon conditions, of which they are unaware or which they perceive only dimly" (ibid., p. 157) could, following clarification of the first clause, easily be interpreted from within a social realist perspective.

Questions can also be asked about the form in which Archer presents arguments concerning micro-macro and agent-structure relations. Morphogenetic methodology's relational component is, as she makes clear, based upon a typology by Münch and Smelser (1987), wherein only one of the seven definitions offered does not invoke some form of size or complexity criteria. The 'outlier' definition comes from Peter Blau (1977), and the synopsis of Blau's (ibid.) position provided by Münch and Smelser (1987) reads: "Micro as social processes that engender relations among individuals and macro as the structure of different positions in a population and their constraints on interaction" (p. 357). Two points regarding Archer's utilisation of Blau's (1977) position deserve consideration.

First, just as it is unnecessary for Archer to cite Lockwood (1964) in support of analytic dualism (since the idea is lodged in Bhaskar's work), so Blau (1977) is not required to sustain a relational conception of micro-macro or agent-structural linkage. *A Realist Theory of Science* (1997) deals overtly and at length with internal and external relations and Archer could easily have adopted and expanded upon Bhaskar's insight, which she does elsewhere in any case, without recourse to Münch and Smelser (1987). Indeed, using Bhaskar in this way would have saved her from having to elasticate, perhaps overly, Blau's (1977) original definition (which is absent from *RST*).

Sticking with Bhaskar would also have allowed her to present a more consistently realist approach and, had Archer followed Bhaskar on this issue then she might (see below) have more fully examined the manner in which differential importance attaches to logical cultural system relations and the situated socio-cultural logics that they generate depending upon whether such relations are internal or external, symmetrical or asymmetrical.

Second, rejecting *all* size and complexity criteria regards micro-macro and agent-structure relations could be considered excessive or unnecessary insofar as other theorists favourably inclined towards realism do not make this move. Layder (1994), for example, recognises the significance and importance of relational criteria in social explanation but he does not reject definitions that employ size or complexity principles.

Concerns about nomenclature or the nature of argumentative construction might be considered quibbles. However, these concerns point towards more fundamental or intriguing 'questions' about morphogenesis and, while the following could be considered overly theoretic, the topics discussed below demanded attention at various times during the write-up of this study and I will therefore assume that these issues are or might potentially be of interest to other researchers who engage with Archer's methodology.

To structure an exploration of these topics the following sub-headings are used: (i) the form and ontological status of cultural system propositions, (ii) hypothesis equivalence and cultural system expositional clarity, (iii) proof by effect and relational strength, (iv) the researcher's position or role in morphogenetic theory and (v) emergence and structural identification. In examining these issues examples or references to cultural system propositions are emphasised. This emphasis or focus is in keeping with the type of explanation outlined in Chapter 2.

The form and ontological status of cultural system propositions

Archer asserts that:

> the CS [cultural system] is distinguished as that sub-set of items to which the law of non-contradiction can be applied – this is propositions, for only statements which assert truth or falsity can be deemed to be in contradiction or to be consistent with one another.
>
> (*RST*, p. 180)

Though complex, this statement is mercifully unambiguous. However, defining the cultural system in this way necessarily leaves much outside its orbit (i.e. culture as *all intelligibilia* – see Chapter 2) and, importantly, cultural system propositional statements and culture more generally need not, according to Archer, share identity. Three points are made here regarding these constructs.

First, we should not presume that propositional cultural system statements asserting truth or falsity claims can or will be verifiable or falsifiable in principle. Thus, self-evidently, although claims such as, for example, *God is omnipotent* can be contradicted, they cannot be verified or falsified. A great deal has been written concerning verification and falsifiability and it is not here necessary to re-engage with that literature. Suffice to say that propositions that can neither be verified or falsified (or, less ambitiously, 'supported' or 'refuted') are, it might be argued, of questionable use value in a research context.

Second, normative or moral propositions (e.g. *it is wrong to steal*) diverge in important respects from propositions that lack an overtly evaluative element (e.g. *two and two equal four*).[8] This difference should not be over-egged and, for example, Putnam would demur. However, it is commonly assumed that normative/moral claims differ from factual or 'fact-like' claims (empiric claims) because, for example, only the latter can, in some circumstances, be sustained or rejected (verified or falsified). This again leaves open the nature of sustenance/rejection or verification/falsification. Yet most commentators maintain or assume a distinction (variously nuanced) between fact and value claims and this potentially creates a problem for researchers who want to advance propositions containing strong normative/moral elements.

Specifically, as noted, Archer emphasises the importance of keeping the cultural system register to those things held to be "true or false in society at any given time or place" (*CAA*, p. xviii). This seems straightforward and, yet, since propositional statements that present largely or purely normative/moral assertions are not fact claims, they are not capable of being deemed true or false and it might therefore be suggested that they are thus 'inadmissible'. Archer does not however wish to exclude normative or moral propositions from the cultural register and in arguing for the emergent nature of the cultural system as a discrete ontological entity she allows that its remit includes "theories, beliefs, values or more strictly the propositional formulations of them" (*RST*, p. 180). This is reasonable and, moreover, by focusing on proposition *formulation* Archer does not contradict any of her previous statements.

Yet while moral/ethical or normative/evaluative tenets can be expressed in propositional statements of the type *x believes that y has value z*, it might have been helpful if Archer had more forcefully stressed that, although propositions embodying normative or moral claims may be perceived as *correct* (at least by some if not all people), the normative or moral content of such propositions is not, to repeat, generally accepted to be *true* in any formal sense. This is a complex topic and various opinions exist on the subject. However, while we can say that it is correct that *y has value z* if by this we mean that *x believes that y has value z* (so *y has value z* is shorthand for the belief of agent *x*), we cannot normally say that it is true that *y has value z*. This aspect of propositional statement construction might have been more fully explained and, with regard to this study I was, for example, very aware of the 'live' nature of this issue when talking about the religious and spiritual beliefs of participants.

Third, putting to one side possible complications thrown up by specific claims containing substantive normative or moral elements, in some instances Archer appears to conflate the expression of non-normative cultural system propositions with truth and/or knowledge (rather than claims *about* truth and knowledge). Propositions of course register those things held to be true or false, but this is not the same as allowing the implication to be given that they *are* true or false. This need not be a problem. However, in the two quotations below, fallible transitive understanding is perhaps (though this might be contested) elided with intransitive reality or 'true' knowledge. If this is occurring then descriptions of 'what is' are not adequately being distinguished from their objects (i.e. the thing that exists and is being described). I may here be wrong. However, if I am correct then this might represent a version of what Bhaskar terms the epistemic fallacy (i.e. ontology's collapse into epistemology).[9]

> all knowledge was certainly activity dependent for its genesis and elaboration. Nevertheless, once recorded it constitutes knowledge without a current knowing subject. It is knowledge because it retains the dispositional character to be understood, though it persists unrecognized, sustaining potential powers (of contradiction and complementarity with other cultural items) which remain unexercised. Ontologically it exists and if the theory is true, if the technique it describes works, or if the belief it articulates is justifiable, these remain the case quite independently of current actors knowing it, using it or believing it. We know that they are real by virtue of their releasable effects.
>
> (*RST*, p. 144)[10]

Archer knows of course that propositions can be factually incorrect. However, just as Bhaskar relies upon or makes use of examples from the physical sciences when arguing for the applicability of critical realist ideas in the social realm, so Archer employs examples that have, at a minimum, the capacity for correct or truthful decipherment. Naturally we want propositions to accurately reference reality. Yet we must not lose sight of the fallible nature of understanding. We must remain alert to the gap that almost always exists between transitive propositional statements of knowledge and the intransitive reality that those statements seek to describe.

> It [cultural system propositional knowledge] exists and if it works, if it is true or false, this is the case independently of agents knowing it. Certainly they can activate it or leave it to gather dust, but its ontological status is not determined by which they do. Knowledge without a knowing subject would be ruled out in elisionism, but would still leave many questioning what the Rosetta Stone was before it was discovered and decoded, yet was capable of decoding.
>
> (*RST*, p. 99)

Archer might be accused in passages such as that cited above of merging epistemological truth claims with the ontological substance that they reference. And, where cultural system propositional statements refer to events (e.g. *decoding* the Rosetta Stone), Archer should perhaps have considered more thoroughly the nature of factual status in explication so that a clearer distinction could be made between transitive description and the intransitive reality described.

Hypothesis equivalence and cultural system expositional clarity

I have already suggested that, insofar as they fail to recognise longstanding debates about the problematic status of events and event identity (see e.g. Casati and Varzi, 2009), neither Bhaskar nor Archer adequately engages with this complex issue. This is potentially important. For, if we grant that "an event cannot be a fact [because] events have positions in space-time, whereas facts do not" (Bennett, 2002, p. 44), then it follows that minor – potentially *very* minor – differences in propositional statements can produce radically divergent fact assertions which allow or permit different event and social explanations to be identified or advanced. Researchers ought therefore to recognise that seemingly trivial variations in the statement of propositional content can produce significant and marked differences in analysis (e.g. mechanism description) and acknowledging the importance of proposition phrasing raises the question or spectre of hypothesis equivalence.

Theory and the data/evidence that theory 'allows' or recognises has value insofar as it supports or suggests error in a hypothesis, model or propositional claim about 'what is' or 'might be' (I here run together hypothesis with propositional claims). Each of these elements (theory, data/evidence and hypothesis/proposition) is intimately connected. However, not only are the linkages between these elements of understanding fiendishly difficult to articulate. It is also the case that, to repeat, since understanding is perforce always fallible, theory and data/evidence rarely if ever 'ultimately' or 'finally' proves or disproves a hypothesis (broadly defined as an explicit or implicit model or set of ideas/propositions concerning the physical or social world).

That said, if we grant that sustainable and defendable (good enough) rather than 'final' linkages between theory, data/evidence and hypotheses are possible, then we should also acknowledge that hypothesis credibility is enhanced when diverse evidences are available in support of that hypothesis (Lipscomb, 2008). This is intuitively sensible, it is a claim that upholds epistemological relativism and it satisfies the 'requirements' of logic:

> All other things being equal, the hypothesis (H) that a given treatment retards the advance of a given disease in all patients is more highly confirmed by 100 positive instances that include men and women, young and old, than by 100 positive instances consisting exclusively of men between 35 and 45 years of age.
>
> (Lange, 2007, p. 31)

Support for the value of diverse evidence, in this instance regarding positive instances of disease treatment, here rests on agreement regarding the *relevance* of evidence (its role or function) in 'good enough' (though this is question begging) hypothesis confirmation and, indeed:

> while certain "inductivist" accounts of scientific procedure seem to assume that relevant evidence, or relevant data, can be collected in the context of an inquiry prior to the formulation of any hypothesis, it should be clear upon brief reflection that relevance is a relative concept; experiential data can be said to be relevant or irrelevant only with respect to a given hypothesis; and it is the hypothesis that determines what kind of data or evidence are relevant for it.
>
> (Hempel, 1945, p. 3)

Arguably, Hempel's insight can inform our understanding of the linkages between theory, data/evidence and hypothesis. Further, it is an insight that, potentially, challenges the way we think about morphogenetic propositional construction.

Let us grant that 'relevance' in the above quotation captures or points towards the *relationship* between theory, data/evidence and hypothesis (derived propositional claim). This relationship cannot be arbitrary (Achinstein, 2010) and hypotheses or propositions generated by the triumvirate of theory-data-evidence must be relevant to that triumvirate. Moreover, regards their formulation (wording), equivalently formulated hypotheses or propositions *must* (a deliberately strong term) be equally relevant to their underpinning data/evidence if illogic or ludicrousness is to be avoided. Put another way, it would be irrational if different data/evidence(s) were required for equivalent but differently formulated versions of the same hypothesis/proposition.

The 'equivalence condition' as Hempel labelled it is mainly associated with natural or physical science. However, equivalence applies to social science in general and morphogenetic theory in particular insofar as its potential absence (the absence of equivalence) generates awkward questions about the adequacy of hypothesis or proposition formulation. It has already and repeatedly been stressed that propositional claims of the sort presented in this study (e.g. see p. 91) must be carefully crafted for, if we are to take them seriously, then the significance of textual or linguistic factors in descriptions of social reality should be recognised (Gauker, 2006).

However, we ought also to acknowledge that propositional claims in morphogenetic theory derive or emerge from analysis and, the key point here, once formulated they direct the researcher's attention towards identifying additional supportive or supplemental data/evidence. Problematically though, a hypothesis or propositional claim can almost always be worded in more than one way and subtle semantic or textual nuances between formulations may push researchers to seek different subsidiary evidence(s).

Further, since hypotheses (broadly defined to include propositional claims) exist within interlocking frameworks of ideas and since, within these frameworks, the conceptual endpoint of one hypothesis or hypothesis set forms the starting premise of another hypothesis set (Hempel, 1945), then epistemological relativists must be cognisant of the threat to logic that occurs when radically different and possibly incommensurable supportive criteria and arguments are confused. That is, since it would be illogical to require equivalence to apply to some parts of an argument but not to others, logic requires that equivalence be maintained throughout analysis. Hempel (ibid.), from a non-critical realist perspective, emphasises the dangers that exist when conflicting epistemological premises are conjoined without adequate consideration.

The implications of Hempel's (ibid.) equivalence condition for Archer's morphogenetic theory is now apparent. Hempel's (ibid.) ideas regarding interlocking hypotheses sets readily map onto morphogenetic modelling and, in particular, the application of analytic histories (where, for example, it is assumed that T^4 of one 'cycle' becomes T^1 in the next – described in this book, p. 22). Further, if structures (social and cultural) occupy an ontological realm whose existence is demonstrated tautologically through the situated logics they create for agents then, insofar as intransitive structures are identified by or with transitive cultural and/or social system propositional statements, minor or unintended differences in the wording of these propositional statements can generate starkly different impressions of the structural realm and, as stated, researchers may in such instances be directed to look for different supporting evidences (which appears foolish).

As both knowledge and truth claims *and* as interest bearers, it is crucial to morphogenetic theory that the cultural and social systems denote realms that are irreducible to 'present tense' agency and this requirement feeds Archer's assertion that cultural and social system strata exist independently of agential awareness or use. Turning to look just at the cultural system, this is to be "distinguished as that sub-set of items to which the law of non-contradiction can be applied – that is propositions" (*RST*, p. 180). And this system is described as residing, both figuratively and actually, within humanity's "Library" (*RST*, p. 98). However, four points require clarification here.

First, although non-truthful and non-factual (non-justifiable) cultural system propositions can provide agents with interests, Archer does not clarify the relationship between false interests and false consciousness (which may perhaps be easily merged). This is a different issue to that described above. Second, where agents are accused of acting upon false or mistaken interests, Archer does not address the question of who is to adjudicate between contested interpretations or the criteria that should be used in judgement. Third, Archer concedes that genuine contradictory and complementary propositions/logics need not be influential. It is a Bhaskarian and/or critical realist orthodoxy that intransitive mechanisms/powers need not be actualised as or in empiric events and, even when empirically realised, these events can escape transitive human understanding (they may not be recognised). However, relations that are never identified and which never generate 'realised' interests are, by definition, unable to demonstrate status via effect and their ontological standing therefore remains indeterminate (albeit that observation of erratically actualised mechanisms may hint at the existence or presence of an otherwise hidden reality). Fourth, the significance of negative realities (negative causation) is recognised but perhaps under-explored in *RST* where, in relation to the cultural system register, it is feasible that a dearth of developed propositional knowledge may be as influential, if not more influential, than actual (existing) contradictions or complementarities.

Anything that muddies or complicates our understanding of the ontological status of cultural or social structures is problematic for researchers who wish to pin down the philosophic/theoretic basis and form of morphogenetic explanation. The disputed position of correspondence theory in critical realism and Groff's (2004) commentary on the lack of an adequate theory of truth or justification in Bhaskar's thinking perhaps underlie some of the ambiguity noted above. Pointing towards the possibility that mutually under-theorised elements exist within the work of Archer and Bhaskar illustrates where additional conceptual work is required.

Proof by effect and relational strength

Putting to one side the circular nature of arguments for ontological status by proof from effect or consequence, Archer here employs a form of reasoning that is integral to critical realism. Nevertheless, she asserts rather than demonstrates that the cultural system takes the form described and even using her own vocabulary it might be suggested that the cultural system contains (i) more logical relations, (ii) different forms of relations or that (iii) some relations may be more significant or powerful than others.

Regarding points i and ii above, Archer suggests proof by outcome only for the existence of certain cultural system powers and, although we can infer from this that a more general cultural realm exists, it must also be conceded that the nature or 'shape' of this thing awaits clarification. Thus the four cultural system logical relations and their situated socio-cultural logics may not capture the complexity or extent of actual concrete relations and logics. Archer recognises that alternative relations and logics could be proposed to extend or develop the four ideal types described (see Chapter 2).[11] Yet she does not explore, for example, relations involving non-binary proposition sets or their differential impact upon socio-cultural interaction.[12]

Further, as regards point iii above, perhaps due to an over-reliance or over-emphasis on Münch and Smelser (1987), Archer might be accused of inadequately distinguishing between internal and external relations vis-à-vis logical cultural system relations despite self-evident differences between them. For example, contingent compatibilities have, at least initially, no necessary logical relation but are opportunistically connected by agents in socio-cultural interaction. In Bhaskarian parlance they may be, in the first instance, externally related, whereas all other relations are internal and symmetric or internal and asymmetric. Bhaskar claims that internal relations carry greater explanatory force than external relations and Archer should perhaps have developed this aspect of her methodology further since, in practical application, researchers need to link the identification of forms of relations (cultural and social structural) pertaining at T^1 with their relative significance in order to inform explanations of emergence.

The researcher's position or role in morphogenetic theory

While acknowledging the influence of "investigator's constructs" (*RST*, p. 178) on the research process, Archer fails to engage sufficiently with the impact of preconceived or distracting researcher values/interests in analysis. This is odd. A great deal of attention has been given to this and kindred topics and, in relation to irrationality or bias, Tversky and Kahneman's (1974) seminal work on 'heuristics and biases' is now an established part of the social science cannon. (And more recent work by Alexander (2012) or Kahneman (2012) plough similar furrows). The impact of *investigator constructs* upon morphogenetic enquiry must therefore be considered.

Although Archer somewhat confusingly states that: "the existence of effects cannot serve to explain origins" (*RST*, p. 167), accurate structural identification is vital in morphogenetic theory and, to facilitate this activity, individual or corporate agential actions, occurring between T^2 and T^3, are used to direct researchers to abductively (retroductively or retrodictively) generate data/evidence for structures at T^1.[13] This process was hopefully demonstrated in Chapter 4. However, clarifying the situation at T^1 inevitably introduces extra-research assumptions regarding past relations – e.g. as background theories, etc., (see Chapter 2) – and these vital but also potentially confounding assumptions must be recognised.

Archer acknowledges that socio-cultural and/or social interaction between T^2 and T^3 cannot be discussed without reference to T^1's conceptual framework. And, as noted, morphogenetic theory emphasises the theoretical nature of explanation by demanding that explanation must *always* begin with structural identification. However, it is difficult not to think that an element of circularity enters research practice at this point. Specifically, Archer suggests that "transcendental arguments" (*RST*, p. 177) can identify cultural and social structures at T^1 and, yet, identification presumably relies upon the interpretation of socio-cultural and social-interactions at T^2/T^3 *and* researchers are enjoined to identify structural formation at T^1 *before* they interpret agential interaction at T^2/T^3.

So what steers interpretative activity? Archer largely ignores the difficulty investigators face in situating their value and other choices within the research process and, with regard to structural recognition at T^1, she sidesteps the significance of researcher subjectivity in analysis. The problem for researchers wishing to use morphogenetic theory is that, since "all data and observations are theory-laden, none are value-neutral" (Porpora, 2006, p. 66) and researcher values-interests thereby inevitably influence temporal and structural identification. The question then is – by how much and in what ways?

Stern (2000), from a non-realist standpoint, highlights the perceiver's (here researcher's) role in perception for, to be identified, the concepts, things or objects of perception must already, though not necessarily pre-conceptually, exist or have been identified as object attributes by the perceiver. Gorner (2000) makes an analogous point and, in an exposition of Gadamerian hermeneutics, notes that meaning-making or understanding never occurs acontextually because it is always impossible to escape "one's own horizon [and] one's own horizon is not a contingent property of an abstract self [it] is constitutive of one's being" (ibid., p. 148).

These are not new problems. Researchers do not or rarely approach their study objects in states of dispassionate apatheia (nor should they necessarily). Yet realists assert that it *is* possible to transitively reach out towards intransitive reality and, in this process, they need to be mindful of the disruptive role that unrecognised presumption can take. Thus morphogenetic theory not only aims to identify "structures as emergent properties, it must also supply an analytical history of their emergence which accounts for why matters are so and not otherwise" (*RST*, p. 167). Researchers therefore elaborate upon agential explanations (variously garnered) and they do not merely or simply re-describe agential explanation. However, in going 'beyond' agential explanation it is not clear how, in the absence of established and justifiable rationales (i.e. some degree of consensus), explanation can achieve and sustain widespread approval for the resulting findings (assuming this is a desirable or 'good thing'). Other interpretations are always possible and, while Archer may legitimately anticipate that her audience will be familiar with the inconclusive and theory laden nature of description and inquiry – this is a well-rehearsed truism – the tentativeness that this situation breeds sits uneasily alongside realism's bold ambition.

A review of Groff's (2004) critique of Bhaskar on the theoretician's contribution to theory development beneficially illustrates how Archer trails Bhaskar in failing to address important questions regarding the researcher's contribution to understanding.

With regard to the role and place of cognition and language in critical realist theory, Groff (2004) cites or raises Hilary Putnam's (1981) distinction between metaphysical and internal realism. Bhaskar associates critical realism with metaphysical realism as defined by Putnam. However, Groff (2004) problematises Bhaskar's position by arguing that metaphysical realism, which underplays the theoretician's contribution to explanation, is criticised by Putnam. Groff (ibid.) suggests that Putnam's critique of, and Bhaskar's identification with, metaphysical realism are both flawed. She instead proposes that critical realism can accommodate Putnam's insight, denied by metaphysical realism, that causal explanation incorporates cognitive or intentional elements. In addition, Groff (ibid.) claims that causal explanations inevitably introduce inquirer (researcher) interests and explanation is therefore always "inherently intentional" (p. 59). Groff (ibid.) distances herself from Putnam's ontological assertions. However, she clearly allows that Putnam's focus on the dual nature of knowledge (i.e. that it is both a mediated product and mediator) is valid, recognised by Bhaskar, but, in vital respects, under-explored in either *RTS* or *PN* (*The Possibility of Naturalism*) (Lipscomb, 2006a).

Archer is of course fully aware of knowledge's mediated character. However, as stated, Archer does not, in *RST* or *CAA*, meaningfully engage with the dilemma that theoretician or researcher generated interests (biases) present in or for the process of mediation. And, if we allow that logical relations at T^1 cannot (or can only rarely) be identified without introducing preconceived researcher ideas concerning those relations, then we must also grant that subjective criteria play a part (large or small) in the identification process. That the researcher's gaze introduces personally held opinions regarding cultural and socio-structural relations (e.g. regarding which relations are likely to exist as well as their relative significance) is unsurprising. Yet if, as Bhaskar asserts, it is in principle possible for transitive human explanations to make sense of intransitive reality and if, as Archer declares, morphogenetic theory can employ analytic histories to reliably describe social flux or stasis, then the contribution or input of the researcher cannot be ignored (see Chapter 3).

Problematically, if social realists believe that reality is structured, stratified and emergent and if they believe that retrospectively if not prospectively social explanation but not prediction is feasible – then it is important to maintain that, from a morphogenetic perspective, analytic histories cannot encompass purely capricious or whimsical time periods, that they should delineate material from immaterial logical relations and that the events described should have identity or substance. Archer does state, somewhat ambiguously, that temporal intervals will be determined by investigators according to the "problem in hand" (*RST*, p. 76). However, Carter (2000) acknowledges that the choice of where to "slice" (ibid., p. 94) history is somewhat "arbitrary" (ibid., p. 98) and, in this study, it will be recalled that the time frames in use were problematised at the beginning of Chapter 4.

Archer demands unconditional assent on the part of users to "each and every" (*RST*, p. 168) morphogenetic principle albeit that the four principles by which "practical application" (*RST*, p. 168) of morphogenetic theory is to be achieved do not clarify, bar researcher fiat, how the beginning (T^1) or end (T^4) of any particular analytic cycle is to be identified, or whether incomplete or ongoing cycles can be described using this theory. Archer might usefully have given more attention to these issues. And, since it is recognised that agents may be ignorant of or misled about their interests, the relative absence of reflection around kindred methodological issues vis-à-vis researchers is surprising.

Understanding the researcher's contribution within the explanatory process may perhaps be clarified if Geertz's distinction between "the need to grasp and the need to analyse" (1973, pp. 24–25, cited in Hammersley, 2005a, p. 17) is considered. Interpretation or grasping and analysis are, of course, intimately referential or Janus-faced (it would be foolish to draw too distinct a line between them). Nonetheless, it might be suggested that Archer's focus upon the analysis of relations and interactions pertaining within and between structure and agency inadvertently sidesteps or overlooks the problem of interpretation. Thus, as described, *RST* and *CAA* provide limited guidance on how structures can be identified (grasped) by their emergent influences upon agency and, although

Archer is correct in stating that "we do not identify structures by interviewing people about them" (*RST*, p. 177), her lack of engagement with the problem of interpretation is problematic since researchers are thereby pushed to assume Nagel's (1986) "view from nowhere" with regard to their object(s) of study.

In *Structure, Agency and the Internal Conversation* (2003a) Archer does speak to some of the problems associated with interpretation. Here she examines the possibility that tacit assumptions regarding the homogeneity of individual reasoning may be mistaken and in *Culture and Agency* she discusses and dismisses idealist or postmodern concerns regarding translation and incommensurability. Yet morphogenetic theory does not explicitly survey, for example, discourse analysis (broadly defined) or the place of narrative structure in the construction of analytic histories (Sayer, 2000). No rationale is given for these lacunae. However, similarities with Bhaskar's reluctance to engage with issues around terminology and language use could be noted and it might be wondered whether Archer avoids these issues because, in part, she perceives a need to distance morphogenetic theory from positions (e.g. idealism) that do take such matters seriously. From within the realist frame it is left to theorists such as, for example, Joseph and Roberts (2003) and López (2003) to address the indeterminate nature of language use.

Emergence and structural identification

The difficulty I am suggesting morphogenetic theory encounters with structural identification at T^1 reproduces or embodies problems inherent in abductive (retroductive/retrodictive) analysis. These problems are exacerbated by Archer's imprecise definition and use of the concept of emergence and they have, at their heart, the problem of the researcher's role in research practice.

Archer employs the term emergence in Bhaskar's sense (i.e. referring to the emergence of new strata) when ephemeral and inconsequential contextual happenings are contrasted with "a special sub-class [of such happenings] that is emergent properties, whose differentiating features are relative endurance, natural necessity and the possession of causal powers" (*RST*, p. 167).[14] However, she also refers to emergence as the product of the interplay of entities which themselves possess ontologically distinct emergent properties and while this definition can encompass emergence in Bhaskar's sense, it may also simply refer to the outcome of structural and agential interplay through analytic cycles (i.e. outcomes that need not represent new or distinct strata). Indeed, at several points in Archer's writing structure and emergence appear to become interchangeable terms and this ambiguity is reminiscent of Groff's (2004) suggestion that Bhaskar permits the concept of emergence to carry multiple, overlapping and divergent meanings. Within Archer's work the descriptor differentiates between at least two separate processes (see above) and lucidity would have been advanced if this had been acknowledged. As stated, the effects of definitional imprecision are most keenly felt when, at T^1, researchers are entreated to identify structures (the outcome of interplay between contexts, mechanisms and agential interaction in previous analytic cycles) as well as operative emergent generative mechanisms. In this process, it is vital for the practical applicability of morphogenetic theory that theoreticians should be able to clearly distinguish contexts from mechanisms. Yet social realists differ markedly about how this feat is to be accomplished (Lipscomb, 2006c).

Summation

The challenges to morphogenetic and critical realist theory that are identified above are, in many respects, simply those which confront *all* sociological theory. Thus, all sociologies must engage with questions such as: What forms of explanation are defendable? What do concepts and language actually depict? How is causation and/or change to be described?

The problematic and general nature of these questions must be acknowledged and it would be inappropriate and not a little silly to single out morphogenetic theory for failing to resolve the riddles that beset all forms of social inquiry. Archer, like Bhaskar, does create avoidable difficulties (e.g. through the use of imprecise concepts). Yet the very lucidity of Archer's (and Bhaskar's) reasoning makes these shortcomings evident. Realism, "unlike some other approaches, is upfront about its ontological presuppositions" (New, 2001, p. 43) and it thus compares favourably with alternative theories that decline to engage in the detail or substance of the sorts of question described above.

Thus despite the problems or issues identified here, morphogenetic theory makes considerable headway in developing Bhaskar's insights concerning causality and the relational nature of social relations into a workable if imperfect (what isn't?) model for use by researchers. Morphogenesis remains at a high level of abstraction. However, Archer acknowledges this and insofar as she shifts critical realism from philosophy towards methodology critics should acknowledge that, while her endeavours remain tentative (and understandable difficulties are encountered), overall, her enterprise or 'project' is nonetheless remarkably successful. Indeed, by beginning to move from the rarefied ontological heights into the lowlands of methodological and practical implementation, Archer and those who use her work cannot but butt up against the sorts of problem described in this chapter for, as Bourdieu (1990) notes, only those who refuse to get their "hands dirty in the kitchens of [actual] research" (p. 19) can maintain the purist or aristocratic demeanour of abstract theoreticians.

To conclude, Bhaskar identifies defects in Humean empiricism and Kantian idealism and from this critique he constructs a realist philosophy for science that, while open to challenge, nonetheless generates valuable insights for theorists and researchers. Bhaskar (like Archer) no doubt overstates the deficiencies in other perspectives so that his own position might be better delineated and, outside of literal positivist empiricism and uncompromising idealism, realists should perhaps concede that alternative doctrines generate powerful insights of their own. Indeed, Rescher (2002) takes this more measured line when he argues, in terms which flatter and recognise the contribution of metaphysicians like Bhaskar, that:

> when discordant doctrines [namely idealism and empiricism] manage to maintain themselves over many generations – it transpires that there is really much to be said on all sides and that the most appropriate and tenable view of the matter is one that somehow manages to combine the best elements of both. Accordingly, the challenge that confronts the metaphysician in such cases is the shaping of a more complex doctrine that manages to effect a higher synthesis among the conflicting contentions by introducing whatever distinctions and sophistications are needed to achieve a reconciliation that accommodates the strong point of each rival position.
>
> (Rescher, ibid., p. 242)

RTS and *PN* present a version of this *higher synthesis*. However, as suggested, theoretical gaps remain to be plugged in critical realist philosophy and, warning against overly inflated ambition (i.e. warning against the illusion that theory can ever be 'final') Hedström (2005) notes that: "Believing that theories can accurately represent reality in all its complexity is an empiricist illusion" (p. 38).

With regard to morphogenetic theory, Archer has developed an authoritative and useful set of conceptual tools to guide exploration in the social realm and, in so doing; she reconfigures philosophic realism to create the framework of a plausible methodology. A great deal still needs to be done before researchers can simply turn to and apply morphogenetic-morphostatic theory in the same way that other theories and techniques are currently utilised. And, compared with non-realist or less nuanced approaches, the complexity of ideas associated with morphogenesis inevitably forecloses upon easy 'accessibility'.

Morphogenetic methodology has been used to describe relations and interaction between large corporate groupings over substantial time periods. On the other hand morphogenesis or stasis may equally be identified "in a sports club or 'defensive associations' in a parish church" (*RST*, p. 274). The study described in this book focuses on one such 'small' organisation and, in hope rather than expectation, I would like to think that the work has three merits. First, it contributes to the developing corpus of realist and morphogenetic research. Second, it adds something to hospice and palliative care literature. And, third, it may encourage social researchers and theoreticians working in health and social care to look more closely (and possibly favourably) at realist social theory.

Notes

1 The bracketed upward pointing arrow might here represent the potential of theory 'in use' to inform the development of theory 'in abstract'.

2 Alternatively, this could simply be an instance of confirmation bias.

3 Bhaskar's critique of the role of empiricist theory in physical science is also challenged by, for example, Monod (2004), who argues that post Einstein and Heisenburg, quantum physicists (contra Hume) neither directly observe events nor require that laws rest upon repeatable conjunctions. A similar point is made by Howson (2000) though not in relation to critical realism. Nevertheless, Bhaskar claims that empiricism's apparent predictive achievement within physical science has cloaked

shortcomings or limitations with observation and, quantum physics notwithstanding, this success has amplified empiricism's influence so that its assumptions, regarding causality and the justifiable basis of law-like or generalisable statements, now pervasively inform both the natural and human sciences including those forms of neo-Kantian and idealist human science which ostensibly reject its precepts (Bhaskar, 1998a, 1998b). Exposing inherent flaws within the empiricist tradition can, critical realists maintain, help establish a more satisfactory philosophy for science and, hence, 'better' science (Archer *et al.*, 1998).

4 From a non-critical realist standpoint, Stroud (2000, p. 89) offers an authoritative discussion on the subject of Kantian transcendental idealism and transcendental realism which problematises Bhaskar's interpretation. Alternatively, Kaidesoja (2005), an author sympathetic to realism, suggests that Bhaskar uses "Kantian terms without clarifying their precise meaning" (p. 44) in novel or divergent ways and that, in consequence, the descriptors become "incomprehensible" (p. 45). This, Kaidesoja (ibid.) argues, undercuts or confuses critical realist claims regarding its own transcendental status.

5 It would be interesting here, were space to permit, to place Kail's (2010) argument regards Humean projection against or alongside Groff's (2004) reading of Kant.

6 Kant's *Critique of Pure Reason* (1990 [1781]) is the key text here. Stern (2000) examines the Refutation of Idealism and its relation to realism (non-critical) and Brook (2006) explores realism in the refutation of idealism.

7 Prolegomena to Any Future Metaphysics – First Part of the Main Transcendental Problem: How Is Pure Mathematics Possible? Remark II (Kant, 1783).

8 Although it is analytically important to distinguish first order (ethical) moral and normative from non-moral, non-normative propositions, it should be noted that: "The majority of descriptions of human activities contain explicit or implicit evaluations" (Trusted, 1987, p. 17). These evaluations frequently contain second order (moralising) judgements and separating facts from values is, in practice, often difficult.

9 Bhaskar criticises Hume for allowing that "statements about being can always be transposed into statements about our knowledge of being" (*RTS*, p. 16). This is termed the epistemic fallacy.

10 A presumed typographical error is corrected in this quotation – 'is' appears in place of 'it'.

11 Like Bhaskar, Archer ignores Russell's "canonical account" (Butchvarov, 2002, p. 284) of propositional relations. Butchvarov (ibid.) cites Whitehead and Russell (1962) in stating that: "propositions are either atomic (e.g. 'Socrates *is* human'), or molecular (e.g. 'Socrates is human *and* Plato is human'), or general (e.g. '*All* humans are moral') in respect to their logical form" (p. 284). Significantly, relations between propositional statements can be influenced by the form of their expression (form and content may be variously allied) and ignoring this aspect of argument can produce logical anomalies. As regards the promulgation of 'alternative views', Archer notes that if the basic principles of realism are accepted then disagreements "can flourish about which structures, what types of interplay and what outcomes should be prioritized and how they ought to be analyzed, but without any discord over the nature and format of explanation itself" (*RST*, p. 160).

12 Howson (2000) takes issue with Karl Popper when he notes that

> Popper's idea of 'logical' probability is a function defined on sentences which reflects just the purely logical relations subsisting between them. The trouble with this suggestion is that there seems to be an infinity of such functions, as many indeed as there are functions satisfying the probability axioms.
>
> (p. 96)

Although this comment occurs within a radically different form of discourse it is clearly salient to Archer's thesis.

13 This is not a denial of proof by effect. Archer here wishes to carry the argument that the purpose of retrospective analysis is not simply to identify structures; rather it aims to develop histories of emergence. Carter (2000) makes a similar point when he suggests that at T^1 researchers "need three levels of analysis" (p. 93). These are: (i) identification of structural emergent properties and causal powers, (ii) definition of agential experience and (iii) the linking of structural properties and powers with agential action(s), "the who and where questions" (ibid., p. 93).

14 Alternatively, Elder-Vass (2005a, 2005b) suggests that Archer misuses the term emergence in Bhaskar's sense since *RST* illustrates the concept using examples that more appropriately describe effects by aggregation rather than the emergence of new and ontologically distinct strata. For an extended discussion regarding Archer's use of the concept of emergence and the relation between emergence and social structure see: Elder-Vass (2007a, 2007b), A. King (2007), Porpora (2007) and Varela (2007).

Appendix A: Interview guide

- Re-introduce study: re-explain purpose, aims, methods.
- Does interviewee have any questions?
- Invite interviewee to sign consent form.
- Start tape recorder: ensure interviewee comfortable/ready to proceed.

1 Confirm grade/position/role/title.
2 How long have you worked here?
3 Where were you before coming here?
4 **Change?**
   a Where?
   b How?
   c When?
   d Why?
   e Specifically?
   f Impact on staff?
   g Impact on patients/care?
   h Impact on you – your role – your work/function?
5 **Admissions/discharges**
   a Admission
      i Who do we admit – criteria for admission?
      ii Balance?
      iii Who influences/controls admissions?
   b Discharge
      i Timeliness?
      ii Organisation of?
      iii Reasons for?
      iv Issues?
6 **Consultant differences**
   a Your opinion?
   b Degree – extent – impact – significance?
   c Specifically?
   d Which, if any, approach do you favour?
   e Benefits/problems?

7 **Treatment/interventions**
   a Changes?
   b Specifically?
   c Why occurring?
   d Appropriateness?
      i When appropriate?
      ii When inappropriate?

8 **Spirituality/religion**
   a At study site?
   b Distinguishing spirituality from religion?
   c Changes in practice/attitudes?
   d Significance for hospice?
   e Significance for you?
   f Role, if any, in care?

9 **External relations/consultant attitudes/care standards**
   a Who do we interact with?
   b Why do we interact with them?
      i How is the process of interaction managed?
   c NHS palliative care consultant attitudes to hospices in general and us specifically?
      i Significance – impact – threat?
   d Clinical Governance and Care Standards?
      i Role – significance – meaning for function/activity?

10 **Other**
   a Education?
   b Funding?
   c Future developments?

- Does interviewee have any questions/wish to say anything?
- Is interviewee comfortable with questions/experience?
- Restate – copy transcript to be forwarded following transcription.
- Thank interviewee for participating and conclude.

Appendix B: Pre-coding interview summary A:a

Conversational style allows content display as 'binary contrasts' – A:a, NA, [edit] years service at hospice (arrived [edit] months after opening). Recent drop in hours to PT from FT.

Past:	*Present:*
Quieter (8 beds)	Busier (16 beds + day hospice + outreach + Macs)
Time to talk/socialise	Less time to talk/socialise
Less patients	More patients
Predominantly terminal patients	Mainly palliative patients (active symptom treatment)[1]
Discharge rare (seen as 'success'[2])	(Implication – discharge now common)
Relationships with pts/families 'friends'	Relationships with pts/families 'professional'
Relationships were 'closer'	Relationships now 'distanced'
Less staff (total)	More staff (total)
More staff "on ground"	(Implication – as (a) ratio changes, (b) less 'hands on')
(Implication – less professionalised)	Increased professionalism distances staff from patients/families[3]
More NAs (ratio) bigger role in care	Less NAs (ratio) reduced role/ importance
Less trained nurses	More trained nurses
More cleaners/kitchen staff (ratio)	Less cleaners/kitchen staff (ratio)
Less admin/support staff	More admin/support staff

Past:	*Present:*
High staff camaraderie (crisis)	(Implication – now less camaraderie)
Clinical staff actively fundraise/promote	(Implication – clinical & support staff distinct)[4]
Nursing/NAs share common values	New 'NHS' staff more diverse (different values)
Overt spiritual values expressed	Secular, few spiritual values displayed
Sympathetic to religion	Less sympathetic (hostile?) to religion
Chapel used more	Chapel less utilised
Staff psyche support 'religious'	(Implication – support now secular or fractured/professionalised)
Prayers prior to MDT	Practice abandoned
Bell call to prayers	Practice abandoned
Prayers offered on death	Prayers now covertly offered – limited expression allowed (by whom?)
Less medicalised (talk – pain control)	More medicalised (quicker resort to drugs)
(Implication – poor medical leadership)	Medical leadership improved
Nurses 'freer' to give medication	Nurses 'hands tied' re medications (distinguishes between old/new hands)[5]
Less documentation/bureaucracy	More documentation/bureaucracy

Hospice:	*Hospital:*
Attitude – care	Attitude – cure
Humane	Less humane – pts not treated as people
Personal relationships formed	Depersonalised
Body 'a nice place to be'	Treatment overextended ('worse than disease')
Not turning away from death[6]	Turning away/reluctance to accept death

continued

Hospice:	*Hospital:*
Open awareness (sensitive)	
Pt 'bravery' confronted with death	
Originally seen as 'defeat' by some GPs	
'In beginning' voluntary organisation status valued	(Implication – voluntary status now devalued/nebulous?)
More than a job	(Implication – just a job for some?)
Good aftercare (hoped for)[7]	Poor aftercare (e.g. drug labelling)

Hospice patients:	*Non-hospice patients:*
	Those treating it as hotel (disrespect)
	Dementia – mental illness, mental degeneration (disruptive)

Professionalism rejected emphatically

Attitudinal changes linked to influx of hospital (system) influenced staff

Strong emotional commitment to hospice

Hospice Board – elitist, distant

Notes

1 Change from terminal to palliative admissions current balance is about right.
2 Anomaly? Rare discharge a 'success', need to 'keep them going so they can go home again' – query does this undermine 'acceptance' of death.
3 Increased numbers of professionals contribute to pt/family-staff distancing.
4 Indicates role/professional boundaries originally fluid, implies now fixed/rigid – note relaxed non-medical behaviour of earlier hospice medics. Sadness at loss of camaraderie/aim.
5 Difference in use of drugs noted between old timers and new recruits.
6 Possible anomaly, doctor refers to hospice as 'unit', why embarrassed by name?
7 Wants admin/discharge liaison nurse appointed. Practical aspects of aftercare often ignored.

Appendix C: Pre-coding interview summary B:a

Conversational style discursive and 'layered'. B:a – Nurse [edit]. At hospice approximately [edit] years.

Emotional response to or engagement with suffering prompts choice of nursing career. Early professional/work experience gained in nursing homes (NH) and [edit]. Frustrated by inability to care for patients as would like. Retrained [edit] – became [edit]. Frustration regards care standards provided continued prior to move to hospice. Following move to hospice, B:a able to provide terminal care as wants to.

Death

'Good' death an important concept for B:a. Prefers terminal to respite pts or arranging discharges. Prefers relations 'calm', patient sedated 'calm', not fighting/thrashing, notes that family and respondents' perceptions can vary.

'Bad' death involves uncontrolled symptoms, anger, unresolved personal or family issues, not relaxed. Claims age irrelevant (but note multiple references to aged death as more acceptable/less fearful than youthful death). Vivid descriptions given of frightening symptoms/deaths (faecal vomit and catastrophic bleeds in particular).

Own death fears [edit]

Professionalism and emotional involvement

Emotional involvement deliberately curtailed/limited behind professional 'face' – professionalism used to distance B:a from emotional response (may be involved with/experience two/three deaths per day at hospice). Notes reduction in emotional involvement with rising medical input. Professionalism associated with 'doing' rather than 'feeling'. Notes professional expectations vary between hospice and NH. Conscious focus at hospice on technical/rational knowledge/ aspects of care. Tech/rational skills valued above 'homemaker' skills. Hospice patients have complex needs and their deaths can be vivid and frightening [edit]. Involvement – influenced by likeability of patient, i.e. 'like my own granny'.

Personal fear of cancer. Distinguishes between personal response to horror (revulsion/nausea) and professional ability to cope [edit].

Symptom control

Claims that appropriate knowledge exists to control symptoms so that, personal failings aside, symptom control should be unproblematic. Pain – states that effective pain control requires professionals to tackle psychiatric 'problems' (pain not purely physiological).

Reluctant to articulate concept of total pain (though aware of concept). Term can be a 'cop out'; has potential for misuse.

Hospice patients

Mix generally correct bar qualms about some respite and dementia patients (linked to 'valued' good death). Unprepared to say who should come in/be excluded. Notes that 'nice' patients kept longer than burdensome.

Hospice

Higher staffing ratios, more resources, good medical cover. Privacy in bays problematic. Hospice = public deaths. Younger deaths less accepting (than advanced ages). Old patients watch younger patients die.

Dissent problematic. Conformity valued (by management?). Initiative valued by clinical team. Ideal hospice – single rooms, encourage talk, high staff ratio, good symptom control, good communication, not raising false hope, setting clear boundaries/objectives.

In actuality – communication sometimes lacking, poor nurse/doctor communication (nurse opinions devalued on ward rounds). Lack of 'momentum', nothing definite, drift. Poor management by consultants, patients slide between categories/boundaries – absence of clarity. Poor planning.

Nursing homes

Long-term care fosters 'family'-like atmosphere (their own home). Poor medical (GP) input (cost, attitude). Attempt not to admit to hospital. Privacy in own (or twin) rooms. NH = private deaths. Advanced age associated with acceptance. High emotional involvement (three/four deaths per year).

Professionalism rather than 'professional', claims difference. NH deaths acceptable (not frightening), however – note qualms re inadequate pain/symptom control. Description of NH death somewhat idealised, but more 'hospice' than hospice.

Hospitals

Hospice better (no evidence), superior communication.

Change at hospice

Notes major changes over last two years. Was – more like NH. Now – busier/ more interventionist (more IVs/antibiotics). Suggests doing more may add to patient problems. Interventions (palliative or otherwise) raise patient/family expectations. Danger of giving false hope (when 'little hope' exists). Over-treatment of symptoms may hamper peaceful death. Activity hinders acceptance. Possible reticence on hospice's part to state situation/prognosis (closed awareness?).

Acknowledges separateness of palliative and hospice care, but reluctant to articulate difference.

Consultants

Recognises major difference between consultants. FT Consultant keeps patients longer. Prescription differences (PT Consultant lower initial doses). PT Consultant more interventionist. Disagrees with some of PT Consultant interventions (e.g. inappropriate transfusions). Acknowledges differing nursing preferences for consultant styles.

Personally likes FT Consultant despite being worse boundary 'smudger' than PT Consultant (anomaly). Choice – Do we allow patients too much choice? Should we 'guide' more? (see Change above).

Opiates/euthanasia

We hasten death, but this is not unacceptable. Equivocal regards euthanasia (variable attitude towards).

Against euthanasia in hospice – what we do is "euthanasia enough".

Prepared to equate sedation with euthanasia. Notes differences in nurse medicating – linked with potential for abuse. Yet also believes we can hold back sedation (reticence about offering enough in a timely manner).

Appendix D: Interview coding process – A:a

TpA coding begins when "a label is attached to a section of text to index it as relating to a theme or issue which the researcher has identified as important to his or her interpretation" (King, 2004, p. 257). Following King (2004, 2007), coding did not begin until the researcher was familiar with the interview transcripts. To this end recordings were replayed, transcripts were re-read and notes were made (Appendices B and C). Familiarisation enabled the researcher to formulate provisional ideas or proto-theories regarding (i) individual transcripts, (ii) relations between transcripts and (iii) relations between transcripts and observed practice. Familiarisation also facilitated (iv) reflection on the relationship between interview derived proto-theory and morphogenetic theory. To illustrate both the labelling process and the importance of pre-coding interpretation a short passage from the interview with participant A:a (Nursing Assistant) is examined.

quietness busyness **physical size**

staff numbers

medicalisation

social and/or emotional engagement

A:a Well it was, well for one it was much quieter than it is now, much quieter (emphasis). The whole, you know, I mean we were only open for eight beds. We used to have four staff in the morning and three in the afternoon and three on the night and that was it. And it was like two trained and two auxiliaries, or perhaps more than that, two trained and three auxiliaries in the morning and one trained and two auxiliaries in the afternoon and one trained and two auxiliaries at night. And so it was very much a (pause). Not so medical (emphasis). You know it was very much well we'll go and ask the trained staff if you can have something, you know, but if you want me to sit here and have a chat, if that might help. And sometimes it did, sometimes the drug wasn't necessary; it was just let's sit and hold your hand and have a talk.

INTERVIEWER: So did they have an on site doctor all the time?

A:a Yes, yes they did.

INTERVIEWER: But you felt you didn't go to them as often as we do now, or do you feel you relied less upon the prescription charts?

A:a Yes but they (pause), I mean they were written up for pain killers, they were written up for morphine. You know, for anti-emetics and all that sort of thing. They were written up for them and they could have them if they wanted to. But it just seemed there were a lot of us on the ground and you know a lot more socialising, sitting on the bed chatting, sitting on the bed show us your knitting, and you know sitting on the bed and playing scrabble.

ocial and/or emotional ngagement

staff numbers staff ratios

INTERVIEWER: So by implication we don't do that so much now?

A:a No, no we don't.

INTERVIEWER: When did it change then?

staff numbers recruitment

A:a (Pause) I suppose as we got more and more patients, as we started to take in more and more sicker patients and then we started taking in more trained staff. And the trained staff were coming mainly from the hospital where you don't sit down playing scrabble (laughs), or crosswords, you don't you know, you don't sit there giving somebody a massage or spending time curling their hair or what have you. You know, that's, that's what changed; it became more of a (pause) medical job. I don't know what the words are.

syness mission ractice

edicalisation

social and/or emotional engagement

INTERVIEWER: You wrinkle your nose when you say that I take it from the way you say it, that you place a high value on the way it was to begin with?

Nursing assistant-registered nurse

A:a (Pause) Yes, but then, you know I'm coming from an auxiliary's point of view, not from a medical. I mean look at the work we're doing here now it's far more palliative than terminal isn't it. I mean then it was terminal care.

ospice/ alliative rkloads

Hospice/ palliative status

Interviewee A:a begins by emphasising how much quieter the hospice used to be and thus, by implication, it is now busier. Quietness is put down to size "we were only open for eight beds" and linked to staff attitudes or behaviours "but if you want me to sit here and have a chat, if that might help". The hospice was, in its early period, "not so medical" and staff engaged with patients in what might be termed emotionally therapeutic socialisation (i.e. massage, playing scrabble and hair curling). This past is then juxtaposed against seven overlapping features of current practice: changes in the ratio of nursing auxiliaries and registered nurses; the admission of more and "sicker" patients; staff recruitment from environments where unhurried socialisation is impractical; increasing busyness; a move from terminal to palliative care and medicalisation. Further, implicit or unarticulated assumptions about nursing assistant-registered nurse interaction and the relative workload involved in terminal and palliative (symptom control) care may also be discernable.

In the exemplar passage (above), identifying labels (notated on transcripts by a mixture of overlapping coloured markings and scribbled margin comments) referenced 'quietness', 'busyness', 'physical size', 'social and/or emotional engagement', 'admission practice', 'recruitment', 'staff numbers', 'staff ratios', 'medicalisation' and 'hospice/palliative status'. Provisional or tentative labels are also posted against 'nursing assistant-registered nurse interaction' and 'hospice/palliative workloads' (the provisional nature of these labels is here illustrated by the use of dotted lines and italicised scripts).

Some comments carry multiple labels. This is termed parallel coding. Parallel coding occurs when "the same segment is classified within two (or more) different codes at the same time" (King, 2004, p. 258). Parallel coding occurs in the above passage when two labels, 'quietness' and 'busyness', are attached to the opening phrase (current busyness is implied). Parallel coding is also apparent in the template created for A:a (Appendix F). Here comments about increasing treatment/interventions are linked to staff recruitment. These data are situated under the first level codes 'Change' *and* 'Treatment/interventions'.

Labels describe data. However, following Chapter 3, labels do not simply arise from data; rather they are suggested by thematically informed pre-coding interview proto-theory as well as broader philosophic/theoretic considerations. Pre-coding transcript familiarisation had, in this instance, forewarned the researcher that A:a and other participants linked together changes such as staff ratios/numbers and recruitment to increasing medicalisation and treatment/intervention use. Familiarisation facilitates the interpretive process when, in examining a single passage, the researcher is, as stated, cognisant of its place within the transcript as a whole, its relation to other transcripts and observed practice. Textual (transcript) analysis is thus aided by factors external to the interview 'segment' under review (this aspect of interpretation is developed further in Appendix E). For example, in the passage above, the label 'staff ratios' can only be attached because subsequent comments by A:a make it clear that this is what she was referring to (the key word here is "us" – i.e. "us" auxiliary nursing assistants) and, below, interviewer-interviewee familiarity allowed affective revelation by A:a to highlight the significance or meaningfulness of what was being said. Thus, in response to the question, "Do we still get to know them [patients] as well as we used to?" A:a replies "No" and suggests that such interaction "isn't part of it", hospice activity, "any more".

A:a No. No. We got to know them a lot (pause), a lot better because we had more time. You know there weren't all these people about.

INTERVIEWER: Why don't we have time? We have very good patient-staff ratios?

A:a Yeah (pause). Why don't we? (Pause) Well because that, that isn't part of it any more. That *was* it (emphasis). That isn't (pause) [it now].

This excerpt suggests that an emotional distancing has occurred between staff and patients. The literal meaning of these comments is clear and yet the emotional or affective 'weight' captured in the interview recording is lost in transcription. Through inflection and wavering tonality a tremendous sadness is conveyed to the listener at this point. A:a may not have revealed this distress to an unfamiliar researcher and, even had this occurred, without knowing the respondent an unfamiliar researcher may not have appreciated the importance of such expression. Pre-coding familiarisation alerted the researcher to the significance of this and similar passages in advance of formal coding; it helped to suggest the sorts of labels that might usefully be employed and it demonstrated that data analysis benefits from consideration of extra-textual factors. It is a strength of Template analysis that it encourages such consideration and, as in the above instance, such consideration allows due significance to be given to emotional as well as literal (textual) statements.

Morphogenetic (level 2) theory allows (see Chapter 3) that unequal rates of change may occur between, for example, social and cultural structures and the expression and interpretation of data/labels were influenced by this possibility. In the exemplar passage it was supposed that suggestive evidence for just this form of differential morphogenesis might be apparent (level 3 theory). Grand conclusions cannot of course be drawn from short transcript excerpts such as those presented above. Nonetheless, the consistency and coherence of the interpretation allowed by the use of these labels is demonstrated internally, within the transcript, both by the repeated use of these labels in describing subsequent passages (albeit that, in Template analysis, frequency does not equal salience) and the closeness or ease of 'fit' between labels and template themes. Externally, the utility of these labels is demonstrated by their ability to interpret data across transcripts.

As will be noted, it is not claimed that A:a's narrative is itself consistent or coherent – though it appears to be – rather, emphasis is placed on the consistency and coherence of the *interpretation* allowed by theoretically informed label use. This does not concede that coding 'merely' produces an interpretation. It recognises rather that, for realists who reject correspondence theories of truth, transitive explanations of intransitive reality are always and necessarily interpretations.

Following formal labelling, Template analysis orders similar labels or codes "together to produce more general higher-order codes [and this] hierarchical coding allows the researcher to analyse texts at varying levels of specificity" (King, 2004, p. 258). Appendix F lists six levels of code for A:a. These range from high first level codes such as 'Change within the hospice' (level 1) through to more specific lower level codes such as 'claims need to keep hospice spirit alive' (level 3). As will be noted, the description of data in Appendix F does not use the 'bulleted' labels described earlier. Rather, more descriptive phrases are employed and this change reflects the requirement that template coding captures the entirety of an interview. That said, although the exemplar passage describes only a small fragment of the interview, data/evidence from this passage clearly informs Appendix F at several points.

For example, starting with the above identified data labels (quietness, busyness, physical size, etc.) and working 'upwards' it was possible to maintain and incorporate additional themes into the interpretation of A:a's narrative so that, in the researcher's opinion, a more comprehensive picture of her position is captured. Thus, as can be seen (Appendix F), under the general heading 'Change within the hospice' and three second level codes (i) 'was quieter, now busier', (ii) 'professionalisation – role change' and (iii) 'staff-patient relations, much of the data from the exemplar passage is reproduced.

Appendix E: Interview coding process – B:a

Here emphasis is placed on the suggestion that interpretation is best accomplished when transcript data are: (i) read in the round (rather than being disaggregated), (ii) placed in context of the interview as a whole and (iii) related to comments made in other interviews. Where this occurs, analysis of the exchange supports and extends initial template themes. The exchange described below was prefaced by a query regarding participant B:a's (Nurse) nursing home experience.

B:a Well, well, if, we have, we have better staffing. We have, but in nursing homes you often are looking after people you've known for very many years often. And they are very much part of the family (pause). And to be fair the carers and the staff feel it very greatly when people do die (*emphasis*) (pause). And I think the difference is that there, there is very little, trying to stop anybody dying. Or, I think symptom control, I think pain control is bad (*emphasis*) in nursing homes because GPs often don't want to know. And if you call in a specialist they don't particularly want to be bothered to come out to a nursing home. And there are cost implications that, that they ask to be paid to come out and give an opinion. And that, often the nursing homes can't do that and you find that people are dying on paracetamol (pause). Which is (laughs) a very good drug (laughs), but you've got someone who (pause). You're using all of the other methods, you're using (pause) positioning of the patient who's, you're using wheat bags, you're using heat, you're using (pause) massage, you're using lots of other, you, you have to be very, very inventive because often you can't get MSTs[1] or, because of cost implications to the GPs who really can't be bothered with (pause) with, to visit nursing homes. I find, I did find that very frustrating (*emphasis*). But here I find it amazing because everything is thrown at people like [Patient] to make sure that things are good. And that was one of the things I found very frustrating in nursing homes (pause). In a nursing home it's a bit like they're dying in their own homes. They've often been with us a long time, like I said. So consequently they, they often die with, in their own bed, with their possessions around them. They're in a place they've known as home, often. With people around them that they recognise, or don't recognise as family. There's certainly (pause), I don't know, I think they feel (pause).

We try very hard not to send them into hospital. We feel very strongly that they should die at home, as in their home (pause). Dying here I think can be a little bit (pause) hospitalised and a bit (pause) medicalised (pause). I think we do our best if a family stays. And obviously they can have as many people around them as they like. But (pause) often, well certainly in the four bedded areas (pause), the families I'm sure, and the patients themselves are quite aware of the deaths going on in the next beds. And that sort of thing. In nursing homes, we did use to make sure that people had their privacy. They often all had single rooms anyway. So it was perhaps always private, their deaths. Whereas here sometimes the deaths are a little bit public (pause). And then again, of course, (pause) people in nursing homes tended to be of, of an age when (pause) not only did they accept it perhaps themselves, but also the people in the nursing home could. Here (pause), I find that some of the, with the age differences, you've got some, an older person watching a younger person die. Or, visa-versa, it's (pause) perhaps, it can be much more frightening, here. Whereas in a nursing home, in a way, they did expect to die.

INTERVIEWER: You said that in the nursing home (pause), it was their home (pause), you'd known them for some time, and when they died, you felt it keenly. Whereas here, if, how does that compare with here?

B:a (Pause). I don't allow myself to feel a great deal here. To me, clearly this is a different ball game (pause). There, that was their home and we got very involved with them (pause). So that, there, they were a little bit like, to use, a little bit like our grannies and granddads. It was, it was a home, yeah. And we tried to make it homely. Here (long pause), that was still professional, it was, I was still a professional person. But here I find it different; I find it more, more (pause) perhaps because it is more medicalised. Because we do more things (pause). Perhaps because it's a more professional team generally and there's a lot more going on. I don't know (pause). I've very rarely been affected by anybody dying here (pause). I don't think it's because I'm hard (pause). I just think it's (pause). When I came here it is what I came here for and to do. And I, I, I'd known those people for perhaps three or four years. I'd watched them get more poorly. Whereas here, they're often admitted more poorly and (pause). I can't explain it, it's different, but I don't get as close. Whether that's because I consciously don't get as close because we have so many and I, emotionally I don't think anyone would be able to hack it if you felt every death (pause). But certainly if you're having two or three in a day (pause).

At one level several of the labels used to code interviewee A:a's (Appendix D) transcript are applicable here. Thus, "we have better staffing" was labelled 'staff numbers' and "Dying here I think can be a little bit hospitalised and a bit medicalised" was labelled 'medicalisation'. New labels are also introduced. For example, in the first paragraph 'GP/pain' was applied to comments regarding perceived GP failings and the statement "everything is thrown at" was labelled 'resource'. The extract's interpretive significance is, however, not revealed in line by line or close labelling (though this occurred). Rather, the extract's significance becomes apparent when read as a whole. It can then be seen to expose values and ideas about nurse-patient relations, good or desirable forms of death and changed hospice practice *through* the juxtaposition of commentaries on nursing home and hospice deaths.

Thus, despite recognising that pain control may be suboptimal and resources limited, B:a idealises nursing home deaths. Reflecting personal values articulated elsewhere in the interview B:a notes that nursing home deaths occur privately in "single rooms". People die "in their own bed, with their possessions around them" and, when it occurs, death is expected and accepted. Importantly, patients are "people you've known for very many years. And they are very much part of the family." Consequently, when they die, "the staff feel it very greatly". Such deaths are infrequent and B:a quantifies this by later noting that two or three a year may be normal.

At the hospice it is, in contrast, common to have "two or three" deaths a day. These deaths lack privacy. They are "public" and occur in un-homely bays where "patients are quite aware of the deaths going on in the next bed". Significantly, for B:a, emotional engagement is reduced. Contra her nursing home experience, B:a states that "I don't allow myself to feel a great deal here" and "I've rarely been affected by anybody dying here." These comments are somewhat disingenuous since it is quite evident from subsequent passages (edited to prevent over-exposure) that B:a, like others, is profoundly affected by witnessed violent and traumatic hospice deaths. Nevertheless, the number and forms of death experienced at the hospice necessitate that, for B:a, conscious boundaries be erected against exposing emotional engagement and, to manage this exposure it is later suggested that "I feel here [at the hospice that] I use my 'professional' head (pause) in a way almost as a (pause) wall to hide behind, to keep me from getting too involved."

Situated within the interview, these comments may be interpreted as a critique of change that uses the running juxtaposition of nursing home-hospice difference as a plot or narrative device. Thus, for example, later in the interview B:a notes that "When I first came here it was closer to (pause) a nursing home death than it is now." B:a also states that "I seem to remember that when I first came here, we, we (pause) we did things for them, but then we seemed to know when to call it a day." Now however, increasing treatment/interventions, although palliative in intent, cannot but "give them hope when there isn't any (pause) hope". Indeed, the hospice currently seems "to treat quite actively and (pause) I don't think that does anything to get, to give somebody a nice, a peaceful death". Again, the censure of current hospice practice is contrasted with nursing home care where "they just seemed to accept the fact that they were dying, as did the family, because that's what was happening everyone was very accepting of that" and B:a thus links change at the hospice with more active treatment/interventions, the potential giving of false hope, professionalisation and personal emotional withdrawal or boundary setting.

Looking across transcripts, this interpretation is bolstered insofar as Appendix D describes, for A:a, kindred changes at the hospice regarding busyness, a rise in the number of high dependency patient admissions and increases in the number and complexity of treatment/interventions. A:a talks about an influx of acutely trained staff whereas B:a does not. Nevertheless, A:a specifically mentions forms of low or non-technical therapeutic intervention (e.g. massage) that mirror B:a's comments on the use of massage, positioning and heat pads to relieve discomfort and A:a reports upon forms of developing professionalisation that, accompanying these changes, encourage or are synonymous with emotional disengagement. Further, allied sentiments about the direction of change, treatment/interventions and staff-patient relations are echoed by other clinically based nurses.

Respondent E:a, for example, made comments that appear to 'confirm' or support the opinions offered by A:a and B:a. E:a is a nurse who worked at the hospice in its early years and, following a break, more recently. She stated that for the early hospice:

E:a The level of medical intervention was far less. I always, we used to be able to feel that our patients died peacefully, I don't anymore (pause). They were loved. We used much less in the way of intervention. We would never have had sub-cut[2] fluids up. We never had an IV.[3] We weren't allowed to give blood it was different (emphasis) the atmosphere was different. The atmosphere was much more homely. Much less like a hospital.

The recurrent ubiquity of similar expressions among *some* respondents does not mean that personal experience validates external reality – the authenticity of extra-linguistic reality cannot meaningfully be 'voted' upon – and contradictory viewpoints were also expressed – nevertheless, insofar as the interpretation of respondent comments offered here is coherent within and across transcripts, the reader may perhaps have some confidence in the interpretation offered.

B:a's interview template (Appendix G) recognises the nursing home-hospice distinction by the inclusion of a new theme labelled 'NH and hospice care'. In this way the initial template is extended albeit that some of the issues illustrated by this dichotomy are parallel coded under other headings such as 'Medicalisation' and 'Professionalisation – role change'. At master template (Appendix H) level the 'NH and hospice care' theme is, as stated in Chapter 3, lost, since other interviewees did not raise this distinction in this way. Nevertheless, key elements from B:a, A:a and E:a's commentaries (as well as others) appear under the heading 'Change within the hospice' and subsidiary headings 'Treatment/interventions' and 'Professionalisation' and, in this way, the substance of these interpretations is maintained.

Template coding, interpretation or analysis occurs at a variety of levels. The place of pre-coding interpretation and line by line labelling was described in Appendix D. Here, emphasis is placed on the argument that interpretation also requires that interpreters look beyond the transcript details so that interviewee comments may be understood 'in the round'. Contextualisation is provided by 'placing' interviewee comments within the 'frame' of the transcript as a whole as well as other transcripts/observations. Contextualisation here enables B:a's nursing home-hospice contrast or dichotomy to be seen as a narrative device through which ideas about change and the consequents of change can be articulated. This interpretation then allows morphogenetic theory to overtly re-enter the analytic process and, for example, it might be suggested that B:a describes structural changes that 'outstrip' the socio-cultural (S-C) 'position' or values of B:a and other clinicians. Suggestions regarding differential morphogensis and agential socio-cultural interaction are made simply to illustrate how Template coding may inform morphogenetic theory and sufficient evidence is not supplied here to substantiate such proposals.

Notes

1 Morphine sulphate tablet – an analgesic.
2 Subcutaneous.
3 Intravenous infusion.

Appendix F: Template A:a

Code levels

1 2 3 4 5 6

Change within the hospice

- Was quieter, now busier
  - Sicker patients – greater willingness to intervene medically
  - Different patients
- Professionalisation – role change
  - Unwelcomed – increasing focus on treatment/interventions
  - Unwelcomed – distances staff from patients/families
  - Unwelcomed – greater role specialism/separateness
    - Respondent more involved in hospice activity when less professionalised
      - During 1980s financial crisis – respondent involved in fund raising – moral/camaraderie then good
        - Financial crisis necessitated practice changes (equipment use)
  - Claims need to keep hospice spirit alive
  - Now more 'upstairs people' and relatively fewer 'downstairs people'
    - More 'form filling' – a shift away from patient care
- Staff relations change with increasing numbers of staff
- Staff relations change with changing staff ratios
  - Auxiliaries – decline in ratio compared with nurses
    - Auxiliaries less active in MDM[1]
    - Auxiliaries disempowered from wider hospice involvement
  - Nurses – influx from local state sector
    - Differences between behaviours/attitudes of old and new recruits
  - Doctors – medicalisation
    - More doctors – medical staff have more power relative to nurses

New doctors and nurses – nurses and doctors coming from acute backgrounds – nurses less willing/able to act on own initiative – inability to intervene to relieve pain without medical input

Staff-patient relations change (used to 'know' patients more) – less involved in personal care with increasing staff numbers

Less than adequate care attributed to recent influx of hospital staff (discharge medications)

Treatment/interventions

Rise in interventions linked to increased staff numbers and recruitment from NHS

Rise in interventions linked to change from terminal to palliative care

Rise in specific interventions – example, blood used

Spirituality/religion

Overtness of spiritual/religious dimension lost

Bell no longer rung

Experiences 'loss' at changed situation

Decline in overt spirituality/religiosity linked with new influx of staff from NHS

More focus on symptom palliation, less focus on event of death or suffering

Prayers on death – now offered covertly

Open awareness

Increased

Reticence of some early medical staff to use term hospice

Patient groups

Were terminal – now palliative care

Paradoxically, respondent appeared to prefer old regime but would not want to turn away non-terminal patients

People with mental health problems and those with dementia not suitable hospice patients

Inappropriate patients or patient behaviours recognised

Consultant differences

Consultant differences acknowledged – FT Consultant a 'soft touch'

Hospice management

Trust board – a distant relationship

Note

1 MDM – Multidisciplinary meeting.

Appendix G: Template B:a

Code levels

1 2 3 4 5 6

- **Change within the hospice** (often juxtaposed against nursing home care)
    - Significant change observed in two years
        - Defined as move away from nursing home (NH) type care
        - New patient needs recognised
            - Higher dependency admissions
        - New medical responses possible
        - New forms of care initiated (more treatment/interventions)
            - New care changes staff-staff and staff-patient relationships
    - Professionalism
        - Hospice becoming more professional – care becoming more professional
        - In contrast to NH professional behaviour, hospice professionalism:
            - Promotes technical competence (doing skills)
            - A response to changing patient needs
            - A response to medical willingness to meet those needs
            - Allows emotional disengagement/protection
                - Disengagement welcomed – response to multiple violent deaths
        - More active patient management required
            - Decision making – poor when 'passive', when patients kept for no purpose
    - Rising expectations on part of public/patients/families

- **Treatment/interventions**
    - Interventions increasing (e.g. – more IVs, antibiotics, etc.)
    - Interventions may inadvertently engender unfounded/false hope
        - Paradox between intervening to ameliorate symptoms (good) and raising false expectations about delaying impending death (bad)
            - Contrast good NH practice (accepting inevitable death) with confused messages given out by proactive hospice stance
    - Treatments may continue for too long – difficulty or failure in withdrawing and/or defining boundaries/limits

Consultant differences

Consultant differences acknowledged

Paradox – respondent wants more active management of patient admissions but prefers less active consultant style on medication use and patient communication

Criticism of active consultant for offering patients options that they cannot emotionally refuse; "clutching at straws"

Believes less interventionist consultant generally preferred by nursing staff

Proactive consultant innovative (good)

Discharge

Problems with discharges – quick readmission – poorly managed

Distinguishes between liked and disliked patients (disliked discharged more speedily)

Communication

Communication and personal skills valued by patients – not just technical skills

Challenges crude ideas about open awareness (emphasises need for privacy – "properly private things")

Danger of engendering false hope (need to make treatment refusal acceptable)

Call for communicative clarity when discussing options with patients – need to set expectational boundaries – encourage patients to get out when able

Notes occasional poor doctor-nurse communication

Leadership/management

Need to take lead in managing admission duration and treatment goals – notes occasional current problems

Lack of medical lead – lack of clarity (results in overly long patient stays and delayed discharges)

Moral imperative to manage admission goals/aims on patients' behalf

Currently failing to manage some patients effectively – in particular – changes in patient status (respite – symptom control – palliative – terminal) poorly managed

Top heavy management

Sedation

Not enough sedation sometimes given – possibly should sedate for reasons other than pain

Concedes opiate use life shortening

Willing to consider euthanasia but probably not at hospice "what we do here is euthanasia enough"

Accepts that terminal sedation a form of euthanasia (functional death)

Nurse differences – some give more opiates than others – open to abuse

Patient groups

Terminal patients – favoured patient group

Access – despite preference for terminal patients – respondent unwilling to deny access to non-terminal patients

Respite and MND patients – admission suitability questioned

Death fears

Strong personal interest in death

Fear of death – hospice deaths often violent and nasty [edit]

Good death – peaceful, calm, sedated, family appreciative

Bad death – lack of equanimity rather than age related (however, NH deaths distanced by age)

Coping with death – difference between professional and private reactions

NH and hospice care

Hospice staff less emotionally involved with patients than NH staff

Respondent emotionally detached at hospice

Explanation for detachment – high patient turnover and number of deaths

Professionalism a bulwark against emotional involvement

Professional 'face'/expectations vary between hospice and NH

NH staff lack hospice resources and must be inventive in tackling pain/ symptoms

Death in NH – a death in the family

Hospice death comparatively medicalised and interventionist compared with NH death

NH death less public than hospice death

NH death expected and accepted (age important) – hospice death may be more unwelcome/violent

Hospice and hospital care

Belief that hospice care superior to hospital care

More staff

More openness and honesty (however, see comments on engendering false hope)

More time

Criticism

Hospice reluctant to seek or accept criticism

Hospice management do not like "boat rockers"

Appendix H: Master template

Code levels

1 2 3 4 5 6

Structures and institutions

State/NHS relations – hostile environment, hospice perceives that its interests are threatened – conscious engagement with external bodies to protect interests

- Department of Health
  - Clinical Governance
    - Burdensome
    - Little/no benefit to hospice
    - Resource wasteful
  - Care Standards Act
    - Requires compliance
    - Will align hospice and NHS practices
    - Means to control hospice activity
- PCT[1]
  - County Palliative Care Directorate
    - New Consultant Chair
      - Hostile to study site:
      - Controlling – wish to make hospice more accountable to state sector
        - Financial levers
        - Organisational levers
- NHS Palliative Care Consultants
  - Hostile to hospices in general and study site as local manifestation
- GPs
  - Relations initially difficult – now greatly improved
    - Referrals 'patchy'
    - Not always appropriate
- Macmillan nurses
  - Historically 'mixed'/antagonistic relationship

Demographic relations

Admissions

Sicker

Physically more dependent than was once case
Later (from acute sector, from community)
Sooner (family support reduced)
Changing referral patterns
Migrant workers

Discharges

Family support reduced – some discharges delayed
More complex

Relations within the hospice

Organisational re-designation as SPCU[2] (2000) – pro- and anti-change groups emerge at hospice consequent to change

Hospice (historic)

Less busy

Holistic care valued

Non-physical and physical care awarded equal attention
Spirituality important to all
Terminal care plus symptom control

SPCU

Busier

Specialist rather than holistic
Physical care predominates
Spirituality a speciality
Symptom control plus terminal care

Patients

Increasing dependency (patients' sicker)
Physical needs predominate

Staffing

New staff from acute sector

Compared to past – new staff orientated to:

Treat/intervene more
Use more medications
Use medications in different ways

Compared to past – new staff are not orientated to:

'Stand back' from life sustaining treatment/interventions
Engage emotionally – act independently
New nurses more reliant on medical direction

Consultant differences

- FT Consultant – GP background
    - Non-interventionist
    - Pain medication 'generous'
    - Slow to discharge
    - Traditional admission criteria
    - Focus within institution
        - Unproblematic relationship with hospice
- PT Consultant – acute background
    - Interventionist
    - Pain medication 'parsimonious'
    - Quick to discharge
    - Non-traditional admission criteria
    - Focus external to institution
        - PT at hospice
        - Problematic relationship with hospice
        - Sees hospice care as inequitable, elitist, unaccountable

Treatment/interventions

- Increasing use of treatment/interventions
    - Reasons for increasing use of treatment/interventions
        - New treatment/interventions available
        - New willingness to use treatment/interventions
        - Change in institutional designation
            - Palliative rather than hospice
                - Function – symptom control
        - Less value placed on non-clinical interventions

Admissions – discharges

- *Admissions*
    - More high dependency patients being admitted
    - Favoured patients
    - Nurses question suitability of some admissions
        - Mental health
        - Dementia
- *Discharges*
    - Conflict
        - End stage patients

Professionalism

- Professionalism perceived to be increasing – needed to:
    - Manage large organisation
        - Fundraising
        - Future planning
    - Successfully meet State/NHS expectations/demands

Professionalism – perceived problems:
- Specialisation allows staff to withdraw from aspects of care
- Creates barriers to staff-patient relations
- Creates barriers within organisation
- Volunteers seen as unprofessional

Bureaucratisation
- Necessary to:
  - Protect hospice future
  - Meet external demands
- Problematic because:
  - Specialisation distances workforce

Medicalisation

More doctors doing more doctoring
Changes in staff ratios
Staff from acute backgrounds
Resistance from long service nurses

Spiritual/religious issues

Religious withdrawal
- Overt religious expression diminishing
  - Dog collar seen as problematic
  - Prayer bell no longer rung
  - Relatively few formal religious services
  - Prayers no longer offered following death
  - Chapel to relocate and lose most Christian iconography

Secularisation and increasing treatment/interventions
- Focus of activity shifting to treatment/interventions

Secularisation and professionalisation
- Role specialisation – spiritual matters responsibility of clergy

Secularisation and recruitment
- New nursing staff less spiritually aware than earlier recruits

Spiritual values
- Differentiate care in hospice from State/NHS
  - Spiritual branding
- Give purpose to activity
  - Define purpose for symptom control
  - Gives meaning to death

Notes

1 Primary Care Trust.
2 Specialist Palliative Care Unit.

References

Abendroth, M. and Flannery, J. (2006) Predicting the risk of compassion fatigue. *Journal of Hospice and Palliative Nursing*. 8(6), 346–356.

Abu-Saad, H. H. and Courtens, A. (2001) Models of palliative care. In Abu-Saad H. H., with contributions from Courtens, A., eds. *Evidence-Based Palliative Care: Across the Life Span*. Oxford: Blackwell Science, pp. 14–24.

Achinstein, P. (2010) *Evidence, Explanation, and Realism*. Oxford: Oxford University Press.

Ahmed, N., Bestall, J. C., Ahmedzai, S. H., Payne, S. A., Clark, D. and Noble, B. (2004) Systematic review of the problems and issues of accessing specialist palliative care by patients, careers and health and social care professionals. *Palliative Medicine*. 18(6), 525–542.

Alcock, P. (1996) *Social Policy in Britain: Themes and Issues*. London: Macmillan Press.

Alexander, J. (2012) *Experimental Philosophy: An Introduction*. Cambridge: Polity Press.

Alexander, J. C., Giesen, B., Münch, R. and Smelser, N. J., eds. (1987) *The Micro-Macro Link*. London: University of California Press.

Alexander, P. (2004) An investigation of inpatient referrals to a clinical psychologist in a hospice. *European Journal of Cancer Care*. 13(1), 36–44.

Allsop, J. (1995) *Health Policy and the NHS: Towards 2000*. Longman Social Policy in Britain Series. Second edn. London: Longman.

Aoun, S. M. and Kristjanson, L. K. (2005) Challenging the framework for evidence in palliative care research. *Palliative Medicine*. 19(6), 461–465.

Archer, M., Bhaskar, R., Collier, A., Lawson, T. and Norrie, A. (1998) *Critical Realism: Essential Readings*. Critical Realism: Interventions Series. London: Routledge.

Archer, M. S. (1972) Introduction. In Archer, M. S., ed. *Students, University and Society: A Comparative Sociological Review*. London: Heinemann Educational Books, pp. 1–35.

Archer, M. S. (1990) Human agency and social structure: a critique of Giddens. In Clark, J., Modgil, C. and Modgil, S., eds. *Anthony Giddens: Consensus and Controversy*. Basingstoke: Falmer Press, pp. 73–84.

Archer, M. S. (1995) *Realist Social Theory: The Morphogenetic Approach*. Cambridge: Cambridge University Press.

Archer, M. S. (1996) *Culture and Agency: The Place of Culture in Social Theory*. Revised edn. Cambridge: Cambridge University Press.

Archer, M. S. (2000) *Being Human: The Problem of Agency*. Cambridge: Cambridge University Press.

Archer, M. S. (2002) Realism and the problem of agency. *Journal of Critical Realism*. 5(1), 11–20.

Archer, M. S. (2003a) *Structure, Agency and the Internal Conversation*. Cambridge: Cambridge University Press.

Archer, M. S. (2003b) The private life of the social agent: what difference does it make? In Cruickshank, J., ed. *Critical Realism: The Difference it Makes*. Routledge Studies in Critical Realism. London: Routledge, pp. 17–29.

Archer, M. S. (2004a) Models of man: the admission of transcendence. In Archer, M. S., Collier, A. and Porpora, D. V., eds. *Transcendence: Critical Realism and God*. Critical Realism: Interventions Series. London: Routledge, pp. 63–81.

Archer, M. S. (2004b) Western mysticism and the limits of language. In Archer, M. S., Collier, A. and Porpora, D. V., eds. *Transcendence: Critical Realism and God*. Critical Realism: Interventions Series. London: Routledge, pp. 92–108.

Archer, M. S. (2007) *Making our Way through the World: Human Reflexivity and Social Mobility*. Cambridge: Cambridge University Press.

Archer, M S., Collier, A. and Porpora, D. V. (2004) *Transcendence: Critical Realism and God*. Critical Realism Interventions Series. London: Routledge.

Arksey, H. (2002) Combining informal care and work: supporting carers in the workplace. *Health and Social Care in the Community*. 10(3), 151–161.

Armstrong, D. (1994) *Outline of Sociology as Applied to Medicine*. Fourth edn. Oxford: Butterworth-Heineman.

Arraf, K., Cox, G. and Oberle, K. (2004) Using the Canadian Code of Ethics for registered nurses to explore ethics in palliative care research. *Nursing Ethics*. 11(6), 600–609.

Ashworth, P. (2000) Editorial: nurse-doctor relationships: conflict, competition or collaboration. *Intensive and Critical Care Nursing*. June. 16(3), 127–128.

Baert, P. (1998) *Social Theory in the Twentieth Century*. Cambridge: Polity Press.

Ballatt, J. and Campling, P. (2011) *Intelligent Kindness: Reforming the Culture of Healthcare*. London: RCPsych Publications.

Barry, J. and Jones, C. (1991) Introduction. In Barry, J. and Jones, C., eds. *Medicine and Charity Before the Welfare State*. London: Routledge, pp. 1–13.

Bass, M. (2006) *Palliative Care Resuscitation*. Chichester: John Wiley and Sons Ltd.

BEN PCT – Birmingham East and North NHS Primary Care Trust (2007) *Proposals for Developing End of Life Care Services Across Birmingham East and North Primary Care Trust: Public Consultation 1st October 2007 to 11th January 2008*. Birmingham: Birmingham East and North NHS Primary Care Trust.

Bennett, J. (2002) What events are. In Gale, R., ed. *Blackwell Guide to Metaphysics*. Blackwell Philosophy Guides Series. London: Blackwell Publishing, pp. 43–65.

Bergene, A. C. (2007) Towards a critical realist comparative methodology: context-sensitive theoretical comparison. *Journal of Critical Realism*. 6(1), 5–27.

Berger, P. L. and Luckmann, T. (1991) *The Social Construction of Reality: A Treatise in the Sociology of Knowledge*. London: Penguin.

Bergman, L. (2006) Spirituality: a glowing and useful term in search of a meaning. *Omega: Journal of Death and Dying*. 53(1–2), 5–26.

Bernstein, R. J. (1979) *The Restructuring of Social and Political Theory*. London: Methuen and Co.

Bhaskar, R. (1989) *Reclaiming Reality: A Critical Introduction to Contemporary Philosophy*. London: Verso.

Bhaskar, R. (1997) *A Realist Theory of Science*. Second edn. London: Verso.

Bhaskar, R. (1998a) The logic of scientific discovery. In Archer, M., Bhaskar, R., Collier, A., Lawson, T. and Norrie, A., eds. *Critical Realism: Essential Readings*. Critical Reslism: Interventions. London: Routledge, pp. 48–103.

Bhaskar, R. (1998b) *The Possibility of Naturalism: A Philosophical Critique of the Contemporary Human Sciences*. Third edn. Critical Realism Interventions Series. London: Routledge.

Biswas, B. (1993) The medicalization of dying: a nurse's view. In Clark, D., ed. *The Future for Palliative Care: Issues of Policy and Practice*. Buckingham: Open University Press, pp. 132–139.

Blau, P. M. (1977) *Inequality and Heterogeneity*. New York: Free Press.

Bouchal, S. R. (2007) Moral meanings of caring for the dying. In Johnson, N. and Scholler-Jaquish, A., eds. *Meaning in Suffering: Caring Practices in the Health Professions*. Volume 6 – Interpretive Studies in Healthcare and the Human Sciences. Wisconsin: The University of Wisconsin Press, pp. 232–275.

Bourdieu, P. (1990) *In Other Words: Essays Towards a Reflective Sociology*. Translation by Adamson M. Oxford: Polity Press.

Bowles, M. J. and Benjamin, I. S. (2001) ABC of the upper gastrointestinal tract: cancer of the stomach and pancreas. *British Medical Journal*. 323(7326), 1413–1416.

Bradshaw, A. (1996) The spiritual dimension of hospice: the secularization of an ideal. *Social Science and Medicine*. 43(3), 409–419.

Brook, A. (2006) Realism in the refutation of idealism. In Metareligion [online]. Available from: www.meta-religion.com/Philosophy/Biography/Immanuel_Kant/realism_in_the_refutation_of_ide.htm [Accessed 6 March 2006].

Bruera, E., Neuman, C., Brenneis, C. and Quan, H. (2000) Frequency of symptom distress and poor prognostic indicators in palliative care patients admitted to a tertiary palliative care unit, hospices, and acute care hospitals. *Journal of Palliative Care*. 16(3), 16–21.

Bruera, E., Delima, L., Woodruff, R. and Doyle, D. (2004) Editorial – International Association for Hospice and Palliative Care (IAHPC): working to improve access to palliative care. *Palliative Medicine*. 18(6), 491–493.

Bruner, J. S. (1990) *Acts of Meaning: The Jerusalem-Harvard Lectures*. Harvard: Harvard University Press.

Bryman, A. (2007) Barriers to integrating quantitative and qualitative research. *Journal of Mixed Method Research*. 1(1), 8–22.

Buckingham, R. W. (1996) *The Handbook of Hospice Care*. Foreword by Hurzeller, R. J. New York: Prometheus Books.

Buckley, W. (1967) *Sociology and Modern Systems Theory*. New Jersey: Prentice Hall.

Butchvarov, P. (2002) Metaphysical realism and logical nonrealism. In Gale, R., ed. *Blackwell Guide to Metaphysics*. Blackwell Philosophy Guides Series. London: Blackwell Publishing, pp. 282–302.

Byrne, D. (2004) Complex and contingent causation – the implications of complex realism for quantitative modelling. In Carter, B. and New, C., eds. *Making Realism Work: Realist Social Theory and Empirical Research*. Critical Realism Interventions Series. Abingdon: Routledge, pp. 50–66.

Byrne, D. S., Harrison, S., Keithley, J. and McCarthy, P. (1985) *Housing and Health*. London: Gower.

Callahan, R. R. (2005) Holistic home hospice: caring for a dying father – a family hermeneutic exemplar. *Home Health Care Management and Practice*. August. 17(5), 365–369.

Callister, L. C., Bond, A. E., Matsumura, G. and Mangum, S. (2004) Threading spirituality throughout nurse education. *Holistic Nursing Practice*. May/June. 18(3), 160–166.

Campbell, R. T. (2005) Care Standards Act 2000 [online]. Available from: www.carelaw.co.uk/articles/carestandards.htm [Accessed 20 March 2008].

Canagarajah, S. (2005) Rhetoricizing reflexivity. *Journal of Language, Identity and Education*. 4(4), 309–315.

Carr, G. (2008) Changes in nurse education: delivering the curriculum. *Nurse Education Today*. 28(1), 120–127.

Carter, B. (2000) *Realism and Racism: Concepts of Race in Sociological Research*. Critical Realism Interventions Series. London: Routledge.

Carter, B. (2003) What race means to realists. In Cruickshank, J., ed. *Critical Realism: The Difference it Makes*. Routledge Studies in Critical Realism. London: Routledge, pp. 148–160.

Casati, R. and Varzi, A. C. (2009) *50 Years of Events: An Annotated Bibliography 1947 to 1997* [online] Available from: www.pdcnet.org/pages/Products/electronic/eventsbib.htm [Accessed 13 March 2013].

Cavendish, R., Konecny, L., Naradovy, L., Luise, B. K., Como, J., Okumakpeyi, P., Mitzeliotis, C. and Lanza, M. (2006) Patients' perceptions of spirituality and the nurse as a special care provider. *Holistic Nursing Practice*. January/February. 20(1), 41–47.

Cihelkova, D. (2013) Subjectivity NOT statement and NOT APA! *The Qualitative Report*. 18(19), 1–5.

Clark, D. (1994) Editorial: at the cross-roads: which direction for the hospices? *Palliative Medicine*. 8(1), 1–3.

Clark, D. and Seymour, J. (1999) *Reflections on Palliative Care*. Facing Death Series. Buckingham: Open University Press.

Clark, D. and Wright, M. – with Łuczak, J. and in association with Fürst, C. J. and Sauter, S. (2003) *Transitions in End of Life Care: Hospice and Related Developments in Eastern Europe and Central Asia*. Facing Death Series. Buckingham: Open University Press.

Clark, D., Malson, H., Small, N., Mallett, K., Neale, B. and Heather, P. (1997) Half full or half empty? The impact of health reform on palliative care services in the UK. In Clark, D., Hockley, J. and Ahmedzai, S., eds. *New Themes in Palliative Care*. Facing Death Series. Buckingham: Open University Press, pp. 60–74.

Clark, D., ten Have, H. and Janssens, R. (2002) Conceptual tensions in European palliative care. In ten Have, H. and Clark, D., eds. *The Ethics of Palliative Care: European Perspectives*. Facing Death Series. Buckingham: Open University Press, pp. 52–65.

Clouder, L. (2003) Becoming professional: exploring the complexities of professional socialization in health and social care. *Learning in Health and Social Care*. 2(4), 213–222.

Cobb, M. (2001) *The Dying Soul: Spiritual Care at the End of Life*. Facing Death Series. Buckingham: Open University Press.

Cohen, L., Manion, L. and Morrison, K. (2000) *Research Methods in Education*. London: Taylor and Francis.

Coleman, P. G. (2004) Older people and institutionalised religion. In Jewell, A., ed. *Ageing, Spirituality and Well-being*. London: Jessica Kingsley Publishers, pp. 101–112.

Collier, A. (1994) *Critical Realism: An Introduction to Roy Bhaskar's Philosophy*. London: Verso.

Collier, A. (1999) *Being and Worth*. Critical Realism Interventions Series. London: Routledge.

Collier, A. (2004) Emancipation, social and spiritual. In Archer, M. S., Collier, A. and Porpora, D. V. *Transcendence: Critical Realism and God*. Critical Realism: Interventions. London: Routledge, pp. 168–176.

Confoy, M. (2002) The contemporary search for meaning in suffering. In Rumbold, B., ed. *Spirituality and Palliative Care: Social and Pastoral Perspectives*. Oxford: Oxford University Press, pp. 22–37.

Connor, S. R. (1998) *Hospice: Practice, Pitfalls and Promise*. London: Taylor and Francis.

Coombs, M. and Ersser, S. J. (2004) Medical hegemony in decision making – a barrier to interdisciplinary working in intensive care? *Journal of Advanced Nursing*. 46(3), 245–252.

Corner, J. and Dunlop, R. (1997) New approaches to care. In Clark, D., Hockley, J. and Ahmedzai, S., eds. *New Themes in Palliative Care*. Facing Death Series. Buckingham: Open University Press, pp. 288–302.

Costello, J. (2004) *Nursing the Dying Patient: Caring in Different Contexts*. Basingstoke: Palgrave Macmillan.

Coyle, J. (2002) Spirituality and health: towards a framework for exploring the relationship between spirituality and health. *Journal of Advanced Health*. 37(6), 589–597.

Creswell, J. W. (1998) *Qualitative Inquiry and Research Design: Choosing Among Five Traditions*. London: Sage.

Cruickshank, J. (2003a) Introduction. In Cruickshank, J., ed. *Critical Realism: The Difference it Makes*. Routledge Studies in Critical Realism. London: Routledge, pp. 1–14.

Cruickshank, J. (2003b) Underlabouring and unemployment: notes for developing a critical realist approach to the agency of the chronically unemployed. In Cruickshank, J., ed. *Critical Realism: The Difference it Makes*. Routledge Studies in Critical Realism. London: Routledge, pp. 111–127.

Cupitt, D. (1984) *The Sea of Faith: Christianity in Change*. London: British Broadcasting Corporation.

Danermark, B., Ekström, M., Jakobsen, L. and Karlsson, J. Ch. (2002) *Explaining Society: An Introduction to Critical Realism in the Social Sciences*. Critical Realism Interventions Series. London: Routledge.

D'Antonio, P. (2006) History for a practice profession. *Nursing Inquiry*. 13(4), 242–248.

Davies, J., ed. Berger, B. and Carlson, A. (1993) The family: is it just another lifestyle choice? The IEA Health and Welfare Unit. Choice in Welfare No. 15. London: IEA.

Davies, K. (2003) The body and doing gender: the relations between doctors and nurses in hospital work. *Sociology of Health and Illness*. 25(7), 720–742.

Davis, C. G., Wortman, C. B., Lehman, D. R. and Silver, R. C. (2000) Searching for meaning in loss: are clinical assumptions correct? *Death Studies*. 24(6), 497–540.

Deakin, N. (1994) *The Politics of Welfare: Continuities and Change*. Hemel Hempstead: Harvester Wheatsheaf.

Deakin, N. (2000) 'Putting narrow-mindedness out of countenance': the UK voluntary sector in the new millennium. Civil Society Working Paper 4. January 2000. [online]. Available from: www.lse.ac.uk/collections/CCS/pdf/CSWP/cswp4.pdf [Accessed 13 April 2008].

Dean, K. (2006) Agency and dialectics: what critical realism can learn from Althusser's Marxism. In Dean, K., Joseph, J., Roberts, J. M. and Wight, C. *Realism, Philosophy and Social Science*. Basingstoke: Palgrave Macmillan, pp. 123–147.

Dean, K., Joseph, J., Roberts, J. M. and Wight, C. (2006a) Realism, Marxism and method. In Dean, K., Joseph, J., Roberts, J. M. and Wight, C. *Realism, Philosophy and Social Science*. Basingstoke: Palgrave Macmillan, pp. 1–31.

Dean, K., Joseph, J., Roberts, J. M. and Wight, C. (2006b) *Realism, Philosophy and Social Science*. Basingstoke: Palgrave Macmillan.

Dekkers, W., Sandman, L. and Webb, P. (2002) Good death or good life as a goal of palliative care. In ten Have, H. and Clark, D., eds. *The Ethics of Palliative Care: European Perspectives*. Facing Death Series. Buckingham: Open University Press, pp. 106–125.

Dein, S. (2006) *Culture and Cancer Care: Anthropological Insights in Oncology*. Facing Death Series. Buckingham: Open University.

Denscombe, M. (1998) *The Good Research Guide: For Small-Scale Social Research Projects*. Buckingham: Open University Press.

DH – Department of Health (1997) *The New NHS: Modern Dependable*. Cm 3807, HMSO. London: Department of Health.

DH – Department of Health (1998) *A First Class Service: Quality in the New NHS*. HMSO. London: Department of Health.

DH – Department of Health (1999) *Clinical Governance: Quality in the New NHS*. HMSO. London: Department of Health.

DH – Department of Health (2000) *The Care Standards Act*. HMSO. London: Department of Health.

DH – Department of Health (2001) *Independent Health Care National Minimum Standards Regulations*. HMSO. London: Department of Health.

DH – Department of Health (2005) *DH 2005 No 375 (W.36) (C.17). Social Care, England and Wales: The Care Standards Act 2000 (Commencement No 21) Order 2005*. Signed S. J. Ladyman, Parliamentary Under-Secretary of State Department of Health (25 February 2005) [online]. Available from: www.opsi.gov.uk/legislation/wales/wsi2005/20050375e.htm [Accessed 7 July 2008].

Doll, R. and Boreham, J. (2005) Recent trends in cancer mortality in the UK. *British Journal of Cancer*. 92(7), 1329–1335.

Douglas, C. (1992) For all the saints. *British Medical Journal*. 29 February. 304(6826), 579.

Downward, P. and Mearman, A. (2007) Retroduction as mixed-methods triangulation in economic research: reorienting economics into social science. *Cambridge Journal of Economics*. 31(1), 77–99.

Doyle, D. (1993) Palliative medicine – a time for definition? *Palliative Medicine*. 7(4), 253–255.

Doyle, D. (2003) Editorial. *Palliative Medicine*. 17(1), 9–10.

Drevdahl, D., Philips, A. and Taylor, J. Y. (2006) Uncontested categories: the use of race and ethnicity variables in nursing research. *Nursing Inquiry*. 13(1), 52–63.

Drew, N. (2006) Bridging the distance between the objectivism of research and the subjectivity of the researcher. *Advances in Nursing Science*. 29(2), 181–191.

Dusek, V. (2006) *Philosophy of Technology: An Introduction*. Oxford: Blackwell Publishing.

Earle, S. (2005) What is health? In Denny, E. and Searle, E., eds. *Sociology for Nurses*. Cambridge: Polity, pp. 47–65.

Elias, N. (1978) *What is Sociology?* London: Hutchinson.

Elder-Vass, D. (2005a) Emergence and the realist account of cause. *Journal of Critical Realism*. 4(2), 315–338.

Elder-Vass, D. (2005b) Personal communication – 14.06.05. Electronic communication subsequent to discussion at British Sociological Association, Realism and Empirical Research Study Group Meeting, 01.06.05, Birkbeck College, London.

Elder-Vass, D (2007a) For emergence: refining Archer's account of social structure. *Journal for the Theory of Social Behaviour*. 37(1), 25–44.

Elder-Vass, D. (2007b) Social structure and social relations. *Journal for the Theory of Social Behaviour*. 37(4), 463–477.

Elder-Vass, D. (2008) Integrating institutional, relational and embodied structure: an emergentist perspective. *The British Journal of Sociology*. 59(2), 281–299.

Elsayem, A., Swint, K., Fisch, M. J., Palmer, J. L., Reddy, S., Walker, P., Zhukovsky, D., Knight, P. and Bruera, E. (2004) Palliative care inpatient service in a comprehensive cancer center: clinical and financial outcomes. *Journal of Clinical Oncology*. 22(10), 2008–2014.

Engholm, P. (1999) *The Possibility of Naturalism* twenty years on. *Alethia*. April. 2(1), 23–29.

Etzioni, A. (1995) *The Spirit of Community: Rights, Responsibilities and the Communitarian Agenda*. London: Fontana.

Exley, C. and Allen, D. (2007) A critical examination of home care: end of life care as an illustrative case. *Social Science and Medicine*. December. 65(11), 2317–2327.

Fay, B. (2000) Winch's philosophical bearings. *History of the Human Sciences*. 13(1), 50–62.

Fennell, G., Phillipson, C. and Evers, H. (1994) *The Sociology of Old Age*. Buckingham: Open University Press.

Fernandez, J. W. (1991) Introduction: confluents of inquiry. In Fernandez, J. W., ed. *Beyond Metaphor: The Theory of Tropes in Anthropology*. Stanford, CA: Stanford University Press, pp. 1–13.

Field D. (1994) Palliative medicine and the medicalization of death. *European Journal of Cancer Care*. 3(2), 58–62.

Field, D. and James, N. (1993) Where and how people die. In Clark, D., ed. *The Future for Palliative Care: Issues of Policy and Practice*. Buckingham: Open University Press, pp. 6–29.

Field, F. (1997) The welfare debate: managing self-interest, self-improvement, altruism. In Askonas, P. and Frowen, S. F., eds. *Welfare and Values: Challenging the Culture of Unconcern*. Basingstoke: Macmillan, pp. 165–175.

Finch, J. and Mason, J. (1993) Filial obligations and kin support for elderly people. In Bornat, J., Pereira, C., Pilgrim, D. and Williams, F., eds. *Community Care: A Reader*. Basingstoke: Open University Press; Macmillan, pp. 96–106.

Fitzsimmons, D., Hawker, S. E., Simmonds, P., George, S. L., Johnson, C. D. and Corner, J. L. (2005) Nurse-led models of chemotherapy care: mixed economy or nurse-doctor substitution? *Journal of Advanced Nursing*. 50(3), 244–252.

Fleetwood, S. (2008) *Working Paper 9 – Institutions and Social Structures: Some Clarifications*. Centre for Employment Studies Research. Bristol Business School. University of the West of England.

Flynn, N. (1996) A mixed blessing? How the contract culture works. In Hanvey, C. and Philpot, T., eds. *Sweet Charity: The Role and Workings of Voluntary Organisations*. London: Routledge, pp. 58–68.

Fogelin, R. J. (2009) *Hume's Skeptical Crisis: A Textual Study*. Oxford: Oxford University Press.

Foggo, B. A. (2006) The hospice: a place to die or just passing on? *Progress in Palliative Care*. 14(3), 109–111.

Foss, C. and Ellefsen, B. (2002) The value of combining qualitative and quantitative approaches in nursing research by means of triangulation. *Journal of Advanced Nursing*. 40(2), 242–248.

Fountain, A. (1999) Ethnic minorities and palliative care in Derby. *Palliative Medicine*. 13(2), 161–162.

Gamble, A. (1995) The weakening of social democracy. In Loney, M., Bocock, R., Clarke, J., Cochrane, A., Graham, P. and Wilson, M., eds. *The State or the Market: Politics and Welfare in Contemporary Britain*. Second edn. London: Sage in association with the Open University, pp. 259–272.

Gann, N. (1996) *Managing Change in Voluntary Organizations: A Guide to Practice*. Buckingham: Open University Press.

Garfinkel, H. (1984) *Studies in Ethnomethodology*. Oxford: Polity Press.

Gauker, C. (2006) Scientific realism as an issue in semantics. In Greenough, P. and Lynch, M. P., eds. *Truth and Realism*. Oxford: Clarendon; Oxford University Press, pp. 125–136.

Geertz, C. (1973) *The Interpretation of Cultures: Selected Essays*. New York: Basic Books.

Gellner, E (1968) Holism versus individualism. In Brodbeck, M, ed. *Readings in the Philosophy of the Social Sciences*. New York: Macmillan, pp. 254–268.

George, R. and Sykes, J. (1997) Beyond cancer? In Clark, D., Hockley, J. and Ahmedzai, S., eds. *New Themes in Palliative Care*. Facing Death Series. Buckingham: Open University Press, pp. 239–254.

Giddens, A. (1976) *New Rules of Sociological Method: A Positive Critique of Interpretive Sociologies*. London: Hutchinson.

Giddings, L. S. (2006) Mixed-methods research: positivism dressed in drag? *Journal of Research in Nursing*. 11(3), 195–203.

Gjerberg, E. and Kjølsrød, L. (2001) The doctor-nurse relationship: how easy is it to be a female doctor co-operating with a female nurse? *Social Science and Medicine*. January. 52(2), 189–202.

Glaser, B. and Strauss, A. (1968) *Time for Dying*. Chicago: Aldine.

Goffman, E. (1990) *The Presentation of Self in Everyday Life*. London: Penguin Books.

Gorner, P. (2000) Gadamer's Philosophical Hermeneutics. In Gorner, P. *Twentieth Century German Philosophy*. Oxford: Oxford University Press, pp. 129–158.

Gracia, D. (2002) Palliative care and the historical background. In ten Have, H. and Clark, D., eds. *The Ethics of Palliative Care: European Perspectives*. Facing Death Series. Buckingham: Open University Press, pp. 18–33.

Graham, H. (1993) Feminist perspectives on caring. In Bornat, J., Pereira, C., Pilgrim, D. and Williams, F., eds. *Community Care: A Reader*. Basingstoke: Open University Press; Macmillan, pp. 124–133.

Green, D. G. (1993) *Reinventing Civil Society: The Rediscovery of Welfare Without Politics*. IEA Health and Welfare Unit: Choice in Welfare Series No 17. London: The Institute of Economic Affairs.

Green, D. G. (1996) *Community Without Politics: A Market Approach to Welfare Reform*. IEA Health and Welfare Unit. Choice in Welfare No 27. London: The Institute of Economic Affairs.

Griffiths, J., Ewing, G., Rogers, M., Barclay, S., Martin, A., McCabe, J. and Todd, C. (2007) Supporting cancer patients with palliative care needs: district nurses' role perceptions. *Cancer Nursing*. 30(2), 156–162.

Griffiths, L. (2001) Categorising to exclude: the discursive construction of cases in community mental health teams. *Sociology of Health and Illness*. 23(5), 678–700.

Groff, R. (2004) *Critical Realism: Post-positivism and the Possibility of Knowledge*. Routledge Studies in Critical Realism. London: Routledge.

Gronow, A. (2008) The over- or the undersocialized conception of man? Practice theory and the problem of intersubjectivity. *Sociology*. April. 42(2), 243–259.

Guest, J. F., Ruiz, F. J., Greener, M. J. and Trotman, I. F. (2006) Palliative care treatment patterns and associated costs of healthcare resource use for specific advanced cancer patients in the UK. *European Journal of Cancer Care*. 15(1), 65–73.

Gunn, T. J. (2003) The complexity of religion and the definition of 'religion' in international law. *Harvard Human Rights Journal*. Spring. 16(1), 189–215.

Habermas, J. (2008) *Between Naturalism and Religion: Philosophical Essays*. Translated Cronin, C. Cambridge: Polity Press.

Haldane, J. J. (2002) A Thomist metaphysics. In Gale, R. M., ed. *The Blackwell Guide to Metaphysics*. Oxford: Blackwell Publishing, pp. 87–109.

Hammersley, M. (1990) What's wrong with ethnography? The myth of theoretical description. *Sociology*. 24(4), 597–616.

Hammersley, M. (2005a) Complexity and qualitative research: thick description versus analytic induction. Personal communication. Unpublished draft paper (dated 3 February 2005) presented at British Sociological Association, Realism and Empirical Research Study Group Meeting 09.02.05.

Hammersley, M. (2005b) Realism, causality and quantitative research. Personal communication. Unpublished draft paper of a transcript of a talk given at a British Sociology Association Realism and Social Research Study Group Meeting, held at Birkbeck College, London, February, 2005. British Sociological Association, Realism and Empirical Research Study Group Meeting 01.06.05.

Hammersley, M. and Atkinson, P. (1995) *Ethnography: Principles in Practice*. Second edn. London: Routledge.

Hampshire, S. (1960) *Thought and Action*. London: Chatto and Windus.

Hardcastle, M. A., Usher, K. J. and Holmes, C. A. (2005) An overview of structuration theory and its usefulness for nursing research. *Nursing Philosophy*. 6(4), 223–234.

Harding, R., Easterbrook, P., Higginson, I. J., Karus, D., Raveis, V. H. and Marconi, K. (2005) Access and equity in HIV/AIDS palliative care: a review of the evidence and responses. *Palliative Medicine*. 19(3), 251–258.

Harris, J. (1985) *The Value of Life: An Introduction to Medical Ethics*. London: Routledge and Kegan Paul.

Hatfield, G., ed. (1997) *Prolegomena to Any Future Metaphysics: With Selections from the Critique of Pure Reason*. Cambridge: Cambridge University Press.

Healthcare Commission (2008) *Information for Healthcare Providers* [online]. Available from: www.healthcarecommission.org.uk/serviceproviderinformation/independenthealthcareprivateandvoluntary/regulation.cfm [Accessed 28 April 2008].

Heath, C., Luff, P. and Svensson, M. S. (2003) Technology and medical practice. *Sociology of Health and Illness*. 25, 75–96.

Hedström, P. (2005) *Dissecting the Social: On the Principles of Analytical Sociology*. Cambridge: Cambridge University Press.

Help the Hospices (2008) *The End of Life Care Strategy for England: How the Government Could Change the Way we Die*. Report and Summary Recommendations from the Hospice Movement. September 2007. Help the Hospices [online]. Available from: www.helpthehospices.org.uk/documents/report_end_of_life_care.pdf [Accessed 15 April 2008].

Hempel, C. G. (1945) Studies in the logic of confirmation (I). *Mind: A Quarterly Review of Psychology and Philosophy*. 213, 1–26.

Henery, N. (2003) Constructions of spirituality in contemporary nursing theory. *Journal of Advanced Nursing*. 42(6), 550–557.

Hermsen, M. A. and ten Have, H. A. M. J. (2004) Pastoral care, spirituality, and religion in palliative care journals. *American Journal of Hospice and Palliative Medicine*. 21(5), 353–356.

Hinton, J. (1967) *Dying*. Harmondsworth: Pelican Books Inc.

Hirst, M. (2001) Trends in informal care in Great Britain during the 1990's. *Health and Social Care in the Community*. 9(6), 348–357.

Hockley, J. (1997) The evolution of the hospice approach. In Clark, D., Hockley, J. and Ahmedzai, S., eds. *New Themes in Palliative Care*. Facing Death Series. Buckingham: Open University Press, pp. 84–100.

Hockey, J. (2001) Changing death rituals. In Hockey, J., Katz, J. and Small, N., eds. *Grief, Mourning and Death Ritual*. Facing Death Series. Buckingham: Open University Press, pp. 185–211.

Hodgson, G. M. (2006) What are institutions? *Journal of Economic Issues*. March. XL(1), 1–25.

Hoefler, J. M. (2000) Making decisions about tube feeding for severely demented patients at the end of life: clinical, legal, and ethical considerations. *Death Studies*. April–May. 24(3), 233–254.

Holliday, A. (2005) How is it possible to write? *Journal of Language, Identity and Education*. 4(4), 304–309.

Hope, R. A., Longmore, J. M., Hodgetts, T. J. and Ramrakha, P. S. (1993) *Oxford Handbook of Clinical Medicine*. Third edn. Oxford: Oxford University Press.

Horner, J. S. (1998) Ethics and the public health. In Chadwick, R. and Levitt, M., eds. *Ethical Issues in Community Health Care*. London: Arnold, pp. 34–50.

Howson, C. (2000) *Hume's Problem: Induction and the Justification of Belief*. Oxford: Oxford University Press.

Hume, D. (1955) *An Inquiry Concerning Human Understanding: with a supplement – An Abstract of A Treatise on Human Nature*. Hendel, C. W., ed. The Library of Liberal Arts. New York: Bobbs-Merrill.

Hume, D. (2004) *A Treatise of Human Nature: Being an Attempt to Introduce the Experimental Method of Reasoning into Moral Subjects*. Book One – Of the Understanding [online]. Available from: www.ecn.bris.ac.uk/het/hume/treat.htm [Accessed 17 December 2004].

Ingleton, C., Clark, D. and Skilbeck, J. (2001) Needs assessment for palliative care: three projects compared. *Palliative Medicine*. 15(5), 398–404.

Jackson, L. (2007) Promoting health for communities. In Wills, J., ed. *Vital Notes for Nurses: Promoting Health*. Oxford: Blackwell Publishing, pp. 154–174.

James, N. and Field, D. (1992) The routinization of hospice: charisma and bureaucratisation. *Social Science and Medicine*. June. 34(12), 1363–1375.

Janssens, R., ten Have, H., Broeckaert, B., Clark, D., Gracia, D., Illhardt, F.-J., Lantz, G., Privitera, S. and Schotsmans, P. (2002) Moral values in palliative care: a European comparison. In ten Have, H. and Clark, D., eds. *The Ethics of Palliative Care: European Perspectives*. Facing Death Series. Buckingham: Open University Press, pp. 72–86.

Jewell, A., ed. (2004) *Ageing, Spirituality and Well-being*. London: Jessica Kingsley Publishers.

Johnson, N. and Scholler-Jaquish, A., eds. (2007) *Meaning in Suffering: Caring Practices in the Health Professions*. Series – Volume 6: Interpretive Studies in Healthcare and the Human Sciences. Wisconsin: The University of Wisconsin Press.

Jones, A. M. (2003) Changes in practice at the nurse-doctor interface. Using focus groups to explore the perceptions of first level nurses working in an acute care setting. *Journal of Clinical Nursing*. January. 12(1), 124–131.

Jones, H. (1994) *Health and Society in Twentieth-Century Britain*. Harlow: Longman.

Joseph, J. and Roberts, J. M., eds. (2003) *Realism, Discourse and Deconstruction*. Routledge Studies in Critical Realism. London: Routledge – Taylor & Francis.

Julian of Norwich (1998) *Revelations of Divine Love (Short text and long text)*. Translation: Spearing E. Introduction: Spearing, A. C. London: Penguin Books.

Kahneman, D. (2012) *Thinking, Fast and Slow*. London: Penguin Books.

Kaidesoja, T. (2005) The trouble with transcendental arguments: towards a naturalization of Roy Bhaskar's early realist ontology. *Journal of Critical Realism*. 4(1), 28–61.

Kail, P. J. E. (2010) *Projection and Realism in Hume's Philosophy*. Oxford: Oxford University Press.

Kant, I. (1990) *Critique of Pure Reason*. Translator Meiklejohn, J. M. D. London: Prometheus Books.

Kastenbaum, R. (2000) *The Psychology of Death*. Third edn. Springer Publishing. London: Free Association Books.

Kearney, M. (2000) *A Place of Healing: Working with Suffering in Living and Dying*. Oxford: Oxford University Press.

Kendall, J. and Knapp, M. (1995) A loose and baggy monster: boundaries, definitions and typologies. In Smith, J. D., Rochester, C. and Hedley, R., eds. *An Introduction to the Voluntary Sector*. London: Routledge, pp. 66–95.

King, A. (2007) Why I am not an individualist. *Journal for the Theory of Social Behaviour*. 37(2), 211–219.

King, N. (2004) Using templates in the thematic analysis of text. In Cassell, C. and Symon, G., eds. *Essential Guide to Qualitative Methods in Organizational Research*. London: Sage, pp. 256–270.

King, N. (2007) Template analysis. University of Huddersfield [online]. Available from: www.hud.ac.uk/hhs/research/template_analysis/intro.htm [Accessed 13 November 2007].

King, N., Thomas, K., Bell, D. and Bowes, N. (2003) *Evaluation of the Calderdale and Kirklees Out of Hours Protocol for Palliative Care: Final Report*. Primary Care Research Group. School of Human and Health Sciences. University of Huddersfield.

Kinn, S. and Curzio, J. (2005) Integrating qualitative and quantitative research methods. *Journal of Research in Nursing*. 10(3), 317–336.

Kirkland, K. (1996) In trust: the changing role of trustees. In Hanvey, C. and Philpot, T., eds. *Sweet Charity: The Role and Workings of Voluntary Organisations*. London: Routledge, pp. 93–110.

Kleinman, D. L. (2005) *Science and Technology in Society: From Biotechnology to the Internet*. Key Themes in Sociology Series. Oxford: Blackwell Publishing.

Kristjanson, L. J., Aoun, S. M. and Yates, P. (2006) Are supportive services meeting the needs of Australians with neurodegenerative conditions and their families? *Journal of Palliative Care*. Autumn. 22(3), 151–157.

Kübler-Ross, E. (1973) *On Death and Dying*. London: Tavistock/Routledge.

Kukathas, C. and Pettit, P. (1990) *Rawls: A Theory of Justice and its Critics*. Cambridge: Polity Press.

Lange, M. (2007) Introduction to Part II. In Lange, M., ed. *Philosophy of Science: An Anthology*. Blackwell Philosophic Anthologies Series. Oxford: Blackwell Publishing, pp. 25–33.

Lavoie, M., Blondeau, D. and Koninck, T. D. (2008) The dying person: an existential being until the end of life. *Nursing Philosophy*. 9(2), 89–97.

Lawton, J. (2000) *The Dying Process: Patient's Experiences of Palliative Care*. London: Routledge.

Layder, D. (1990) *The Realist Image in Social Science*. London: Macmillan.
Layder, D. (1994) *Understanding Social Theory*. London: Sage.
Layder, D. (1997) *Modern Social Theory*. London: UCL Press.
Leat, D. (1995) Funding matters. In Smith, J. D., Rochester, C. and Hedley, R., eds. *An Introduction to the Voluntary Sector*. London: Routledge, pp. 157–189.
Leplin, J. (2004) A theory's predictive success can warrant belief in the unobservable entities it postulates. In Hitchcock, C., ed. *Contemporary Debates in Philosophy of Science*. Oxford: Blackwell, pp. 117–132.
Levering, B. (2006) Epistemological issues in phenomenological research: how authoritative are people's accounts of their own perceptions? *Journal of Philosophy of Education*. 40(4), 451–462.
Lewis, J. (1996a) The boundary between voluntary and statutory social service in the late nineteenth and early twentieth centuries. *The Historical Journal*. March. 39(1), 157–177.
Lewis, J. (1996b) What does contracting do to voluntary agencies. In Billis, D. and Harris, M., eds. *Voluntary Agencies: Challenges of Organisation and Management*. Basingstoke: Macmillan Press, pp. 98–112.
Lewis, J. (1999) The voluntary sector in the mixed economy of welfare. In Gladstone, D., ed. *Before Beveridge: Welfare Before the Welfare State*. The IEA Health and Welfare Unit: Choice in Welfare No 47. London: The Institute of Economic Affairs, pp. 10–17.
Liamputtong, P. (2007) *Researching the Vulnerable: A Guide to Sensitive Research Methods*. London: Sage Publications.
Lipscomb, M. (2003) Suffering – hospice care's hidden heritage? *Progress in Palliative Care*. 11(4), 195–199.
Lipscomb, M. (2006a) Book Review: Groff, R. (2004) *Critical Realism, Post-positivism and the Possibility of Knowledge*. Routledge. *Nursing Philosophy*. 7(2), 104–105.
Lipscomb, M. (2006b) Rebutting the suggestion that Anthony Giddens's Structuration Theory offers a useful framework for sociological nursing research: a critique based upon Margaret Archer's *Realist Social Theory*. Critical response. *Nursing Philosophy*. 7(3), 175–180.
Lipscomb, M. (2006c) Review essay. Realist theory in research practice – making realism work: realist social theory and empirical research. Carter, B. and New, C., eds. (2004). With response commentary from Carter, B. and New, C. *Journal of Critical Realism*. 5(2), 363–379.
Lipscomb, M. (2008) Mixed method nursing studies: a critical realist critique. *Nursing Philosophy*. 9(1), 32–45.
Lipscomb, M. (2010a) Events and event identity: under-explored topics in nursing. *Nursing Philosophy*. 11(2), 88–99.
Lipscomb, M. (2010b) Participant overexposure and the role of researcher judgement. *Nurse Researcher*. 17(4), 49–59.
Lipscomb, M (2012) Abductive reasoning and qualitative research. *Nursing Philosophy*. 13(4), 244–256.
Lishman, A. (2003) Conclusions. In Monroe, B. and Oliviere, D., eds. *Patient Participation in Palliative Care: A Voice for the Voiceless*. Oxford: Oxford University Press, pp. 193–195.
List, C. and Pettit, P. (2011) *Group Agency: The Possibility, Design, and Status of Corporate Agents*. Oxford: Oxford University Press.
Lockwood, D. (1964) Social integration and system integration. In Zollschan, G. K. and Hirsch, W., eds. *Explorations in Social Change*. Introduction by Martindale, D. London: Routledge and Kegan Paul, pp. 244–257.

Löfmark, R., Mortier, F., Nilstun, T., Bosshard, G., Cartwright, C., van der Heide, A., Norup, M., Simonato, L. and Onwuteaka-Philipsen, B. (2006) Palliative care training: a survey of physicians in Australia and Europe. *Journal of Palliative Care*. Summer. 22(2), 105–110.

Longworth, G. (2012) Sharing thoughts about oneself (draft paper). *Proceedings of the Aristotelian Society*. CXIII(1), 1–18 [online] Available from: www.aristoteliansociety.org.uk/the-proceedings/the-programme/guy-longworth/ [Accessed 16 March 2013].

López, J. (2003) Critical realism: the difference that it makes, in theory. In Cruickshank, J., ed. *Critical Realism: The Difference it Makes*. Routledge Studies in Critical Realism. London: Routledge, pp. 75–89.

López, J. and Scott, J. (2000) *Social Structure*. Buckingham: Open University Press.

Mackay, L. (1993) *Conflicts in Care: Medicine and Nursing*. London: Chapman and Hall.

Macleod, R. (2003) Forum: wisdom and the practice of palliative care. *Journal of Palliative Care*. Summer. 19(2), 123–126.

Madill, A., Jordan, A. and Shirley, C. (2000) Objectivity and reliability in qualitative analysis: realist, contextual and radical constructionist epistemologies. *British Journal of Psychology*. 91(1), 1–20.

Maggs-Rapport, F. (2001) 'Best research practice': in pursuit of methodological rigour. *Journal of Advanced Nursing*. 35(3) 373–383.

Malpas, J. (2005) Hans-Georg Gadamer. *Stanford Encyclopedia of Philosophy* [online]. Available from: http://plato.stanford.edu/entries/gadamer/ [Accessed 10 January 2008].

Mandelbaum, M. (1959) Societal facts. In Gardiner, P., ed. *Theories of History: Readings from Classical and Contemporary Sources*. New York: Free Press, pp. 476–488.

Manias, E. and Street, A. (2001) Nurse-doctor interactions during critical care ward rounds. *Journal of Clinical Nursing*. July. 10(4), 442–450.

Marsland, D. (1996) Community care as an alternative to state welfare. *Social Policy and Administration*. September. 30(3), 183–188.

McCormack, B. (2003) Research nursing practice: does person-centredness matter? *Nursing Philosophy*. 4(3), 179–188.

McGuire, A., Fenn, P. and Mayhew, K. (1991) The economics of health care. In McGuire, A., Fenn, P. and Mayhew, K., eds. *Providing Health Care: The Economics of Alternative Systems of Finance and Delivery*. Oxford: Oxford University Press, pp. 5–45.

McKechnie, R. C. (2006) What does the literature tell us about death, dying and palliative care for people with intellectual disabilities? *Progress in Palliative Care*. 14(6), 255–259.

McLennan, G. (2009) 'FOR science in the social sciences': The end of the road for critical realism? In Stones, R. and Moog, S. eds. (2009) *Nature, Social Relations and Human Needs: Essays in Honour of Ted Benton*. Basingstoke: Palgrave-Macmillan.

Mearman, A. (2008) Personal communication. Critical realism and mixed methods. UWE Critical Realist Workshop 13.02.08.

Merrell, J. (2000) Ambiguity: exploring the complexity of roles and boundaries when working with volunteers in well woman clinics. *Social Science & Medicine*. 51(1), 93–102.

Meystre, C. J. N., Burley, N. M. J. and Ahmedzai, S. (1997) What investigations and procedures do patients in hospices want? Interview-based survey of patients and their nurses. *British Medical Journal*. 315(7117), 1202–1203.

Miles, B. M. and Huberman, A. M. (1994) *Qualitative Data Analysis: An Expanded Sourcebook*. Second edn. London: Sage.

Miller, A. (2002) Realism. *Stanford Encyclopedia of Philosophy* [online]. Available from: http://plato.stanford.edu/entries/realism/ [Accessed 24 May 2004].

Mino, J.-C. and Lert, F. (2005) Beyond the biomedical model: palliative care and its holistic model. *HEC Forum*. September. 17(3), 227–236.

Mohan, K. (2004) Eastern perspectives and implications for the West. In Jewell, A., ed. *Ageing, Spirituality and Well-being*. London: Jessica Kingsley Publishers, pp. 161–179.

Mola, G. D. (1997) Palliative home care. In Clark, D., Hockley, J. and Ahmedzai, S., eds. *New Themes in Palliative Care*. Facing Death Series. Buckingham: Open University Press, pp. 129–141.

Monod, E. (2004) Einstein, Heisenberg, Kant: methodological distinction and conditions of possibilities. *Information and Organization*. 14(2), 105–121.

Morgan, D. L. (2007) Paradigms lost and paradigms regained: methodological implications of combining qualitative and quantitative methods. *Journal of Mixed Method Research*. 1(1), 48–76.

Morgan, P. (1999) Farewell to the family? Public policy and family breakdown in Britain and the USA. The IEA Health and Welfare Unit. Choice in Welfare No. 21. Second edn. London: Institute of Economic Affairs.

Morris, J. (2005) *Independent Hospices in Wales: A Consumer Perspective*. Cardiff: Welsh Consumer Council.

Mueller, M. (2004) Involvement and (potential) influence of care providers in the enlistment phase of the informed consent process: the case of AIDS clinical trials. *Nursing Ethics*. 11(1), 42–52.

Münch, R. and Smelser, N. J. (1987) Relating the micro and macro. In Alexander, J. C., Giesen, B., Münch, R. and Smelser, N. J., eds. *The Micro-Macro Link*. London: University of California Press, pp. 356–387.

Murphy, F. (2005) Preparing for the field: developing competence as an ethnographic field worker. *Nurse Researcher*. 12(3), 52–60.

Mutch, A. (2004) Book review: *Structure, Agency and the Internal Conversation* by Margaret Archer. *Journal of Critical Realism*. 3(2), 384–389.

Nader, L. (1972) Up the anthropologist – perspectives gained from studying up. In Hymes, D., ed. *Reinventing anthropology*. New York: Pantheon Books, pp. 284–311.

Nagel, T. (1986) *The View from Nowhere*. Oxford: Oxford University Press.

Narayanasamy, A. (2007) Palliative care and spirituality. *Indian Journal of Palliative Care*. 13(2), 32–41.

Neale, J. C., Goulden, J. W., Allan, S. G., Dixon, P. D. and Isaacs, R. J. (2004) Esophageal stents in malignant dysphasia: a two-edged sword? *Journal of Palliative Care*. Spring. 20(1), 28–31.

Nelson, C. D. (2005) Crafting researcher subjectivity in ways that enact theory. *Journal of Language, Identity and Education*. 4(4), 315–320.

Nelson, C. J., Rosenfeld, B. J., Breitbart, W. and Galietta, M. (2002) Spirituality, religion, and depression in the terminally ill. *Psychosomatrics*. May/June. 43(3), 213–220.

Nettleton, S. (1995) *The Sociology of Health and Illness*. Cambridge: Polity Press.

New, C. (2001) Realising the potential: the ESCR Seminar Series on Social Realism and Empirical Research. *Journal of Critical Realism (incorporating Alethia)*. May, 4(1), 43–47.

Newell, R. and Burnard, P. (2006) *Research for Evidence-Based Practice*. Oxford: Blackwell Publishing.

Núñez Olarte, J. M. (2003) Cultural difference and palliative care. In Monroe, B. and Oliviere, D., eds. *Patient Participation in Palliative Care: A Voice for the Voiceless*. Oxford: Oxford University Press, pp. 74–87.

Oliver, D. P., Porock, D. and Courtney, K. (2005) Patient and family involvement in hospice interdisciplinary teams. *Journal of Palliative Care*. Winter. 21(4), 270–276.

Oneschuk, D., Moloughney, B., Jones-Mclean, E. and Challis, A. (2004) The status of undergraduate palliative medicine education in Canada: a 2001 survey. *Journal of Palliative Care*. Spring. 20(1), 32–37.

Osborne, S. and McLaughlin, K. (2004) The cross-cutting review of the voluntary sector: where next for local government-voluntary sector relationships? *Regional Studies*. 38(5), 573–582.

Oughtibridge, D. (1998) Under the thumb. *Nursing Management*. January. 4(8), 22–24.

Outhwaite, W. (1990) Realism, naturalism and social behaviour. *Journal for the Theory of Social Behaviour*. December. 20(4), 365–377.

Paley, J. (2005) Phenomenology as rhetoric. *Nursing Inquiry*. 12(2), 106–116.

Paley, J. (2008a) Philosophy and palliative care. *Nursing Philosophy*. 9(2), 75–76.

Paley, J (2008b) Spirituality and nursing: a reductionist approach. *Nursing Philosophy*. 9(1), 3–18.

Paley, J. (2008c) Spirituality and secularization: nursing and the sociology of religion. *Journal of Clinical Nursing*. February. 17(2), 175–186.

Parker-Oliver, D., Bronstein, L. R. and Kurzejeski, L. (2005) Examining variables to successful collaboration on the hospice team. *Health and Social Work*. 30(4), 279–288.

Parkes, C. M. (1986) *Bereavement: Studies of Grief in Adult Life*. Foreword Bowlby, J. Second edn. London: Routledge.

Pawson, R. (1989) *A Measure For Measures: A Manifesto for Empirical Sociology*. London: Routledge.

Pawson, R. (2006) *Evidence-based Policy: A Realist Perspective*. London: Sage.

Pawson, R. and Tilley, N. (1997) *Realistic Evaluation*. London: Sage.

Pellatt, G (2003) Ethnography and reflexivity: emotions and feelings in fieldwork. *Nurse Researcher*. 10(3), 28–37.

Pennycook, A. (2005) Performing the personal. *Journal of Language, Identity and Education*. 4(4), 297–304.

Pesut, B. (2008a) A conversation on diverse perspectives of spirituality in nursing literature. *Nursing Philosophy*. 9(2), 98–109.

Pesut, B. (2008b) A reply to 'Spirituality and nursing: a reductionist approach' by John Paley. Dialogue. *Nursing Philosophy*. 9(2), 131–137.

Polit, D. F. and Beck, C. T. (2006) *Essentials of Nursing Research: Methods, Appraisal, and Utilization*. Sixth edition. London: Lippincott Williams and Wikins.

Porpora, D. (2006) Methodological atheism, methodological agnosticism and religious experience. *Journal for the Theory of Social Behaviour*. 36(1), 57–75.

Porpora, D. (2007) On Elder-Vass: refining a refinement. *Journal for the Theory of Social Behaviour*. 37(2), 195–200.

Portenoy, R. K. and Bruera, E., eds. (2003) *Issues in Palliative Care Research*. Oxford: Oxford University Press.

Porter, S. (1993) Critical realist ethnography: the case of racism and professionalism in a medical setting. *Sociology*. November. 27(4), 591–609.

Porter, S. (1998) *Social Theory and Nursing Practice*. Sociology and Nursing Practice Series. Basingstoke: Palgrave.

Porter, S. and Ryan, S. (1996) Breaking the boundaries between nursing and sociology: a critical realist ethnography of the theory-practice gap. *Journal of Advanced Nursing*. 24(2), 413–420.

Potter, G. (2003) Critical realist strengths and weaknesses. [Review of book: Cruickshank, J., ed. (2003) *Critical Realism: The Difference that it Makes*. London: Routledge] *Journal of Critical Realism*. November. 2(1), 161–165.

Powell, M. (1992) Hospital provision before the National Health Service: a geographical study of the 1945 hospital surveys. *Social History of Medicine*. 5(3), 483–504.

Pratschke, J. (2003) Realist models? Critical realism and statistical models in the social sciences. *Philosophica*. 71, 13–38.

Prochaska, F. (1988) *The Voluntary Impulse: Philanthropy in Modern Britain*. London: Faber and Faber.

Putnam, H. (1981) *Reason, Truth and History*. Cambridge: Cambridge University Press.

Quinn, H., Allan, H. and Bryan, K. (2004) An evaluation of dependency: experiences of staff, patients and carers in a UK hospice. *International Journal of Palliative Nursing*. 10(12), 592–599.

Ramanathan, V. (2005a) Situating the researcher in research texts: dilemmas, questions, ethics, new directions. *Journal of Language, Identity and Education*. 4(4), 291–293.

Ramanathan, V. (2005b) Some impossibilities around researcher location: tensions around divergent audiences, languages, social stratifications. *Journal of Language, Identity and Education*. 4(4), 293–297.

Ramberg, B. and Gjesdal, K. (2005) Hermeneutics. *Stanford Encyclopedia of Philosophy*. [online]. Available from: http://plato.stanford.edu/entries/hermeneutics/ [Accessed 7 January 2008].

Randall, F. and Downie, R. S. (1999) *Palliative Care Ethics: A Companion for All Specialities*. Second edn. Oxford: Oxford University Press.

Randall, F. R. and Downie, R. S. (2006) *The Philosophy of Palliative Care: Critique and Reconstruction*. Oxford: Oxford University Press.

Rescher, N. (2002) An idealistic realism: presuppositional realism and justificatory idealism. In Gale, R., ed. *Blackwell Guide to Metaphysics*. Blackwell Philosophy Guides Series. London: Blackwell Publishing, pp. 242–262.

Reynard C. F. B. (1993) Do we need more hospices? Letters. *British Medical Journal*. 26 June. 306(6894), 1754.

Rochester, C. (1995) Voluntary agencies and accountability. In Smith, J. D., Rochester, C. and Hedley, R., eds. *An Introduction to the Voluntary Sector*. London: Routledge, pp. 190–207.

Roessler, J. (2013) The epistemic role of intentions. Paper given 5 November 2012. *Proceedings of the Aristotelian Society* 134th Session. Issue 1. Vol. CXIII.

Rose, D. (2006) *Consciousness: Philosophical, Psychological and Neural Theories*. Oxford: Oxford University Press.

Rosenberg, A. (2001) How is biological explanation possible? *British Journal for the Philosophy of Science*. 52, 735–760.

Roy, D. J. (2004) Editorial: palliative care in a technological age. *Journal of Palliative Care*. 20(4), 267–268.

Rucker, G. M. (2005) Guest editorial: palliative care for the next decade: moving beyond cancer. *Journal of Palliative Care*. Autumn. 21(3), 140–141.

Rumbold, B. (2002a) From religion to spirituality. In *Spirituality and Palliative Care: Social and Pastoral Perspectives*. Oxford: Oxford University Press, pp. 5–21.

Rumbold, B., ed. (2002b) *Spirituality and Palliative Care: Social and Pastoral Perspectives*. Oxford: Oxford University Press.

Ryan, K. R. and McQuillan, R. (2005) Palliative care for disadvantaged groups: people with learning disabilities. *Progress in Palliative Care*. 13(2), 70–74.

Rycroft-Malone, J., Seers, K., Titchen, A., Harvey, G., Kitson, A. and McCormack, B. (2004) What counts as evidence in evidence-based practice? Nursing and health care management and policy. *Journal of Advanced Nursing*. 47(1), 81–90.

Salmon, W. C. (2002) Causation. In Gale, R., ed. *Blackwell Guide to Metaphysics*. Blackwell Philosophy Guides Series. London: Blackwell Publishing, pp. 19–42.

Sandman, L. (2005) *A Good Death: On the Value of Death and Dying*. Facing Death Series. Buckingham: Open University Press.

Sargeant, A., Payne, S., Gott, M., Small, N. and Oliviere, D. (2007) User involvement in palliative care: motivational factors for service users and professionals. *Progress in Palliative Care*. 15(3), 126–132.

Sarkis, J. M. and Skoner, M. M. (1987) An analysis of the concept of holism in nursing literature. *Holistic Nursing Practice*. November. 2(1), 61–69.

Saunders, C. (1990) *Beyond the Horizon: A Search for Meaning in Suffering*. London: Darton, Longman and Todd.

Saunders, C. (1996) A personal therapeutic journey: into the valley of the shadow of death. *British Medical Journal*. 313(7072), 1599–1601.

Saunders, C. (2002a) *Cicely Saunders: Founder of the Hospice Movement. Selected Letters 1959–1999*. Introduction by Clark, D. Oxford: Oxford University Press.

Saunders, C. (2002b) Letter to Dr J. R. Heller. 12 June 1959. In *Ciciely Saunders: Founder of the Hospice Movement. Selected Letters 1959–1999*. Introduction by Clark, D. Oxford: Oxford University Press, p. 14.

Saunders, C. (2002c) Letter to Jack Wallace. 29 October 1959. In *Cicely Saunders: Founder of the Hospice Movement. Selected Letters 1959–1999*. Introduction by Clark, D. Oxford: Oxford University Press, p. 16.

Saunders, C. (2003) *Watch with Me: Inspiration for a Life in Hospice Care*. Sheffield: Mortal Press.

Saunders, C. (2006a) And from sudden death … First published in *Frontier* – Winter 1961. In *Cicely Saunders Selected Writings 1958–2004*. Introduction by Clark, D. Oxford: Oxford University Press, pp. 37–39.

Saunders, C. (2006b) *Cicely Saunders Selected Writings 1958–2004*. Introduction by Clark, D. Oxford: Oxford University Press.

Saunders, C. (2006c) Dying of cancer. First published in *St Thomas's Hospital Gazette*. (1958) 56(2) 37–47. In *Cicely Saunders Selected Writings 1958–2004*. Introduction by Clark, D. Oxford: Oxford University Press, pp. 1–11.

Saunders, C. (2006d) Should a patient know…? First published in *Nursing Times* 16 October 1959, pp. 994–995. In *Cicely Saunders Selected Writings 1958–2004*. Introduction by Clark, D. Oxford: Oxford University Press, pp. 12–20.

Saunders, C. (2006e) Terminal illness. First published in *Proceedings of Health Congress of the Royal Society of Health*. Symposium on 'Teaching, an Aspect of Home Care' 1961, pp. 112–114. In *Cicely Saunders Selected Writings 1958–2004*. Introduction by Clark, D. Oxford: Oxford University Press, pp. 53–56.

Savage, J. (2000) Ethnography and health care. *British Medical Journal*. 2 December. 321. 1400–1402.

Sawyer, R. K. (2002) Nonreductive Individualism: Part 1 – Supervenience and Wild Disjunction. *Philosophy of the Social Sciences*. 32(4), 537–559.

Sayer, A. (2000) *Realism and Social Science*. London: Sage.

Schulman-Green, D (2003) How do physicians learn to provide palliative care? *Journal of Palliative Care*. Winter. 19(4), 246–252.

Seale, C. (1998) *Constructing Death: The Sociology of Dying and Bereavement*. Cambridge: Cambridge University Press.

Seale, C. (1999) *The Quality of Qualitative Research*. Introducing Qualitative Methods Series. London: Sage.

Seddon, N. (2007) *Who Cares?: How State Funding and Political Activism Change Charity*. London: Institute for the Study of Civil Society.

Sell, A. P. F. (1996) *The Philosophy of Religion 1875–1980*. Reprint: Originally published 1988 by Routledge. Bristol: Thoemmes Press.

Seymour, J. (2007) Needs and preferences of patients with diseases other than cancer: the UK experience. *Progress in Palliative Care*. 15(3), 108–112.

Seymour, J., Clark, D. and Marples, R. (2002) Palliative care and policy in England: a review of health improvement plans for 1999–2003. *Palliative Medicine*. 16(1), 5–11.

Seymour, J. E. (2001) *Critical Moments – Death and Dying in Intensive Care*. Facing Death Series. Buckingham: Open University Press.

Sheldon, F. (1997) *Psychosocial Palliative Care: Good Practice in the Care of the Dying and Bereaved*. Cheltenham: Stanley Thornes Publishers.

Silverman, D. (2005) *Doing Qualitative Research*. Second edn. London: Sage Publications.

Simons, L. (2007) Moving from collision to integration: reflecting on the experience of mixed methods. *Journal of Research in Nursing*. 12(1), pp. 73–86.

Simmons, M. (2007) Insider ethnography: tinker, tailor, researcher or spy? *Nurse Researcher*. 14(4), 7–17.

Sjöström, B. (2002) Applying phenomenology in nursing research. *Journal of Advanced Nursing*. 40(3), 339–345.

SMAC/SNMAC – Standing Medical Advisory Committee, Standing Nursing and Midwifery Advisory Committee (1992) *The Principles and Provision of Palliative Care*. London: HMSO.

Small, N. (2003) The changing National Health Service, user involvement and palliative care. In Monroe, B. and Oliviere, D., eds. *Patient Participation in Palliative Care: A Voice for the Voiceless*. Oxford: Oxford University Press, pp. 9–22.

Smith, J. D. (1996) Should volunteers be managed? In Billis, D. and Harris, M., eds. *Voluntary Agencies: Challenges of Organisation and Management*. Basingstoke: Macmillan Press, pp. 187–199.

Smiths Medical (2008) [online]. Available from: www.smiths-medical.com/ [Accessed 14 May 2008].

Stanworth, R. (2004) *Recognizing Spiritual Needs in People Who Are Dying*. Oxford: Oxford University Press.

St Christopher's Hospice and Help the Hopsices (2008) Hospice and Palliative Care Facts and Figures 2005. Hospice Information [online]. Available from: www.hospiceinformation.info/uploads/documents/hospice_&_palliative_care_facts_&_figures_2005.pdf [Accessed 19 April 2008].

Stern, R. (2000) *Transcendental Arguments and Scepticism: Answering the Question of Justification*. Oxford: Oxford University Press.

Stevens, T., Wilde, D., Paz, S., Ahmedzai, S. H., Rawson, A. and Wragg, D. (2003) Palliative care research protocols: a special case for ethical review? *Palliative Medicine*. 17(6), 482–490.

Stienstra, D. and Chochinov, H. M. (2006) Vulnerability, disability, and palliative end-of-life care. *Journal of Palliative Care*. Autumn. 22(3), 166–174.

Stjernsward, J. (1997) The WHO cancer pain and palliative care programme. In Clark, D., Hockley, J. and Ahmedzai, S., eds. *New Themes in Palliative Care*. Facing Death Series. Buckingham: Open University Press, pp. 203–211.

Stoddard, S. (1979) *The Hospice Movement: A Better Way of Caring for the Dying*. London: Johnathan Cape.

Strauss, A. L. (1987) *Qualitative Analysis for Social Scientists*. Cambridge: Cambridge University.

Stroud, B. (2000) *Understanding Human Knowledge: Philosophical Essays*. Oxford: Oxford University Press.

Tadd, V. (1998) Discrimination. In Chadwick, R. and Levitt, M., eds. *Ethical Issues in Community Health Care*. London: Arnold, pp. 92–101.

Tanyi, R. A. (2002) Towards clarification of the meaning of spirituality. *Journal of Advanced Nursing*. 39(5), 500–509.

Taube, A. W., Osinchuk, J. W. and Bruera, E. (2003) Forum: whose responsibility? *Journal of Palliative Care*. Summer. 19(2), 119–122.

Theis, S. L., Biordi, D. L., Coeling, H., Nalepka, C. and Miller, B. (2003) Spirituality in caregiving and care receiving. *Holistic Nursing Practice*. January/February. 17(1), 48–55.

Timmermans, S. and Berg, M. (2003) The practice of medical technology. *Sociology of Health and Illness*. 25(3), 97–114.

Tong, E., Mcgraw, S. A., Dobihal, E., Baggish, R., Cherlin, E. and Bradley, E. H. (2003) What is a good death? Minority and non-minority perspectives. *Journal of Palliative Care*. Autumn. 19(3), 168–175.

Trigg, R. (2001) *Understanding Social Science: A Philosophical Introduction to the Social Sciences*. Second edn. Oxford: Blackwell.

Trusted, J. (1987) *Moral Principles and Social Values*. London: Routledge and Kegan Paul.

Tversky, A. and Kahneman, D. (1974) Judgement under uncertainty: heuristics and biases. *Science*. 185(4157), 1124–1131.

van Hooft, S. (2002) Towards a philosophy of caring and spirituality for a secular age. In Rumbold, B., ed. *Spirituality and Palliative Care: Social and Pastoral Perspectives*. Oxford: Oxford University Press, pp. 38–50.

Varela, C. (2007) Elder-Vass's move and Giddens's call. *Journal for the Theory of Social Behaviour*. 37(2), 201–210.

Walter, T. (1994) *The Revival of Death*. London: Routledge.

Warelow, P. (1996) Nurse-doctor relationships in multidisciplinary teams: ideal or real? *International Journal of Nursing Practice*. March. 2(1), 33–39.

Weaver, K. and Olson, J. K. (2006) Understanding paradigms used for nursing research. Integrative literature reviews and meta-analysis. *Journal of Advanced Nursing*. 53(4), 459–469.

Webb, P., ed. (2000) *Ethical Issues in Palliative Care: Reflections and Considerations*. Manchester: Hochland & Hochland.

West, T. (1990) Multidisciplinary working. In Saunders, C., ed. *Hospice and Palliative Care: An Interdisciplinary Approach*. London: Edward Arnold, pp. 3–13.

Whelan, R. (1996) *The Corrosion of Charity: From Moral Renewal to Contract Culture*. The IEA Health and Welfare Unit: Choice in Welfare No 29. London: The Institute of Economic Affairs.

Whitehead, A. N. and Russell, B. (1962) *Principia Mathematica*. Cambridge: Cambridge University Press.

WHO – World Health Organization (2002) *National Cancer Control Programmes: Policies and Managerial Guidelines*. Second edn. Geneva: WHO.

WHO – World Health Organization (2008) *Definition of Palliative Care* [online]. Available from: www.who.int/cancer/palliative/definition/en/ [Accessed 21 April 2008].

Wight, C. (2006) Realism, science and emancipation. In Dean, K., Joseph, J., Roberts, J. M. and Wight, C. *Realism, Philosophy and Social Science*. Basingstoke: Palgrave Macmillan, pp. 32–64.

Williams, A. (2003) A comment on Sorell's paper from an economics perspective. In Oliver, A., ed. *Equity in Health and Healthcare: Views from Ethics, Economics and Political Science. Proceedings from a Meeting of the Health Equity Network*. London: The Nuffield Trust, pp. 21–24.

Williams, M. and Dyer, W. (2004) Realism and probability. In Carter, B. and New, C., eds. *Making Realism Work: Realist Social Theory and Empirical Research*. Critical Realism: Interventions Series. London: Routledge, pp. 67–85.

Willmott, R. (2003) New Labour, school effectiveness and ideological commitment. In Cruickshank, J., ed. *Critical Realism: The Difference it Makes*. Routledge Studies in Critical Realism. London: Routledge, pp. 128–148.

Winch, P. (1958) *The Idea of a Social Science and its Relation to Philosophy*. Studies in Philosophical Psychology. Eighth impression 1973 (third impression 1963 – minor corrections). London: Routledge and Kegan Paul.

Winch, P. (1970) Understanding a primitive society. In Wilson, B. R., ed. *Rationality: Key Concepts in the Social Science*. Oxford: Basil Blackwell, pp. 78–111.

Wittgenstein, L. (1976) *Philosophical Investigations*. Trans: Anscombe, G. E. M. Oxford: Basil Blackwell.

Wood, D. J., Clark, D. and Gatrell, A. C. (2004) Equity of access to adult hospice inpatient care within north-west England. *Palliative Medicine*. 18(6), 543–549.

Woods, S. (2002) Respect for autonomy and palliative care. In ten Have, H. and Clark, D., eds. *The Ethics of Palliative Care: European Perspectives*. Facing Death Series. Buckingham: Open University Press, pp. 145–165.

Woods, S. (2007) *Death's Dominion: Ethics at the End of Life*. Facing Death Series. Berkshire: McGraw-Hill, Open University Press.

Bibliography

Archer, M., Bhaskar, R., Collier, A., Lawson, T. and Norrie, A., eds (1998) *Critical Realism: Essential Readings*. Critical Realism Interventions Series. London: Routledge.

Carter, B. and New, C., eds (2004) *Making Realism Work: Realist Social Theory and Empirical Research.* Critical Realism Interventions Series. London: Routledge.

Collier, A. (1994) *Critical Realism: An Introduction to Roy Bhaskar's Philosophy.* London: Verso.

Cruickshank, J., ed. (2003) *Critical Realism: The Difference it Makes*. Routledge Studies in Critical Realism. London: Routledge.

Danermark, B., Ekström, M., Jakobsen, L. and Karlsson, J. C. (2002) *Explaining Society: Critical Realism in the Social Sciences.* Critical Realism Interventions Series. London: Routledge.

Dean, K., Joseph, J., Roberts, J. M. and Wight, C. (2006) *Realism, Philosophy and Social Science*. Basingstoke: Palgrave-Macmillan.

Sayer, A. (2000) *Realism and Social Science*. London: Sage Publications.

Index

Page numbers in *italics* denote tables, those in **bold** denote figures.

Taylor & Francis

eBooks

FOR LIBRARIES

ORDER YOUR FREE 30 DAY INSTITUTIONAL TRIAL TODAY!

Over 23,000 eBook titles in the Humanities, Social Sciences, STM and Law from some of the world's leading imprints.

Choose from a range of subject packages or create your own!

Benefits for **you**

- Free MARC records
- COUNTER-compliant usage statistics
- Flexible purchase and pricing options

Benefits for your **user**

- Off-site, anytime access via Athens or referring URL
- Print or copy pages or chapters
- Full content search
- Bookmark, highlight and annotate text
- Access to thousands of pages of quality research at the click of a button

For more information, pricing enquiries or to order a free trial, contact your local online sales team.

UK and Rest of World: **online.sales@tandf.co.uk**

US, Canada and Latin America:
e-reference@taylorandfrancis.com

www.ebooksubscriptions.com

ALPSP Award for BEST eBOOK PUBLISHER 2009 Finalist

Taylor & Francis eBooks
Taylor & Francis Group

A flexible and dynamic resource for teaching, learning and research.